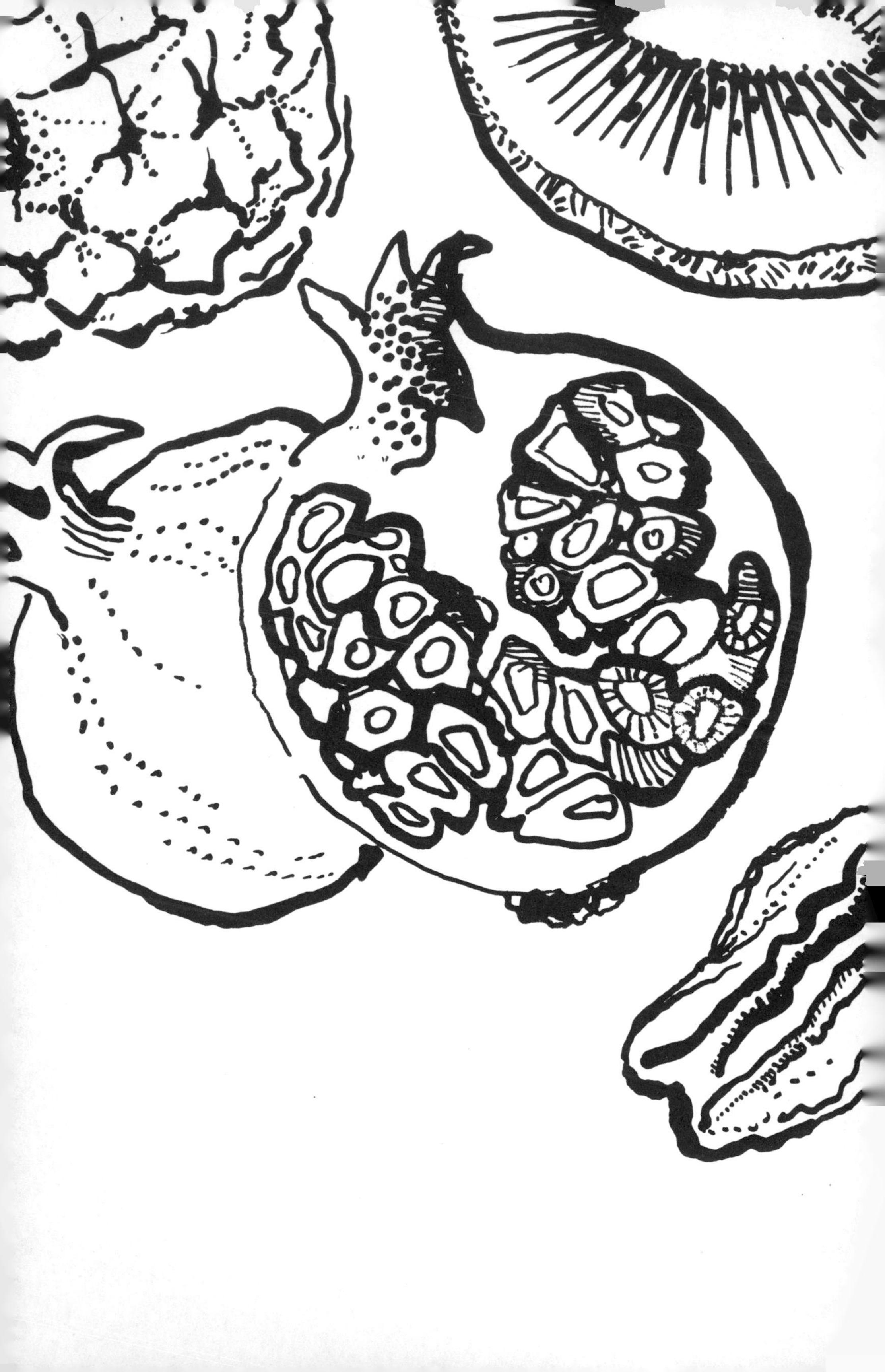

THE FRUIT & NUT BOOK

GAIL DUFF

SIDGWICK & JACKSON
LONDON

ACKNOWLEDGEMENTS

I SHOULD VERY much like to thank the following people for all their help and information.

Daphne MacCarthy, of the British Food Information Service of Food from Britain.

All the staff of the Fresh Fruit and Vegetable Information Bureau.

Caroline Miller of the New Zealand Apple and Pear Marketing Board.

Roger Bartlett of Petty, Wood and Co. Ltd, suppliers of Epicure brand foods.

Paul Setters of the Guernsey Growers Co-operative Ltd.

Jim Saunt, European Technical Manager of the South African Co-operative Citrus Exchange Ltd.

The Citrus Marketing Board of Israel.

First published in Great Britain in 1990 by Sidgwick & Jackson Ltd, 1 Tavistock Chambers, Bloomsbury Way, London WC1 2SG

Designed by Hammond Hammond
Illustrations by Madelaine David

ISBN 0 283 06005 0

Typeset by Rowland Phototypesetting Ltd, Bury St Edmunds, Suffolk
Printed in Great Britain by Mackays of Chatham plc, Chatham, Kent

CONTENTS

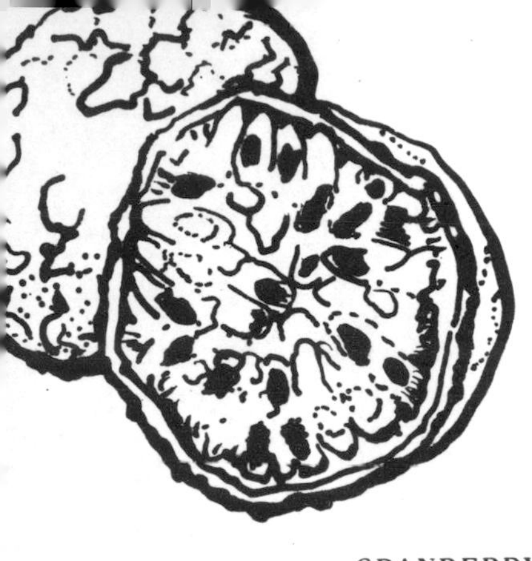

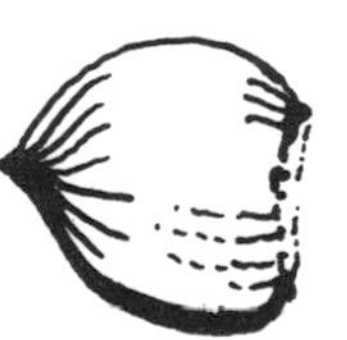

NUTS AND SEEDS

INTRODUCTION

'ARE YOU A fruit and nut case?' I must confess to having been deeply influenced a long time ago by this advertisement on the Tube. I rushed straight from the train, pushed my money into the slot machine and extracted a chocolate bar crammed with nuts and raisins. Now, almost twenty-five years on, I wouldn't give anything for the chocolate bar, but I have a whole kitchen cupboard full of nuts and dried fruits that I munch on while working in the office, and which I use in as many different recipes as possible, both sweet and savoury. I eat an enormous bowl of chopped fresh fruits for breakfast and a large percentage of desserts that I make are fresh-fruit based. For those occasions when there has been no time to concoct a dessert, then an attractively presented arrangement of fresh fruit, the larger, stickier types of dried fruit and an assortment of nuts has often saved the day. Fruits and nuts certainly play an important part in my culinary life. I don't know that I could actually live on them exclusively, but I should certainly be at a great loss without them.

In these days of fast air travel and efficiently refrigerated cargo ships, the supply of fruits that reaches our markets and shops has never been greater, and many fruits that were once available for only a few months can now be bought for the greater part of the year. I don't know whether these extended seasons are good or bad. To me, a cook who has always relied upon fresh ingredients, summer always meant strawberries and peaches. Now I can buy these at Christmas my world has been turned a little upside down. But out-of-season fruits are never quite as good as those that come from nearer home, at what was once the 'right' time of the year, and the prices may be higher, so I never buy them just for the sake of it.

The vast range of different fruits available in any supermarket is something that *should* be taken advantage of. There are so many new varieties appearing which, although they may seem strange now, may be commonplace in a few years time, and it is useful to know how to use them to their best advantage. After all, look what happened to the kiwi fruit. Once strange and exotic, it is now commonplace, inexpensive, and grown in Sussex.

Many of these new fruits yield surprises. Outside they may be dull and uninteresting, but cut them open and what do you find? A peculiar ridged fruit may give a star shape; an orange, thorny outside may be full of deep green seeds; inside a dull, green skin there may be sweet, soft, pink flesh, full of black seeds that look like caviar. These are the carambola, the Kiwano and the pawpaw, and there are many more.

It is all too easy to fall in love with a fruit in a shop but to take it home, treat it in entirely the wrong way and end up by consigning it to the bin in disgust. I once tried to eat a pomelo like an orange, just biting into the large segments, and found it unpleasant, dry and chewy. I candied the peel and threw the rest away. It was some years later that I discovered that I should be peeling each segment, and what a difference it made. The fruit became succulent and full of flavour.

People rarely make the most of nuts. To many, they are a luxury bought in the shell at Christmas, or a snack in a packet at the pub. But nuts are, in fact, an extremely versatile ingredient. They keep well and can be used to make either sweet or savoury dishes.

Many fruits and nuts have been grown since ancient times, and the stories of where they were first grown, how they came to Britain and their original uses are fascinating. It is interesting too, to know where newer fruits come from and why someone decided that they would be a good commercial proposition. I have often found that the more I know about any ingredient, the better I am able to treat it. If I know its country of origin, for example, I know which other ingredients will complement it.

All the recipes in this book are devised to bring out the best qualities of the particular fruits and nuts that they feature. Some, especially those using the newer and more exotic fruits, have been kept very simple so that the special flavours and qualities of the fruits will not be lost.

I hope that my enthusiasm for fruits and nuts will inspire you, that their stories will intrigue you, and that the culinary information and recipes will save your exotic and expensive ingredients from the bin. If *The Fruit and Nut Book* does all these things, then it will have succeeded.

GAIL DUFF

VITAMIN AND MINERAL CHART

FRUITS AND NUTS contain a wide variety of vitamins and minerals. The main ones are listed here, with their specific functions.

VITAMINS

VITAMIN A	Manufactured by the body from carotene, which is found in yellow and red fruits. Ensures good eyesight, particularly in the dark; builds resistance to infections; promotes healthy skin, hair, teeth and gums; promotes growth in children.
B VITAMINS	(these complement each other: each functions best in the presence of the others)
VITAMIN B1	Known as thiamine. Aids the digestion of carbohydrates. Fights both physical and mental stress; ensures the healthy functioning of the nervous system.
VITAMIN B2	Known as riboflavin. Aids in the digestion of carbohydrates, fats and protein. Promotes healthy skin, hair and nails; essential for growth in children.
VITAMIN B6	Known as pyridoxine. Aids in the digestion of protein and fat. Fights mental stress.
VITAMIN B12	Known as cobalamin. Aids in the digestion of all food substances. Maintains a healthy nervous system and is particularly important for concentration, memory and balance. Promotes growth in children. Regenerates red blood cells.
VITAMIN C	Fights infection and fatigue; promotes healing. Necessary after antibiotics to reduce toxic effects.
VITAMIN D	Promotes strong bones and teeth. Works with Vitamins A and C to combat infection.
VITAMIN E	Burns up saturated fats. Promotes healthy skin and hair; said to combat ageing. Promotes bone growth in children.
VITAMIN K	Aids in blood clotting.

MINERALS

CALCIUM	Metabolises iron. Maintains strong bones and healthy teeth; promotes bone growth in children. Ensures healthy reflexes and regular heart beat.
CHLORINE	Aids in digestion and maintaining muscle flexibility.
IODINE	Burns up excess fat to produce energy. Promotes growth and learning ability in children. Good for skin, hair, nails and teeth.
IRON	Builds resistance to disease; prevents fatigue; aids growth in children. Necessary to prevent some types of anaemia.
MAGNESIUM	Relieves indigestion, maintains health of heart and lungs. Fights depression.
MANGANESE	Aids reflexes and memory. Combats fatigue and nervous irritability.
PHOSPHORUS	Aids in metabolism of fats and starches. Promotes healthy teeth and gums; speeds mending of broken bones.
POTASSIUM	Aids in elimination of waste products. Helps maintain healthy blood pressure; ensures adequate oxygen supply to brain. Can combat allergies.
SELENIUM	Keeps muscles and tissues elastic. Ensures good oxygen utilisation.
SULPHUR	Helps to keep skin and hair healthy. Combats bacterial infections.
ZINC	Promotes healing; promotes growth in children. Increases mental alertness. Decreases cholesterol levels in blood.

FRUITS

APPLE

MALUS SPECIES

THERE COULD BE no better fruit to begin with than the apple. It is one of the oldest fruits of all and, in the Western world at least, one of the most loved and most familiar. We feel comfortable with apples. Wherever desirable fruits have appeared in the Bible or in myths and legends, we have named them after this, our most common and abundant fruit, making the stories easier for us who dwell in temperate climates to understand. An apple tempted Eve, golden apples were sought by Hercules in the garden of the Hesperides, and another was said to have started the Trojan war.

All the apples that we know today are descended from several different types of crab apples, which grow wild in Britain and Europe and across to western Asia, and were first enjoyed in Britain in Neolithic times. The Romans much improved them, by grafting and pollinating, to produce larger, sweeter, long-keeping varieties and they established Britain's first apple orchards. After the Romans left, apple trees flourished mainly on monastery land, but it was the Normans who confirmed Britain as an important apple-growing country.

The earliest recorded apple was the pear-shaped pearmain which with the costard apple, a cooking variety which later gave its name to the costermongers of London, remained the most popular during the medieval period. By the fifteenth century pippins, pomewaters and blanderelles had appeared, a great many of which were grown especially for cider. King Henry VIII sent his fruiterer, Richard Harris, to France to learn more about apple cultivation and when he returned he established large orchards at Teynham in Kent, which were a model for the growing and propagation of apples over the next four centuries.

When Europeans started to explore the world, apples went with them. They travelled on the *Mayflower* to America, with Captain Bligh of the *Bounty* to Australia and also to Canada, South Africa and New Zealand.

Over the years, countless varieties of apple have come in and out of favour. Some have disappeared completely, others flourish secretly in corners of old gardens, a few have been developed into commercial successes. The early nineteenth century was the golden age of apples, as it was then that most of our modern varieties were raised.

Pippins were so called because they were originally raised from seedlings grown from pips. In the sixteenth century John apples,

Queenings, Leathercoats and Russetings were all pippin varieties, but the most famous of all, the **Cox's Orange Pippin** was raised by a Mr Cox, at Colnbrook, by the present Heathrow airport, in 1825. It is still the same, a green colour, ripening to yellow with a russet red blush, a crisp yet melting texture and a sweet, almost perfumed flavour.

Mr R A Laxton raised **Laxton's Fortune**, one of the early ripening apples, and **Laxton's Superb**, ready in the late autumn, which is similar to a Cox but sweeter flavoured. One tree bearing shiny red, early ripening apples was discovered quite by chance growing in an Essex garden. Named **Discovery**, it became one of our most successful dessert apples. It is sweet and juicy and remains firm and crisp for up to a week.

The **Worcester Pearmain**, a direct descendant of the early pearmain, ripens in September and October. It is red, streaked with green, with crisp sweet flesh that has a hint of strawberry flavour. It does not keep well, so make the most of it in the autumn.

Egremont Russet is an old variety enjoying a come-back. It has brownish skin, and creamy textured and flavoured flesh. A few years back it was being phased out, but due to popular demand has been brought back. It is best from October to Christmas. After that, if it kept in store, it can develop bitter patches, and is never so good.

Spartan is a new variety which has won several awards over the past few years. It is deep red, fine textured and very crisp, making it a delicious salad apple. **Ida Reds** are very similar, red and shiny, with a firm, crisp flesh and a refreshing tang to the flavour. In complete contrast, **Crispin**, a variety originally from Japan, is light green, sweet and juicy and only available in the autumn.

Golden Delicious apples do not grow only in France. English types have a firmer texture and better flavour.

Of course, even with efficient cold stores, English apples do not last all year and every month there will be apples from other countries on the shelves. New Zealand sends **Cox's** similar to our own and South Africa provides crisp, green **Granny Smiths**. The United States and Canada send the dark, shiny red varieties which include **Red Delicious**, **Starkings** and **Starkrimsons** but these, although they look tempting, often have an unappetising, powdery texture. This may be due to the varieties themselves or to the length of time they have taken to get here. As it is, they are not a patch on our own varieties, but the only true comparison would be to taste one straight from the tree.

We never have to import cooking varieties as our own keep so well. **Grenadiers** come into the shops in August. They are a dull, clear green, slightly flattened in shape with a firm flesh that is better sliced into pies than cooked to purées. **Lord Derbys** are the next to arrive. They are long shaped, tapering towards the base, with ribs running downwards and cook down to a fluffy purée. Last of all comes the **Bramley**, large, bright green, shiny and flushed with red. This is a super apple, ideal for all cooking purposes and, when ripe and mellow, excellent in salads and as a dessert apple with cheese. It keeps exceptionally well and the last ones will come out of the cold store in July just before the first Grenadiers are ready.

Nutrition

Yes, apples really are good for us. They are high in Vitamin C and fibre and low in calories, and the pectin they contain will reduce cholesterol levels in blood, especially if they are eaten regularly.

Buying and storing apples

Great care is now taken to see that apples are in peak condition when they reach the shops so you will rarely find bumps, bruises and blemishes. There is no need to buy more than a week's supply at a time. Store them in a cool, dark cupboard and put only a few at a time into a small fruit bowl. Although a large, bountiful bowlful may look wonderful at the beginning of the week, after a few days in a warm atmosphere, it could be full of wrinkly apples.

If you have your own apple trees, then other methods of storing will be needed. With cooking apples, wrap each one individually in newspaper and store in boxes in a cool place such as a garage. You can also cook them to a lightly sweetened puree for freezing.

Dessert apples can be stored in newspaper in the same way. To freeze, they must be peeled and sliced, soaked for 15 minutes in water to which lemon juice has been added, and then frozen on open trays. Alternatively they can be first poached in a sugar syrup, again with lemon juice added.

Apples in the kitchen

With apples you can always produce a culinary miracle with little cost, and at reasonably short notice.

All the dessert varieties are delicious raw and they go wonderfully with cheese after a meal. Spartans and Ida Reds and all the crisp types go well with Cheddar, Cox's with Stilton, and Russets with the creamy cheeses such as Lymeswold or Brie.

To eat before a meal, apples make pretty salads. Arrange slices in a ring and in the centre put a portion of curd cheese into which you have mixed some parsley or crushed garlic. Apples go well in all kinds of side salads and are best with crunchy ingredients like celery, celeriac, fennel, chicory, and red or white cabbage.

Slices of dessert apple, when cooked, hold their shape well and look attractive as garnishes for desserts or in fruit salads. A Normandy tart, made with rings of apples cooked on a rich pastry base is always made with dessert apples for this reason.

An easily prepared yet impressive dish, can be made by quickly frying slices of dessert apple in butter and glazing with sugar or honey. For every day, serve them as they are, or for a special occasion, flame them in brandy, calvados or rum.

A favourite family winter treat is baked apples. Score them all round with a sharp knife, remove the cores and fill with mixtures of dried fruits, chopped or ground nuts, mincemeat, jam, marmalade, honey or sugar. Stand in a dish with about half an inch (1.5 cm) of water and bake at 400F/200C/gas 6 for 20 minutes or until soft but still holding their shape. Wrap the prepared apple in pastry before baking for an apple dumpling.

Apple pies, puddings, crumbles and turnovers have been baked in English kitchens for centuries. To ring the changes, add dried fruits to the apples, or sweeten them with jams or marmalade. Add other fruits such as blackberries, blackcurrants, quinces or frozen strawberry purée.

To make a thick, sweet, apple purée for pies and other desserts, chop the apples with the peel on, cook them with honey, sugar or jam and then rub them through a sieve. The flavour is so much better than when they are cooked peeled. Fold in whipped egg whites for an apple snow; stir in whipped cream and custard for fool; or make a mousse with egg yolks and cream.

When you are boiling ham, add a sliced cooking apple to give extra flavour. Add diced apple to pot roasts and casseroles of pork or lamb, or lay slices on pork or lamb chops as they grill. Use fried slices of cooking apples to garnish bacon, ham or mixed grills. Add chopped apple to stuffings for goose or duck.

Both dessert and cooking varieties of apples can be made into apple jelly, but cooking types are best for apple cheese. Apples added to chutneys give flavour and body.

Dried apples

Dried apples come from California, Italy and even China.

The fruit is picked when perfectly ripe and then peeled, cored, and sliced by machine. It is either cut into rings, which are most common, or quarters. In order to keep the pale colour and to prevent fermentation, the fruit is exposed to sulphur fumes before being dried in hot air tunnels, graded and packed. It takes 6–9 lb (2.7–4 kg) fresh apples to produce 1 lb (450 g) dried.

According to one fruit importer, once the apples are reconstituted and cooked, 'the bulk of the sulphur dioxide is dispelled into the air'.

Dried apple rings make delicious, chewy substitutes for sweets.

Soak them for at least six hours in fruit juice to make them soft enough for a fruit salad, or cook and purée them to use as a sweetener in cakes, buns and teacakes.

Crab apples

You can still gather crab apples in the wild or you can grow decorative, but nevertheless edible, varieties in your garden. One of the most popular of garden varieties is **John Downy**. The tiny apples look like large red and yellow marbles and, when cooked make a delicious orangy-pink purée or jelly. When they are roasted, the skins look as though they are really blushing.

Crab apples on cultivated trees hang down the centre of the tree and are easy to pick. Although they look most attractive when just ripe, they are best for cooking when they begin to look translucent. They have a mellow flavour and, if eaten raw, are sweeter than a newly picked Bramley. When cooked, their flavour is richer than that of an ordinary cooking apple with a sherbet, effervescent quality.

Other decorative varieties include **Golden Hornet** which are smaller and bright yellow; and **Oldenham Ensis**, which are deep purple.

To cook crab apples, quarter and core them, but leave the peel on, and treat them as ordinary cooking apples.

Chicken livers with apples and cider

A cheap and easily prepared dish, suitable for any occasion. The livers and apples both have a melting texture.

1½ lb (675 g) chicken livers
2 medium dessert apples
1 oz (25 g) butter
1 large onion, quartered and thinly sliced
½ pint (275 ml) dry cider
2 tablespoons chopped parsley
6 sage leaves, chopped

Cut any stringy pieces or green parts from the chicken livers. Quarter and core the apples, and cut into thin, lengthways slices. Melt the butter in a large frying pan over a high heat. Brown the chicken livers quickly, moving them around all the time. Mix in the apples and onion and continue cooking over a high heat in the same way, for about 5 minutes. The livers should be just cooked through.

Pour in the cider and bring to the boil. Add the parsley and sage, and cook over a medium heat for a further 5 minutes, or until the cider is reduced by about three-quarters.

Serve with brown rice cooked in cider.

Serves 4.

Apple and raisin relish

1 large Bramley apple
1 large onion, finely chopped
2 oz (50 g) raisins
¼ teaspoon ground cloves
3 fl oz (90 ml) cider vinegar

A thick, sweet and sharp relish, good with pork chops, sausages, cold roast pork, ham, pork pies and pâtés.

Quarter, core and finely chop the unpeeled apple. Put into a saucepan with the rest of the ingredients. Cover and cook gently on a low heat for 25 minutes, stirring from time to time, until the mixture is thick and pulpy.

Serves 4.

Cheese scone with apple and rum topping

SCONE BASE

12 oz (350 g) wholemeal flour
½ teaspoon fine sea salt
2 teaspoons ground cinnamon
1 teaspoon bicarbonate of soda
6 oz (175 g) butter, plus extra for greasing
6 oz (175 g) curd cheese
½ pint (275 ml) milk

TOPPING

2 lb (900 g) cooking apples
6 oz (175 g) molasses sugar
4 tablespoons rum

This moist scone with an apple topping can be served warm, with cream, as a dessert, or cold as a sweet teatime treat.

Heat the oven to 350F/180C/gas 4. Put the flour into a bowl with the salt, cinnamon and bicarbonate of soda and rub in the butter. Make a well in the centre. Put in the cheese and pour in the milk. Gradually beat into the flour with a wooden spoon, taking flour from the sides of the well. When the mixture is smooth, it should be the consistency of a slightly stiff cake mixture.

Thickly butter an 8 by 12 inch (20 by 30 cm), 2-inch (5 cm) deep tin. Fill with scone mixture, spread out in an even layer. Peel, core and chop the apples and put into a bowl. Mix in the sugar and rum. Spread apples evenly over the scone mixture.

Bake the scone for 1 hour until the apples are a dark, rich brown and the underneath is firm.

Serves 8.

Apple muffins

Eat these semi-sweet muffins plain, or split and buttered.

4 oz (125 g) dried apple rings
½ pint (275 ml) natural apple juice
8 oz (225 g) wholemeal flour
1 teaspoon bicarbonate of soda
3 tablespoons corn oil
1 egg, beaten
4 oz (125 g) raisins

Put the apple rings into a saucepan with the apple juice. Bring gently to the boil, remove from the heat and leave to soak for 2 hours. Drain, reserving juice. Liquidize the apple rings with ¼ pint (150 ml) of the juice.

Heat the oven to 375F/190C/gas 5. Put the flour and bicarbonate of soda into a bowl and make a well in the centre. Put in the apple purée, oil and egg and gradually beat in flour from the sides of the well to make a thick, smooth batter. Stir in the raisins.

Divide the batter between 16 oiled bun tins and bake for 20 minutes, or until risen and firm. Cool on wire racks.

Makes 16.

Spiced apple jelly

Dried apple rings are easier to use in jellies than fresh apples and they have a soft, slightly chewy, texture.

2 oz (50 g) dried apple rings
1½ pints (850 ml) natural apple juice
3 inch (7.5 cm) cinnamon stick
4 cloves
½ lemon, sliced
1 oz (25 ml) gelatin
4 oz (125 g) low fat soft cheese or curd cheese, or ¼ pint (150 ml) double cream
2 tablespoons chopped walnuts

Finely chop the apple rings and put into a bowl. Put the apple juice into a saucepan with the cinnamon, cloves and lemon slices. Bring to just below boiling point, and keep there for 10 minutes. Strain the apple juice over the dried apple and leave for 4 hours.

Drain dried apple, reserving juice. Put the juice into a saucepan and heat to just below boiling point. Pour ¼ pint (150 ml) of the hot juice into a jug, sprinkle in the gelatin and stir until dissolved. Stir the mixture into the rest of the juice.

Arrange the chopped apple in the bottom of a 1½-pint (850 ml) ring mould. Pour in the apple juice. Cool the jelly to room temperature, and refrigerate for 1½ hours to set.

To turn out, dip the base of the mould into hot water. Invert a plate over the top. Turn the mould and plate over together and give them a quick sideways shake. Remove mould. Beat the cheese to a cream, or whip the cream, and pile into the centre of the mould. Scatter with the chopped nuts.

Serves 6.

APRICOT

PRUNUS ARMENIACA, SYN. ARMENIACA VULGARIS

WITH THEIR MILD flavour, soft texture and downy blushing skins, apricots are a fruit of temperate summers. Their season is a short one, confined to the three hottest months of the year, and their very name is a reminder of hot days with meals out of doors, cold summer desserts and savoury dishes flavoured with fruits and summer herbs. Well, it was, until Cape apricots, which are available from November to January, turned our northern hemisphere year upside down.

The apricot came originally from China where it grew wild around Peking, and was first cultivated about 4,000 years ago. From there it was taken along the old silk routes through India to the Far East and through Armenia and Turkey to the Middle East. The ancient Arabs loved apricots and quickly established them around the Mediterranean, particularly in southern Spain. The Romans took them all over Europe, where they grew them in sheltered villa gardens.

It is said that Crusaders brought apricots back with them from the Holy Land, but these surely must have been dried (or perhaps they were seedlings?) for the delicate fresh fruits would never have stood such a journey. Interest in gardening increased in Tudor times and by 1540 they had become a popular garden tree, grown in the Italian fashion against south-facing walls, and they remained so until the decline of the kitchen garden at the beginning of this century. It was about this time that the fruit received its name of apricot, after the Portuguese *albricoque*, meaning early ripening, because it ripened before the peach.

If old cookery books are anything to go by, apricots were an exceptionally popular fruit in English kitchens from the sixteenth century onwards. They were boiled to a purée with sugar to make small, sweet fruit drops, the original fruit jelly sweets; they were preserved and pickled; made into wines and brandies; and dried for winter use. There were egg white cakes called apricot puffs, apricot tarts and creams, and later fritters and blancmange. Even green fruits which refused to ripen were candied or made into compotes.

From Europe, apricots were taken to the United States, South Africa, New Zealand and Australia. Now they are imported into Britain mainly from Spain, France and Italy in the summer and South Africa in November, December and January.

There are many different varieties, each suited best to the country where it has been developed and grown, and these can be divided into two types, those with loose stones that are mainly sold as dessert fruit, and those with clinging stones used mainly for processing. There are also the small, sweet, Hunza apricots, always sold dried, which originate around Afghanistan and Armenia.

Canned apricots are halved, skinned and cooked, before canning in either sugar syrup or a mixture of fruit juices. They can be used in many recipes calling for cooked apricots.

Nutrition

Apricots are exceptionally high in Vitamin A, are rich in potassium and have a high fibre content.

Buying and storing apricots

Apricots should be firm when you buy them, with no tinge of green. Generally speaking, the deeper the colour the riper the fruit. The skin should look smooth and the fruits should give slightly to the touch. If they are too squashy, then they will be over-ripe and floury tasting.

Slightly under-ripe apricots can be ripened off by leaving them for a day or so in a warm room. Fruit at the peak of ripeness should be used as soon as possible, but will keep in the refrigerator in a polythene bag for up to three days.

To freeze apricots, halve and stone them (the stones give an unpleasant flavour if left in). Freeze them plain if they are going to be kept for under two months, or blanch them and pack into a sugar syrup.

Apricots in the kitchen

To stone apricots, run a small, sharp knife around the groove that circles the fruit. The two halves will come away easily from the stone. The stones can be cracked to provide a few kernels that, when poached with the apricots, will give a mild almond flavour to both the fruit and the syrup.

The skin can be left on the apricots for most recipes but when a smooth appearance is required such as in Apricots in a whip (page 25), skinning is sometimes necessary. Put the apricots into a bowl, pour boiling water over them and leave for about two minutes. You should then be able to peel the skin off easily by hand.

Soft, ripe apricots are delicious served plainly as a dessert fruit either alone or with soft, creamy cheeses. Firmer just-ripe fruit are good for summer salads. Try them sliced with lettuce, cucumber and spring onions in a simple oil and vinegar dressing flavoured with chopped mint. For a first course, fill apricot halves with cream or curd cheese to which you have added herbs, chopped nuts or finely diced ham.

Halved apricots can be put raw into pies, tarts and crumbles before they go into the oven, sprinkled with sugar or covered in honey to draw out the flavour. To cook apricots for other recipes, simmer them gently in a sugar or honey syrup for 10 minutes.

Once cooked, apricots can be puréed by rubbing them through a sieve. Set the purée with gelatin, use it as a pancake filling or turn it into a mousse or soufflé.

Apricots can also be used in cooked savoury dishes. In the Middle East they are added to spicy dishes of lamb and rice or cracked wheat. Diced, they can be added to stuffings for chicken or lamb, and slices can be laid on chops or gammon steaks for the last few minutes of cooking.

Apricots can be preserved in syrup or pickled whole. They make an excellent jam which is invaluable for making sweet glazes and sauces. Commercially, they are made into apricot brandy and apricot liqueur and, if you have enough, you can use them for a country wine.

Dried apricots

Varieties of apricot for drying come from California and other parts of the American Pacific coast; from Australia, South Africa, Turkey and Iran. Ideally they should be picked at the peak of ripeness, and should be as large as possible and unblemished.

About twenty years ago, most of the dried apricots sold in Britain were of the variety known as Persian slab apricots which come from Iran. These have a sharp flavour and are always halved before drying. They are excellent for making jam and wine, but have the wrong flavour for the unsweetened dried fruit compotes and salads that have become popular in recent years.

To meet this demand, whole dried apricots produced mainly in California and South Africa have become more common. These are sweet, plump varieties that have been stoned, but left whole.

After picking and stoning, the fruits are briefly treated with sulphur dioxide so that they keep their orange colour and do not go mouldy. They are sun-dried for several days and the process is then finished off in the shade to prevent them from shrivelling and to keep them moist and sticky.

Some health food shops sell Turkish unsulphured apricots and these are definitely the type to buy if you can find them. They are very dark, very sweet and very sticky. They make a delicious substitute for sweets and are wonderful with nuts. They can also be used in all recipes that call for dried apricots.

Both types of whole dried apricot are better if soaked for a long time before use, rather than being simmered, which can spoil their flavour and texture. Put them into a bowl and cover with natural fruit juice, water or a mixture of the two. Leave for about eight hours. You can then mix them with other dried or fresh fruits to make a fruit salad, or purée them as a base for mousses, cheesecakes and other desserts. No sugar will be necessary.

In baking, dried apricots can be used as a sugar substitute. Use the same weight of dried fruits as you would sugar. Bring them to the boil in fruit juice, soak for four hours and then liquidize them. If you have a microwave oven, it is much quicker. Cook in the juice for four minutes and leave to stand for fifteen minutes.

Hunza apricots come from an area that stretches between Iran and the Hunza valley of Kashmir. They are unsulphured, dried complete with their stones and look like wrinkled, dull brown marbles. When soaked for eight hours in fruit juice, they become soft and succulent and can easily be stoned by slitting the stalk end with a sharp knife and squeezing from the opposite end. They are delicious eaten plain with cream or yoghurt.

Minted chicken with walnuts and apricots

one 3–3½ lb (1.3–1.6 kg) roasting chicken
3 tablespoons chopped mint
3 tablespoons chopped chives
¼ pint (150 ml) natural yoghurt
2 tablespoons olive oil
1 garlic clove, crushed
freshly ground black pepper
3 oz (75 g) shelled walnuts
4 oz (125 g) apricots

Lightly flavoured chicken with a rich coating of walnuts and apricots.

Cut the chicken into 8 pieces. In a dish, mix together the herbs, yoghurt, oil, garlic and pepper. Turn the chicken pieces in the mixture, and leave them to marinate for 8 hours at room temperature.

Coarsely grind the walnuts in a blender or food processor. Stone and chop the apricots. Heat the oven to 400F/200C/gas 6.

Take the chicken pieces out of the marinade, put into a flat, ovenproof dish, and bake for 25 minutes. Mix the walnuts and apricots into any remaining marinade. Spoon over the chicken and continue cooking for a further 20 minutes so that the walnut coating becomes browned. Serve straight from the dish.

Serves 4.

Pickled apricots

1 lb (450 g) small, firm apricots
1 teaspoon cloves
1 teaspoon allspice berries
2 inch (5 cm) cinnamon stick
1 dried red chilli
¾ pint (425 ml) white wine vinegar
9 oz (250 g) honey

A sweet-sour, golden pickle, good with pork, ham, lamb and poultry.

Prick the apricots all over with a fork and pack them into a 900 g (2 lb) preserving jar with the spices.

Put the vinegar and honey into a saucepan and stir over a low heat until the honey dissolves. Bring to the boil, and boil for 10 minutes. Pour enough hot syrup into the jar to cover the apricots and leave to cool completely, topping the level up if necessary.

Cover tightly and leave for two weeks before opening.

Apricots in a whip

1 lb (450 g) apricots
8 fl oz (250 ml) medium sweet white wine
3 tablespoons honey
1 sprig sweet cicely, if available
½ oz (15 g) gelatin
¼ pint (150 ml) double cream
¼ pint (150 ml) natural yoghurt
2 egg whites

The deliciously creamy-tasting base of this light-as-air dessert contrasts well with the juicy apricot halves.

Put the apricots into a bowl, cover with boiling water, and leave for 1–2 minutes. Drain the apricots, skin and halve them and remove the stones.

Put the wine and honey into a saucepan and stir over a low heat until the honey dissolves. Bring to simmering point. Add the apricots and sweet cicely, cover, and cook gently for 10 minutes. Lift out and reserve 12 of the best halves. Remove the sweet cicely. Liquidize the remaining apricot halves with the cooking liquid. Return the purée to the pan and reheat gently. Sprinkle in the gelatin and stir until dissolved. Cool the mixture, but do not let it set.

Whip the cream, then whip in the yoghurt. Whip the egg whites until stiff. Fold first the cream mixture, then the egg whites into the purée.

Pour the mixture into an 8-inch (20 cm) diameter, 2-inch (5 cm) deep dish. Leave in a cool place until almost set. Carefully place the remaining apricot halves on top, cut side down, so that they half sink into the whip. Leave to set completely.

Serves 4–6.

Crunchy apricot layer

8 oz (225 g) dried whole apricots
½ pint (275 ml) natural orange juice
4 oz (125 g) quark or other low fat soft cheese
4 tablespoons natural yoghurt or soured cream
3 oz (75 g) porridge oats
2 tablespoons wheatgerm
1 oz (25 g) sunflower seeds
1 oz (25 g) desiccated coconut
4 tablespoons sunflower oil

A creamy, layered dessert with a crunchy topping.

Either soak the apricots in the orange juice for 8 hours, or put into a saucepan with the juice, bring to the boil, remove from heat and leave for 4 hours. Drain (the juice can be used again), and purée. Add the quark and yoghurt or soured cream, and mix well.

Heat the oven to 350F/180C/gas 4. Mix together the oats, wheatgerm, sunflower seeds, coconut and oil. Spread on a baking sheet and bake for 15 minutes or until golden. Leave on the tray until they quite cold and crisp.

Put one-third of the oat mixture in an even layer in the bottom of a deep soufflé dish. Put in half the apricots, another third of the oats, the remaining apricots, and top with the remaining oats. Chill for at least 1 hour before serving.

Serves 4–6.

Hunza apricots in red wine jelly

8 oz (225 g) hunza apricots
¾ pint (425 ml) natural orange or apple juice
½ pint (275 ml) dry red wine
2 inch (5 cm) cinnamon stick
1 blade mace
2 tablespoons honey
½ oz (15 g) gelatin; or agar-agar or other vegetarian gelling agent to set 1 pint (575 ml) liquid

Hunza apricots are so good that they need only the simplest of recipes. Serve this jelly with single cream.

Soak the apricots in the fruit juice for 8 hours. Drain, stone and place in a serving dish. Measure the liquid and if necessary make up to ½ pint (275 ml) with more juice.

Put the juice, wine, spices and honey into a saucepan. Bring to simmering point and simmer for 10 minutes. Remove the spices. Sprinkle in the gelatin or other setting agent and stir until dissolved.

Pour the jelly over the apricots and put it into a cool place or the refrigerator to set.

Serves 6–8.

Lemon and apricot cake

9 oz (250 g) dried, whole apricots
¾ pint (425 ml) natural orange or apple juice
6 oz (175 g) wholemeal flour
1 teaspoon bicarbonate of soda
grated rind of 2 lemons
3 fl oz (90 ml) corn oil, plus extra for greasing
3 eggs, beaten
8 oz (225 g) curd cheese
4 tablespoons no-sugar-added apricot jam
1 oz (25 g) candied peel, in one piece
candied angelica

A pretty cake for a special occasion. The same apricot filling can be used in other cake recipes.

Put the apricots into a saucepan with the juice, bring to the boil, remove from the heat and leave to soak for 4 hours. Liquidize two-thirds of them with ½ pint (275 ml) of the juice.

Heat the oven to 350F/180C/gas 4. Put the flour, bicarbonate of soda and the rind of 1 lemon into a bowl. Make a well in the centre. Pour in the liquidized apricots, oil and eggs and gradually beat in the flour from the sides of the well to make a thick batter. Grease two 7-inch (18 cm) diameter cake tins and divide the batter between them. Bake the cakes for 20 minutes or until firm, and a skewer stuck into the centre comes out clean. Turn them on to wire racks to cool.

Liquidize the remaining apricots with 3 tablespoons of the juice. Beat the curd cheese to a cream and beat in the remaining lemon rind. Spread half the cheese on the underside of one and top with all the liquidized apricots. Spread the remaining cheese on the top of the other cake and decorate with strips of candied peel and angelica. Finally, sandwich the two cakes together. (Assembling the cake in this order prevents the apricots from being squeezed out as the cake is decorated.)

Serves 8.

BABACO

CARICA PENTAGONA

'SOMETHING NEW UNDER the sun', is how the Guernsey Growers Co-Operative Ltd describe this amazing fruit. It is certainly new to British shops, where it appeared only during the late 1980s, but it grew quietly by itself in an Ecuadorian forest for many long years before that.

The babaco is a natural hybrid of two types of mountain papaya. It was introduced commercially to New Zealand and later Australia in the early 1970s. It is now grown outdoors near Rome and under glass on Guernsey. The trees, as you might expect, have a tropical appearance, topped with umbrellas of large leaves, and with clusters of thirty or more dull green, ripening fruits hanging down all round the bark.

The babaco looks rather like an elongated green pepper, slightly wider, at least 10–12 inches (25–30 cm) long and pointed at the bottom. The soft, shiny, thin skin can be any colour from green to bright yellow. Babaco are picked when they are under-ripe and are mostly green with a few yellow patches. At this stage they have a high acidity and very little flavour and should definitely be left for a while. When the fruit reach the shops they should be about 25 per cent yellow. The flavour will still be acid, but the diced flesh can be added to curries and other savoury dishes. By the time the fruit is 95 per cent yellow it is suitable for use in salads, savoury dishes and for cooking to make desserts. Only when the babaco is completely yellow and has developed a sherbet, sweet scent is it be suitable for eating raw.

Cutting a babaco crossways produces an attractive, curved, star shape with a round hole in the centre. The flesh is pale green or yellow-green, depending on the stage of ripeness, and the texture is rather like a soft melon and very juicy. The flavour also depends on the ripeness: when under-ripe it is freshly acid, rather like a cross between a lemon and a melon, with a fresh hint of sherbet and spice. As it ripens the acidity gradually diminishes and a hint of strawberry creeps in.

Nutrition

The babaco is low in calories and high in Vitamins A and C and minerals. It also contains the enzyme papain, which helps to digest meat.

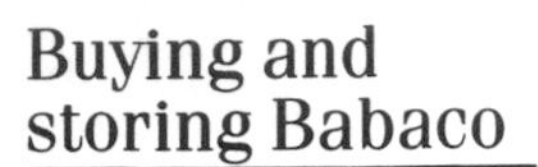

Buying and storing Babaco

Babaco can be stored in a polythene bag in the refrigerator for up to a week. To ripen, leave the fruit in a cool, dark place until it is ready. You can use some of the fruit at one stage of ripening, leaving the rest in a cool, dark place with the cut end covered in cling film and standing on a plate, to ripen off to the next stage.

Babaco in the kitchen

Almost every part of a babaco is edible, including the very thin, soft skin. Wash the fruit and slice off the stalk end and the tip of the point at the bottom. When slicing a perfectly ripe fruit, catch as much of the juice as you can. It is good added to the syrup for a fruit salad.

Diced, under-ripe babaco can be added sparingly to curries, to give a fresh, spicy flavour. It can also be added to fried or sautéed meats and fish to make an unusual relish. Add slices to stir-fried dishes and to fried rice.

Slices of ripe babaco can be overlapped on a plate, given a creamy savoury dressing made with soured cream and herbs, and served as a first course. Serve them instead of lemon wedges with smoked salmon or trout, or with thinly sliced cold cooked meats.

Ripe babaco can also be eaten as a dessert. If you have never tried the fruit before, serve it quite plainly at first. Slice it, and layer the slices in a dish, sprinkled with dark Muscovado sugar. When you have sampled its flavour, add other ingredients to taste such as freshly squeezed orange or lime juice, or a dash of liqueur. Soaked in sugar syrup mixed with its own juice, babaco makes an interesting addition to a fruit salad. Slices can be baked with sweet wine and sugar, and the whole fruit can be filled with a sweet stuffing, wrapped in foil and baked at 375F/190C/gas 5 for 20 minutes.

To make a refreshing drink, remove the skin and liquidize the flesh with sugar to taste and ice cubes.

Turkey strips with babaco

Babaco adds a freshness to this rich dish of turkey.

1½ lb (675 g) boneless turkey breasts
8 slices babaco ¼ inch (6 mm) thick
1 oz (25 g) butter
1 medium onion, finely chopped
½ pint (275 ml) stock
4 tablespoons fromage blanc

Cut the turkey breasts into ½ inch (1.3 cm) wide diagonal strips. Cut each slice of babaco into quarters and remove the seeds. Melt the butter in a large frying pan on a high heat. Brown the turkey strips all over, stirring. Lower the heat, add the onion and cook it until golden brown and the turkey strips are cooked through, stirring frequently. Remove the turkey and onion and keep warm. Add the babaco, fry quickly on both sides and remove.

Raise the heat, pour in the stock, and reduce to half its volume. Take the pan from the heat and stir in the fromage blanc.

Spoon the sauce on to four dinner plates. Place the turkey and onion on top and garnish with the babaco.

Serves 4.

Sweet stir-fried babaco

1 babaco
½ oz (15 g) butter
2 tablespoons honey
2 pieces preserved stem ginger, chopped

A quick and easy dessert with a warming, spicy flavour.

Slice the babaco and cut it into ¾-inch (2 cm) dice. Melt the butter in a large frying pan on a high heat. Put in the babaco and stir-fry it quickly for 30 seconds so it just heats through. Add the honey and ginger, boil up the juices and serve immediately in small dishes.

Serves 4.

BANANA

MUSA SAPIENTUM

BANANAS ARE ONE of nature's convenience foods. Easy to carry, store and eat, sweet and creamy in texture and flavour, they can be turned instantly into all manner of dishes from curries to baby food. Bananas are a good old stand-by, bought every week along with the apples and the potatoes. Yet until the introduction of the steam ships at the very end of the nineteenth century, they were a rare luxury.

Bananas are an ancient fruit, probably one of the first to have been gathered and cultivated. They came originally from India and southern Asia and were grown in the Indus valley some 5,000 years ago. They were also grown in the Middle East and legend has it that the serpent in the story of the Garden of Eden hid in a banana bush and Adam and Eve covered themselves with banana leaves instead of the smaller ones of the fig. From the Middle East, bananas were taken to Africa where they were discovered by Portuguese explorers in the fifteenth century. This hastened their spread throughout the tropical world, to the Canary Islands, the West Indies, tropical America and Hawaii.

The first bunch of bananas to reach Britain arrived in 1633. They had travelled from Bermuda and were put up for display in the herbalist's shop of Thomas Johnson in Snow Hill, London. What state they were in and whether they were edible is not known! For the next 200 years, however, bananas remained rare as there was no ship fast enough to enable them to reach port in good condition. As soon as steam ships came into operation, they were shipped in from the Canary Islands and, with the advent of refrigerated holds in 1901, from the West Indies.

Bananas grow in all warm, windless, humid tropics. They appear on the tree in upward growing hands, with about twelve bananas to each hand and up to the same number of hands clustered together to make a bunch. The 'fingers' of the hand are the small bananas, which are bright green with white, clove-shape flowers on the ends. A large red bulb hangs down from the centre of the bunch which is eaten locally as a vegetable. The bunches are cut when the bananas have reached full size but are still bright green. They are stored and shipped at temperatures of 53–56f (12–13C) and not ripened off until they reach their destination. So we, in the more temperate countries, never get the chance to eat a sun-ripened banana. If we did, we would probably never eat an imported one again.

Many different varieties are grown, for various uses. The larger ones, known as plantains, are sold green and most often eaten as a vegetable. Some are cultivated for fibre with which to make ropes, others because they can be distilled into an alcoholic drink, and others for the large leaves which are used to wrap food while it is being cooked.

Several unusual, recognizable varieties are available in Britain, but you may have to hunt round West Indian and Indian shops to find them. Ladies' Fingers is the sweetest variety of the banana as we know it. The fruits are bright yellow, thin-skinned, short and fat, with white, floury textured flesh. Baby bananas are about 2 inches (5 cm) long with sweet, creamy flesh. There are green cooking bananas which have a mild flavour and are always cooked as a vegetable and red bananas with a deep, maroon-red skin and pink flesh which is soft, sticky and very sweet.

Nutrition

Bananas, like all yellow fruits, are high in Vitamin A. They also contain significant amounts of B Vitamins and some Vitamin C. They are rich in minerals, particularly potassium, but their calorific content is higher than that of most fruits. They are easy to eat and digest and are an ideal first food for babies and young children, who may well like their flavour better than the sharper kinds of fruits.

Buying and storing bananas

If you buy slightly under-ripe bananas, make sure that the skins are a smooth yellow all over with no blemishes, and no brown shading coming from beneath the skin, which may mean that the fruit will be brown before it is fully ripe. If you would prefer ripe bananas and are going to eat them straight away, buy those with firm skins, speckled black or brown. If they are black or dark brown all over they will be excellent for making banana cakes, but the texture will be too floury for them to be pleasant eaten raw.

Store bananas in a cool, dark larder. Under-ripe ones should ripen within the week.

Bananas in the kitchen

Bananas need little preparation, apart from peeling, slicing and, for some dishes, puréeing or sieving. If they are to be sliced and left for some time, sprinkle with a little lemon juice to prevent them from turning brown. Add lemon juice to the purée for the same reason.

Bananas are used most imaginatively in their countries of origin. In the Caribbean they are fried, baked in their skins in the ashes of barbecues, flamed in rum, used as fillings for pancakes and sweet omelettes, made with rum and lime juice into a cocktail known as a banana daiquiri, and baked with pecan nuts and raisins into banana bread which is served, not only with sweet dishes, but with blood puddings, sausages and lime marinated pork. Banana leaves are made into envelopes filled with a mixture of cornmeal, chopped meat, raisins and coconut.

There are countless varieties of bananas in India, where they are more often used as a vegetable than as a dessert. Green bananas are added to vegetable curry, and the small yellow and black varieties stuffed with a sweet-sour mixture of coconut, tamarind juice, sugar and spices and baked.

From West Africa come banana fritters, and a banana gin known as waragi is made in Uganda. In East Africa bananas and plantains are served as a salad with mayonnaise, or puréed and mixed with groundnuts to make cakes. Bananas are fried with cinnamon, grilled with slices of orange, puréed and whipped with eggs into a custard and made into a strong banana wine.

A cheap dessert in Brazilian households is mashed banana mixed with half its volume of Muscovado sugar, freshly grated ginger, ground cloves and cinnamon all mixed and cooked gently over a low fire for a long time. Gradually the sugar caramelises and the mixture becomes very dark. It is set in a loaf shape and served cold and sliced. In Ecuador, banana flour is a staple food made into breads and pastries and said to be more digestible than wheat flour.

Back home we can make banana custard; whip a banana with yoghurt and fruit juice to make a substantial breakfast-time drink; mash bananas and top them with creamy yoghurt and blobs of home made jam;

make them into sandwiches or use the purée as the base for a soufflé.

Try adding diced banana to savoury omelettes and salads, or mash the flesh and mix it with cider vinegar as an unusual salad dressing.

Dried bananas

Dried bananas are delicious: dark, sticky, slightly chewy and full of flavour. They make a nourishing snack and an excellent substitute for sweets. Most of those sold in Britain come from Ecuador and other South American countries, and at times they can be scarce since they are only produced when there are too many fresh bananas to export. No chemicals are used in their preparation. They are sun-ripened, sun-dried in their skins and then peeled before packing.

Banana chips

Banana chips have been specially dried to reduce their moisture content to less than 5 per cent and can be bought on their own or in mixtures of fruits and nuts known as trail mixes. They are most often eaten as a snack, but can be fried in oil and used as a garnish for curries and savoury rice dishes.

Banana and prawn salad

This salad, based on cottage cheese, has a delightful combination of flavours and textures. Serve it as a main course.

1½ lb (675 g) cottage cheese
3 tablespoons tomato purée
2 ripe avocados
2 firm bananas
1 box mustard and cress
6 oz (175 g) shelled prawns

Put the cheese into a bowl and mix the tomato purée in well to give an even pink colour. Peel, stone and dice the avocados. Peel and slice the bananas. Mix into the cheese.

Pile the salad on to a serving plate and garnish with the mustard and cress and prawns.

Serves 4.

Banana and sultana cake

3 ripe bananas
4 oz (125 g) sultanas
6 oz (175 g) vegetable margarine, plus extra for greasing
6 oz (175 g) wholemeal flour
2 teaspoons baking powder
1 teaspoon ground mixed spice
2 eggs, beaten

Little or no sugar is needed in cakes made with very ripe bananas. This one is very moist with a slightly 'puddingy' texture. It can be cooled and eaten like a cake, or served warm as a dessert. It keeps best wrapped in cling film and refrigerated.

Heat the oven to 350F/180C/gas 4. Grease an 8-inch (20 cm) diameter cake tin. Liquidize the bananas or mash and sieve them. Put the sultanas into a small saucepan and just cover them with water. Bring slowly to the boil, simmer for 2 minutes and remove from the heat. Drain, reserving the liquid.

Cream the margarine and gradually beat in the bananas. Mix the flour with the baking powder and mixed spice. Beat it into the margarine and the bananas. Beat in the eggs and 2 tablespoons of the sultana liquid. Mix in the sultanas.

Put the mixture into the prepared tin and bake for 30 minutes, or until brown and firm. Cool the cake in the tin for 5 minutes and turn it on to a wire rack to cool.

BILBERRY AND BLUEBERRY

VACCINIUM SPECIES

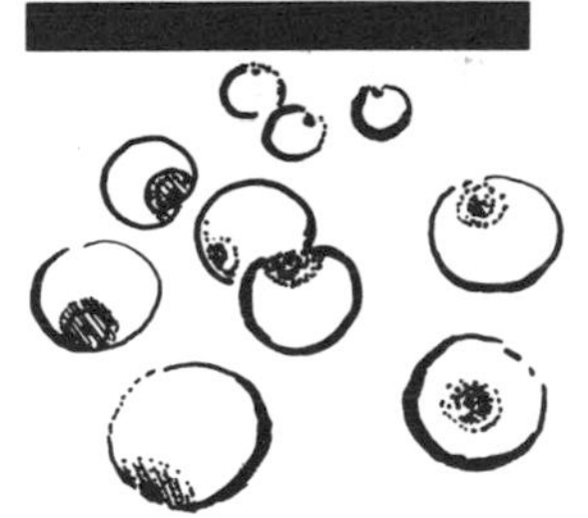

BILBERRY

BILBERRIES AND BLUEBERRIES are both small, dark berries that grow wild in Britain, Europe and the United States. Closely related, they are shrubby members of the heather family and flourish on barren heaths and moorlands.

Bilberries (*V. myrtillus*) are the European species. They are very tiny, about ⅜ inch (1 cm) at the most in diameter, and a dark bluish black. They have never featured greatly in our national cuisine, nor been exploited commercially, although occasionally they have been transplanted into gardens.

The name given in these rich, sharp-tasting berries has varied: blaeberry because they are blue; whinberry because they taste like wine; and hurtleberry, whortleberry or just hurts, because they are the colour of bruises.

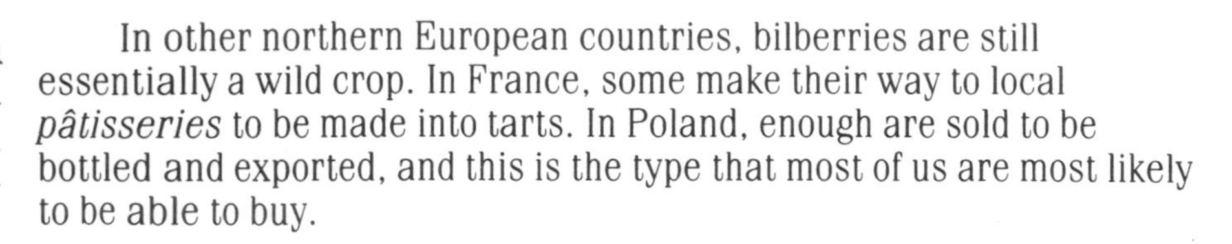

In other northern European countries, bilberries are still essentially a wild crop. In France, some make their way to local *pâtisseries* to be made into tarts. In Poland, enough are sold to be bottled and exported, and this is the type that most of us are most likely to be able to buy.

Nutrition

Bilberries are rich in Vitamin A and potassium, and also contain significant amounts of Vitamin C.

Picking and storing bilberries

Being so small, bilberries are difficult to pick and will stain your fingers, and anything else they touch, a deep purple. Pick them over carefully to remove any leaves or twigs, and use them as soon as possible. Wild fruits don't store as well as cultivated ones.

Bilberries in the kitchen

In Devon, raw bilberries served with sugar and clotted cream were a late summer luxury. They have also been put into tarts and crumbles, either alone or mixed with apples. In France, the cooked fruits, their juices thickened with cornflour or arrowroot, are put into tarts of rich pastry on a *crème pâtissière* base. You can make bilberry sorbet and bilberry mousse, they make good jam and a dark, rich country wine, and their juice diluted with soda water makes a refreshing drink.

Bilberries need very little water when you cook them. Put them into a saucepan with four tablespoons water and 4 oz (125 g) sugar or honey per pound (450 g). Cover, place on a low heat and within fifteen minutes they will be soft and juicy.

BLUEBERRY

Blueberries were gathered by the American Indians who used them fresh and dried. They were quickly discovered by the first settlers and have been prized ever since. Unlike the bilberry, many cultivated varieties have been developed.

Blueberries are generally slightly larger than bilberries, and are usually blue-black with a soft bloom and a mild, sweet, non-acid flavour, rather like that of a gooseberry but without the sharpness. There are many different varieties, some growing in moorland, others in damp, swampy land, and some more adaptable to cultivation. Another name for some of the varieties is huckleberry.

Blueberry plants can now be bought from seedsmen to grow in British gardens. Fresh blueberries are also imported from the United States. They are mostly available in the autumn, but can be bought from specialist shops at other times of the year.

Nutrition

Like bilberries, blueberries are high in potassium and Vitamins A and C.

Buying and storing blueberries

Blueberries are usually bought packed in plastic baskets which keep them from squashing. Their skins should look smooth, and bloom fresh, and the berries should not be too soft. Blueberries will keep for up to a week if they are refrigerated immediately.

Blueberries in the kitchen

Blueberries are one of the few soft fruits that can be eaten raw without sugar. They are delicious with creamy yoghurts and soured cream. Even when you cook them, there is no need to add sugar, simply stewing them gently with four tablespoons of water will make them soft and juicy. Their flavour when cooked, however, can be a little bland, so freshen it with the juice of half a lemon per pound (450 g) of fruit, plus two tablespoons of sugar to counteract the sharpness.

Cooked blueberries can be piled over waffles, used to fill pancakes and used as a basis for sorbets, mousses and fruit fools. Rubbed through a sieve to a purée and then thickened with arrowroot, they make a deep purply-blue sauce which looks delicious spooned over ice-creams or used as a glaze over sharper fruits such as raspberries and strawberries.

Pies, crumbles, steamed puddings and cobbler dishes all suit blueberries. A blueberry pie recommended by Fanny Farmer, the American equivalent of Mrs Beeton, consists of blueberries mixed with sugar and molasses and a pinch of salt, put into an open pastry shell and dredged with flour before baking.

Sweet bilberry soup

1 lb (450 g) bilberries
2 oz (50 g) sugar
1½ pints (850 ml) water
½ teaspoon ground cinnamon
½ tablespoon chopped sweet cicely
½ tablespoon cornflour
¼ pint (150 ml) double cream

Because I was unable to find fresh bilberries when I was writing this book, I have taken this recipe from a book called *Pick, Cook and Brew* by Suzanne Beadell, published by Pelham Books Ltd, 1973.

This is not a soup for the beginning of the meal, but a sweet one to be served as a dessert.

Put the bilberries into a saucepan with the sugar, water, cinnamon and sweet cicely, bring to the boil and simmer for 3–4 minutes or until soft. Sieve or liquidize the bilberries with the juices.

Put the cornflour into a bowl, mix in 3 fl oz (90 ml) of the liquid and return the rest to the saucepan. Warm on a medium heat and stir in the cornflour mixture. Bring the soup to the boil, stirring, and boil until it is clear.

Serve hot or cold, with the cream swirled over the top.

Serves 6.

Blueberry and almond tart

shortcrust pastry made with 4 oz (125 g) wholemeal flour
12 oz (350 g) blueberries
1 tablespoon chopped mint
juice ½ lemon
2 tablespoons clear honey

TOPPING
4 oz (125 g) butter, softened
4 oz (125 g) honey
2 oz (50 g) ground almonds
4 oz (125 g) wholemeal flour
1 teaspoon bicarbonate of soda
grated rind ½ lemon
2 eggs, beaten

This is a variation of an English bakewell tart. The blueberries become soft and plump under a rich, almondy cake mixture.

Heat the oven to 375F/190C/gas 5. Use the pastry to line an 8-inch (20 cm) diameter tart tin. Put in the blueberries and scatter the mint and lemon juice over. Spoon the honey over the top.

Cream the butter with the honey and beat in the almonds. Mix the flour with the bicarbonate of soda and lemon rind and beat them into the butter mixture alternately with the eggs. Spoon the mixture over the blueberries.

Bake the tart for 30–35 minutes or until a skewer inserted in the centre comes out clean. Serve warm.

Serves 4–6.

Blueberry muffins

8 oz (225 g) wholemeal flour
½ teaspoon fine sea salt
½ pint (275 ml) milk
3 oz (75 g) butter
1 oz (25 g) fresh or ½ oz (15 g) dried yeast
2 tablespoons clear honey
1 egg, beaten
10 oz (300 g) blueberries
soured cream for serving

Serve these light, semi-sweet muffins brimming over with dark purple fruits.

Put the flour and salt into a bowl. Warm the milk slightly and add 1 oz (25 g) of the butter. Stir until it melts. Stir in the yeast. If you are using dried yeast, add a teaspoon of honey. Leave the fresh yeast for 5 minutes, the dried for 15 minutes, or until frothy.

Make a well in the flour. Add the egg and gradually beat in flour from the sides of the well. Add the honey and gradually beat in the milk and yeast mixture to make a thick batter. Leave the batter in a warm place for an hour, by which time bubbles should be appearing on the surface. Mix in 6 oz (175 g) of the blueberries.

While the muffin mixture is rising, put the remaining blueberries into a saucepan with 4 tablespoons water. Cover, and set on a low heat. Bring them gently to the boil and simmer for 10 minutes, or until soft and juicy. Take from the heat and keep warm.

Use remaining butter to grease a griddle or a heavy frying pan and some muffin rings. Set the griddle on a low to medium heat. Put the muffin rings on to the griddle and half fill with the batter. Cook the muffins until the underside is browned and the top just set. Remove the rings, turn the muffins, and brown the other side. Remove the muffins, keep warm and cook the rest in the same way.

To serve, top each muffin with cooked blueberries and a large spoonful of soured cream.

Any muffins not eaten straightaway can be cooled, stored in a polythene bag, and reheated later under the grill or in a microwave oven.

Makes 10.

BLACKBERRY, DEWBERRY AND CLOUDBERRY

RUBUS SPECIES

BLACKBERRY

If someone were to ask me 'What is your favourite fruit?', I should probably say the blackberry. The plant is a generous one, despite its thorns, and the ripe fruit are versatile, with a flavour reminiscent of hot country lanes in late summer and chilly autumn evenings all rolled into one. Blackberries are the most abundant and most loved of all wild fruits.

The blackberry has always been first and foremost a wild fruit, native to Britain, Europe and the United States. It can also now be found in Australia, New Zealand and South Africa, having probably been taken there by the first white settlers. Blackberries were gathered in the Bronze Age and have been plentiful ever since, rambling over wastelands and heaths.

Blackberries were often the only fresh fruit available to country people and so were put to the fullest use. Not only were they made into numerous sweet dishes, they were added to bread and cakes as a substitute for currants, used in countless remedies and even made into a dye for lilac stockings. Their leaves were used as a substitute for tea. They have some wonderful country names such as black-blegs, black-spice, doctor's medicine, gatter berry and mooches, all used in different localities.

There are many different varieties of blackberry. Some are commercially grown by nurserymen to produce larger juicier fruits, but who really wants to pay for blackberries when picking them is so enjoyable?

Nutrition

The anti-scorbutic (scurvy prevention) properties of blackberries were recognized a long time ago, and they are indeed a rich source of Vitamin C and also of potassium.

Picking, buying and storing blackberries

Take a curved stick to pull the bramble arches towards you and wear wellington boots to prevent your feet and legs from scratches. Put your blackberries into a flat, open basket or plastic box rather than a carrier bag, to prevent them from becoming squashed. If a blackberry is so soft that it squashes in your fingers, eat it – it will be delicious. Do not put it with the others or it will make them soft as well. Pick only fruits that are black all over and succulent-looking. Hard, red ones are of no use at all.

When buying blackberries, make sure they look fresh and bright and ripe but firm.

Blackberries will keep for a day in a cool place and two days in the refrigerator. The easiest way to freeze them is to spread them on trays until hard, then pack them 8 oz (225 g) at a time into polythene bags.

Blackberries in the kitchen

The sweetest, juiciest blackberries grow on the very tips of the stems and are the first to ripen. These are the ones for eating raw, with brown sugar and cream.

Blackberries and apples are almost inseparable in many people's minds, a marriage brought about originally through necessity. Early ripening apples were scarce and had to be bought. Blackberries were free, and would pad them out admirably. Nowadays we often put fewer blackberries than apples into pies, but originally this was the other way round. You can make blackberry and apple pies, crumbles, turnovers, cakes and cobblers; or cook and purée them together for mousses and fruit fools.

You can sieve the cooked fruits and thicken them with arrowroot to make a rich purple, cold fruit soup. Many a country larder has stores of blackberry jam and jelly laid down for the winter, and the berries will also produce a delicious, rich red wine.

You can add blackberries to salads of poultry, cook them with meat, and make them into pickles and savoury sauces.

DEWBERRY

Dewberries are wild fruits, closely related to the blackberry and similar in appearance. They are most common in eastern England and are generally smaller than blackberries, black, but covered in a fine bloom and with fewer segments. If you can compare them, you will find that they have a more delicate flavour.

CLOUDBERRY

The cloudberry is a low-growing plant related to the blackberry which grows on high ground in Scotland, Scandinavia, North America and Canada. It is also called the Arctic cloudberry, yellowberry or baked apple berry.

Those growing in North America and Canada are a bright orange-red and taste like baked apples when they are ripe. The Scandinavian type, which can also be found in Scotland, is like an orange-yellow blackberry. The pips are large and the flavour is rather like caramel. It is an excellent source of Vitamin C. Should you ever come across any cloudberries, treat them like blackberries.

Pigeon breasts with blackberry sauce

breasts of four pigeons, each in two pieces
1 oz (25 g) butter
1 medium onion, finely chopped
7 fl oz (200 ml) stock, ideally made from the pigeon carcasses
7 fl oz (200 ml) dry red wine
2 tablespoons red wine vinegar
8 oz (225 g) blackberries
bouquet of sage and thyme

Blackberries give a savoury sauce just the right touch of sharpness to go with rich meats.

Skin the pigeon breasts. Melt the butter in a frying pan on a high heat. Brown the pigeon breasts well on both sides (about 5 minutes). Remove, and keep warm. Pour off all but a thin film of fat from the pan and replace on a medium heat. Add the onion and stir it until browned. Pour in the stock, wine and wine vinegar and bring to the boil. Put in 6 oz (175 g) of the blackberries and the bouquet garni. Boil gently until the liquid has reduced by half. Strain the contents of the pan, pressing down hard on the blackberries and onion.

Return the sauce to the cleaned pan and simmer it for 2 minutes. Cut the pigeon breasts into very thin slices. They should be very tender but pink in the middle. Spoon a portion of the sauce on to each of four plates. Arrange the slices of pigeon breast on the sauce and scatter the blackberries over the top.

Serves 4.

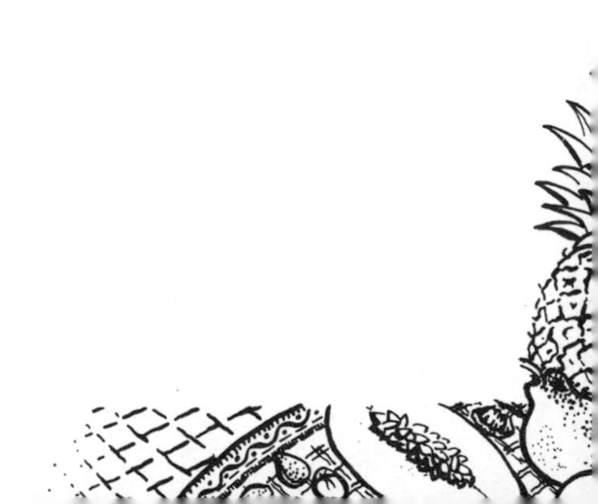

Blackberry and apple curd

12 oz (350 g) cooking apples
8 oz (225 g) blackberries
2 tablespoons clear honey
2 eggs, beaten
¼ pint (150 ml) thick, full cream natural yoghurt
3 fl oz (90 ml) double cream
¼ nutmeg, grated

The eggs, yoghurt and cream in this simple dessert make a creamy textured curd with the warm autumn flavour of blackberries.

Heat the oven to 400F/200C/gas 6. Peel and chop the apples. Mix them with the blackberries and honey. Place in an 8 inch (20 cm) diameter 2 inch (5 cm) deep tart dish.

Gradually beat the eggs into the yoghurt. Beat in the cream and then the nutmeg. Pour the mixture over the blackberries and apples.

Bake for 20 minutes, or until the curd is set and beginning to brown on top. Serve warm.

Serves 4–6.

CAPE GOOSEBERRY

PHYSALIS PERUVIANA, PHYSALIS PERUVIANA EDULIS AND OTHER SPECIES

CAPE GOOSEBERRIES ARE nature's perfect garnish. They are small, golden coloured berries, about ⅝ inch (1.5 cm) in diameter, encased in a thin Chinese lantern that can be peeled back to give the fruit wings. Their flavour is akin to tomato and yet there is a mellow, gooseberry-like quality as well. They are neither sweet, nor sharp, but fresh and slightly bitter.

Cape gooseberries are also called by their Latin name of physalis besides being known as golden berries, Andean cherry, cherry tomato, winter cherry and Chinese lantern. They are closely related to the Chinese lantern plants that are grown in Britain to provide winter flower decorations, and also to tomatoes.

The Cape gooseberry came originally from Peru, Mexico and other parts of South America and has been cultivated for over 200 years in South Africa (hence the name), and in France and around the Mediterranean since the late eighteenth century. There are about 100 different varieties, many of which are edible, and plants are now sold that will successfully fruit in British gardens.

Not all varieties look or taste the same. Some have larger purple fruits, and the berries of the Mexican ground berry, or tomatillo as it is often called, are large and completely stuck to the outer case, with a sticky texture and mild flavour.

Nutrition

Cape gooseberries are high in Vitamins A and C, phosphorus and calcium.

Buying and sorting Cape gooseberries

Cape gooseberries are sold still encased in their papery calyx which protects them and keeps them fresh. Ideally, they should be loosely packed into small plastic baskets. Kept in a cool place, with the calyx intact, the fruit should keep for up to three weeks. If the weather is hot, store them in the refrigerator for the same amount of time.

If you grow your own fruits you can freeze them whole after first removing the calyx, or you can cook them to a sweetened purée and freeze it in small pots.

Cape gooseberries in the kitchen

To make an instant garnish for cold meats, roast meats or any kind of dessert, carefully tear or snip the papery case along its natural divisions. Fold the separate pieces back and give them a gentle twist.

As an after-dinner treat, Cape gooseberries can be dipped into a fondant icing made with a lightly whipped egg white, a teaspoon of lemon juice and 8 oz (225 g) icing sugar and then left to dry on greaseproof paper. They look extremely attractive among other confectionery and the contrast between the bitter-sweet fruit and the sugary icing is superb. These coated fruits can also be used as cake decorations.

Sliced or whole, Cape gooseberries make interesting additions to salads, particularly to those made with rice or burghul wheat. They can also be sliced and set in aspic jellies. Simmered gently in a light honey syrup with a strip of lemon rind, they make a delicious compote which can be served as it is or puréed for a cake filling. If you have enough, you can make a rich golden jam.

In Mexico, tomatillos are added to the avocado dip known as guacamole and in India they are an ingredient in chutneys.

Haricot bean salad with cape gooseberries

8 oz (225 g) haricot beans
½ oz (15 g) parsley, finely chopped
1 egg yolk
½ teaspoon mustard powder
4 fl oz (125 ml) sunflower oil
4 tablespoons white wine vinegar
24 cape gooseberries
1 green pepper
¼ teaspoon cayenne pepper

Cape gooseberries, with their hint of tomato, go very well with savoury ingredients. Diced cold chicken or turkey can be given the same dressing and relish.

Soak the beans for 6 hours and cook until soft, about 1½ hours. Drain, cool, and mix with the parsley.

Put the egg yolk into a bowl and beat in the mustard powder. Drop by drop, beat in 2 tablespoons of the oil, and then 2 teaspoons of the vinegar. Gradually beat in the remaining oil and then up to 1 tablespoon of the vinegar to taste.

Chop 6 of the Cape gooseberries and put them into a liquidizer with the dressing. Blend until the dressing is smooth.

Finely chop 10 more of the Cape gooseberries and core, seed and finely chop the pepper. Mix these together, adding 2 tablespoons of the vinegar and the cayenne pepper.

Put the beans and parsley on to a large serving plate. Spoon the dressing down the centre and put the pepper relish round the edge. Arrange the remaining Cape gooseberries, whole, on top.

Serves 4.

Chocolate berry fondants

16 Cape gooseberries
4 oz (125 g) ground almonds
1 tablespoon cocoa powder
4 tablespoons honey
2 oz (50 g) desiccated coconut

Instead of coating Cape gooseberries with fondant icing, use this soft, chocolate-flavoured mixture that contrasts beautifully with the fresh fruits. Serve them as after-dinner *petit fours*.

Fold back the leaves on the fruits and twist them slightly to keep them back.

Put the almonds and cocoa powder into a bowl and mix in the honey to make a firm paste. With slightly dampened hands, divide the mixture into 16 portions. Flatten each one slightly and mould it round a fruit. Roll the covered fruits in the desiccated coconut.

Eat within 12 hours of covering so that the fruits stay fresh and firm.

Makes 16.

CARAMBOLA

AVERRHOA CARAMBOLA

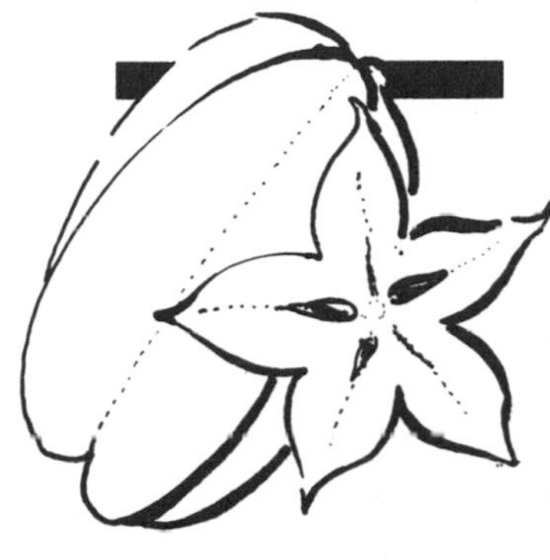

THE CARAMBOLA, or star fruit as it is often called, has been rapidly accepted into British kitchens over the last two years. On first looking at the fruit, it is not particularly remarkable, being about 3–5 inches (7.5–12.5 cm) long and 1½ inches (3 cm) wide; oval, deeply ribbed and a greeny yellow colour. It does, however, have a delicious sweet, fresh scent, but only when you cut it across will you discover the secret of its success. Every slice is in the shape of a perfect, five-pointed star. The carambola tastes good, too. It has a freshening, enlivening effect on the palate and its name comes from the Sanskrit *Karamara*, meaning food appetizer.

The origin of the carambola is uncertain, but it most probably came from Indonesia or Malaysia. It is grown widely in China, India, south-east Asia and Israel, and also in the tropical areas of Australia and the United States, including Hawaii and South America. It was introduced into Europe in the eighteenth century to be grown as a novelty in Victorian hot-houses, and was briefly appreciated at society dining tables, but the rest of the population didn't get to hear of it until fast, modern refrigerated transport made the fruit available to all.

The carambola grows on a small, evergreen tree that both flowers and fruits continuously and so is available all the year round, coming to Britain mainly from Israel.

Nutrition

Carambola are exceptionally high in Vitamin A and potassium, and have significant amounts of Vitamin C, phosphorus and calcium.

Buying and storing carambola

Carambola should ideally be a light, translucent green and the skin smooth and slightly bloomed. As they age, their skin turns yellow and eventually wrinkles. They maintain their flavour at this stage, but should be used immediately. Once the points of the deep ridges begin to turn brown the flavour will have lost its freshness.

A fresh, green carambola will keep in the refrigerator for up to five days.

Carambola in the kitchen

The fresh flavour and crisp, juicy texture of this fruit makes it ideal for eating raw. Lay slices on a plate with pâtés or thinly sliced meats as a first course, or add to salads of leafy vegetables or grains. As a snack, slices go well with nuts and cheese.

If you gently poach slices of carambola for five minutes in the syrup for a fruit salad, the syrup will take on a delicious, fresh, fragrant flavour. Add the carambola slices to the rest of the fruit and pour the syrup over while it is still hot.

Carambola can be stir-fried, not just in savoury dishes but to make a dessert. Fry ¼-inch (6 mm) thick slices quickly in butter, add the juice of half an orange, a little dark Muscovado sugar and some raisins and boil them up quickly until the orange and sugar begin to caramelize.

Crystallized carambola slices make an unusual cake decoration. Use 8 oz (225 g) sugar and ½ pint (275 ml) water to make a syrup, and pour it over two sliced fruits. Leave for 24 hours, boil the drained syrup again, and once more pour it over the fruits. Do this three times. On the fourth day, boil up the syrup, put in the slices of fruit and boil until the syrup has completely evaporated. Lift the fruit on to greaseproof paper to dry and leave for a week before packing in a box.

Fried rice with chicken and carambola

8 oz (225 g) long grain brown rice
12 oz (350 g) boneless chicken breasts
2 rashers lean bacon
½ oz (15 g) fresh ginger root
12 spring onions
1 carambola
4 tablespoons sunflower oil
1 garlic clove, finely chopped
3 tablespoons soy sauce

Carambola slices give fried rice a sweet and sour flavour.

Cook the rice in lightly salted, boiling water until tender, about 40 minutes. Drain, rinse with cold water and drain again.

Cut the chicken breasts into small, thin strips. Dice the bacon. Peel and grate the ginger root. Cut the spring onions into 1 inch (2.5 cm) lengths. Thinly slice the carambola.

Heat the oil in a large frying pan on a high heat. Cook the ginger and garlic for 15 seconds. Add the chicken and bacon and stir-fry until the chicken is cooked through. Remove from pan.

Stir-fry the onions and carambola for 1 minute. Remove from pan. Put the rice in the pan, stir in the soy sauce and stir-fry for 1 minute. Add the chicken, bacon, onions and carambola. Stir for 1 minute more, or until everything is heated through.

Serves 4.

Carambola garnish

2 carambola
1 small onion
juice ½ lemon
¼ teaspoon cayenne pepper

Serve with cold meats, cheese and all kinds of salads.

Finely chop half of one carambola. Cut the rest into ¼-inch (6 mm) slices. Finely chop the onion. Mix it with the chopped carambola, lemon juice and cayenne pepper. Pile the chopped mixture on top of the carambola slices.

CAROB

CERATONIA SILIQUA

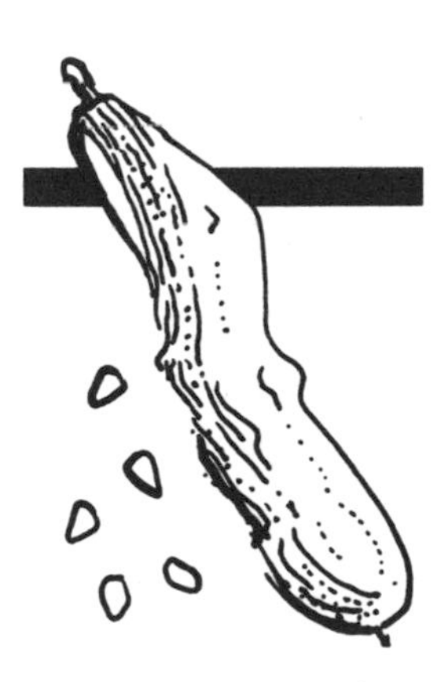

THE DARK BROWN, sweet-scented carob powder bought in health shops would never remind you of a fruit, yet it is the product of one. Carob has become popular as a 'healthy' ingredient in the West over recent years. Until the 1970s it existed in relative obscurity in much of the Western world, only dimly remembered by ex-soldiers who chewed the beans in the desert during the last war.

The carob tree is a large evergreen which grows wild on barren hillsides around the Mediterranean, as well as being cultivated. The varieties were first improved for cultivation by the Arabs and trees were introduced to southern Europe in the sixteenth century for use mainly as animal fodder. They have been grown in the warmer parts of the United States for about 100 years.

The carob fruits, sometimes called locust beans or St John's bread, take the form of glossy brown seed pods, about 12 inches (30 cm) long and 1½ inches (4 cm) wide. They contain a sweet brown pulp and several hard seeds which were once used as weights to measure gold and precious stones. The pulp can be chewed directly from the pods and has a sweet, caramel flavour.

Fresh carob pods are occasionally found in health food shops, but most often we buy carob powder which is made by sieving, roasting and grinding the pulp.

Nutrition

Carob beans are highly nutritious and are said to have sustained John the Baptist in the desert. They contain 8 per cent protein and are rich in B Vitamins, Vitamins A and D and calcium, magnesium and potassium. Unlike chocolate, for which it is used as a substitute, carob contains no caffeine, theobromine or oxalic acid, a substance which renders calcium unavailable to the body. It has less fat and sodium and a higher fibre content and, as it contains a high proportion of fruit sugars, dishes made with it need less sweetening than those made with the more bitter cocoa powder. This is why carob has become so popular in the health food market.

Buying and storing carob

Carob powder should be treated like cocoa powder. It will keep for up to a year in a sealed container in a cool cupboard. Carob bars, which are similar to chocolate bars and come in a variety of flavours, keep for up to six months in the same conditions.

Carob in the kitchen

Carob powder can be used as a substitute for cocoa powder in the same amounts. The amount of sugar in the recipe can be cut by about a quarter. Cakes made with carob turn out a very dark brown, have a slightly stickier texture than those made with cocoa powder and a rich flavour that is a cross between caramel and chocolate.

Carob bars can be used like chocolate bars, but greater care has to be taken when melting them. Always use a double saucepan or a bowl standing in a pan of water and keep the heat low. Use the carob as soon as it has melted as overheating will cause it to curdle and lose its gloss. Splashing water into it will have the same effect.

Semolina and carob moulds

Another no-sugar recipe that is perfectly sweet. The fruity flavour of the apple juice contrasts with the rich carob.

1 pint (575 ml) milk
2 oz (50 g) wholewheat semolina
1 tablespoon instant coffee powder (or coffee substitute)
1 tablespoon carob powder
8 tablespoons concentrated apple juice
natural yoghurt for serving

Warm the milk in a saucepan. Sprinkle in the semolina, coffee powder and carob powder and add the apple juice. Bring the mixture to the boil, stirring. Stir on the heat for 2 minutes or until thick.

Wet the inside of 6 dariole moulds or small soufflé dishes with cold water. Divide the semolina mixture between the moulds. Leave in a cool place to set for 2 hours.

Turn the moulded semolina on to individual plates and spoon natural yoghurt over the top before serving.

Serves 6.

Steamed carob pudding with orange sauce

3 oz (75 g) dried dates
3 fl oz (90 ml) natural orange juice
4 oz (125 g) wholemeal flour
1 teaspoon bicarbonate of soda
2 oz (50 g) carob powder, sieved
4 oz (125 g) vegetable margarine plus extra for greasing
2 eggs beaten

SAUCE

1 tablespoon arrowroot
½ pint (275 ml) natural orange juice

Although this pudding contains no sugar, it is very light and sweet and makes an ideal family dessert.

Finely chop the dates. Place in a saucepan with the orange juice, bring to the boil and simmer for 5 minutes. Liquidize with the juice.

Mix together the flour, bicarbonate of soda and carob powder. Cream the margarine and gradually beat in the liquidized dates. Beat in the flour mixture, alternately with the eggs.

Pour the mixture into a greased, 1½ pint (850 ml) pudding basin. Cover with buttered greaseproof paper and then aluminium foil and tie the cover securely with string, making a handle for easy lifting. Lower the pudding into a saucepan of boiling water. Cover and steam the pudding for 1½ hours, topping up the water when necessary.

To make the sauce, put the arrowroot into a bowl and mix in 6 tablespoons of the orange juice. Bring the remaining orange juice to the boil, stir in the arrowroot mixture and stir until the sauce is thick.

Turn the pudding out of the basin and serve the sauce separately.

Serves 4.

CHERRY

PRUNUS SPECIES

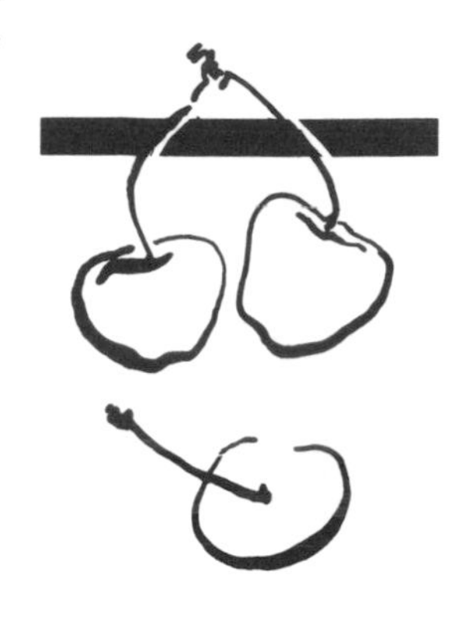

CHERRIES ARE A fruit of summer, arriving in the hottest days of the year and disappearing again before the evenings begin to shorten. Although related to the plum, they are unlike any other fruit; soft, yet firm; sweet but not too sweet, the right size for popping into the mouth of your true love, or for hanging over your ears to make you look like a gypsy.

A Kentish orchard of immensely tall, laden cherry trees with sheep grazing beneath is a wonderful sight, but now all too rare. As the old trees outlived their useful lives, they were cut down to be replaced by those grown on shorter stock, making them easier to pick. The skill of balancing and climbing a tall cherry ladder is all but forgotten.

Cherries have been growing wild for centuries throughout Britain and Europe and across to western Asia. There are basically three types: sweet, sour and hybrids between the two. Altogether there are over 600 varieties. Sour cooking cherries are thought to have originated in Eastern Europe and around the Caspian Sea. Sweet cherries were discovered by the Romans in Asia Minor in about 70BC. They took them wherever they conquered, and it is thought that the British wild cherries were the result of the Roman armies eating cherries as they marched and spitting out the pips on the way. Certainly, by the end of their occupation cherries were well established in Britain.

By the Middle Ages, the poor relied on wild cherries while the rich cultivated them in orchards. Fresh fruit was scarce in those days and when the crop ripened there was great rejoicing. Cherries 'on the ryse' (on the twig) were cried in the streets of London and cherry feasts and cherry fairs held in all the cherry growing areas.

Even with modern cultivation and transport, cherries are still a summer treat. British ones come into the shops around the beginning of July and last until the beginning of August. The French ones arrive earlier and those from Italy, Spain and the United States usually come at the end of our season.

There were once vast orchards of sour cherries in Kent, but they have all but disappeared. Occasionally they are available from greengrocers but most supplies now come from private gardens. **Morello** cherries are the best known of this type. They are small and dark, very juicy but with a sour flavour that makes them impossible to eat raw but ideal for cooking, preserving and wine making. **Amarelles** are another type, slightly less acid than Morellos, lighter coloured on the outside and with an almost yellow flesh.

Of the sweet cherries, there are two basic types, **Geans** (sometimes called Guignes) which are black or red, soft, juicy and very sweet, and **Bigarreaus** (also called Naps or whites) which are a blushing pale yellow with firm flesh. Both make ideal dessert cherries eaten raw, but they can also be cooked.

The hybrids developed from crossing sweet and bitter cherries are known as **Dukes** or **Royals**, and are dual purpose.

Tinned cherries are useful in winter and, unlike many tinned fruits, preserve the flavour of the fresh fruit.

Crystallized or glacé cherries are used for cake making. Traditionally red, they now come coloured green or yellow as well.

Nutrition

Although delicious to eat, cherries are surprisingly low in most nutrients. They contain small amounts of Vitamins C and A and traces of iron and calcium.

Buying and storing cherries

Cherries should be firm, shiny, unbruised and not split. All sweet and Duke cherries should have their stalks still attached. Sour cherries are most often sold without stalks.

If the fruit is in peak condition it should keep well for up to a week in the refrigerator. Leave at room temperature for 30 minutes to bring out their flavour before eating raw.

To freeze cherries, stone them and freeze them on trays before packing into polythene bags. They will keep for six to eight months. Poached and frozen in a sugar syrup, or packed sprinkled with sugar they will keep for up to a year. When freezing in a syrup, use rigid containers as the juice may remain slightly liquid.

Cherries in the kitchen

Stone cherries using a special cherry stoner or by inserting the fine point of a potato peeler or a bent hair pin at the stalk end and twisting it. Keep some stones when you are preserving cherries. When cracked, the kernels will add an almond flavour.

Raw sweet cherries can be added to fruit salads and to leafy green salads. They are also good in salads with diced poultry or lamb.

For cooking and preserving, use Dukes or the bitter varieties. They can be made into fruit compotes and cherry tarts, pies with other soft fruits such as raspberries or redcurrants, fillings for pancakes, pastries and strudels, and toppings for rich buns and croissants. Baked under a rich batter they are a favourite country dessert in both France and England.

For jams and preserves use the bitter cherries. They contain very little pectin, so always add lemon juice to jam. To make cherry brandy, prick the cherries all over without stoning and one-third fill a bottle with them. Cover with sugar and fill the bottle with brandy. Leave for six months, shaking frequently.

Commercially, cherries are made into cherry brandy, which is given an almond flavour by adding some of the crushed stones. From Alsace and the Black Forest comes Kirsch or Kirschwasser, a strong, clear coloured liqueur. Maraschino, also colourless, is made in Yugoslavia and Italy.

Jellied duckling with cherries

A delightful cold dish for summer. The green herbs, browned skin and red cherries shine through the deep crimson jelly.

one 4 lb (3.6 kg) duckling
2 bouquets of mint, thyme and parsley
10 black peppercorns
6 allspice berries
6 juniper berries
giblets of duck
1 small onion, halved
1 small carrot, roughly chopped
1 celery stick, roughly chopped
1 egg white
¼ pint (150 ml) dry red wine
½ oz (15 g) gelatin
4 oz (125 g) black or red cherries
1 tablespoon each chopped thyme, mint and parsley

Heat the oven to 400F/200C/gas 6. Truss the duckling, putting one bouquet garni inside. Crush together the black peppercorns, allspice and juniper berries, and rub into the skin of the duckling. Put the duckling on a rack in a roasting tin and cover it with foil. Roast for 1 hour. Remove the foil and cook for a further 30 minutes or until the skin is brown and the juices run clear when the thicker parts of the meat are pierced with a knife. Leave to cool completely.

While the duckling is cooking, put the giblets, onion, carrot and celery into a saucepan with the remaining bouquet garni and 3 pints (1.7 litres) water. Bring to the boil and simmer for 1 hour. Strain off the stock and return it to the cleaned pan set on a medium heat. Lightly beat the egg white. Whisk it into the stock with a downward movement. Keep whisking until the stock boils and the scum rises to the surface. Strain the stock into a bowl through a tea-cloth.

Put ¼ pint (150 ml) of the strained stock into a saucepan with the wine. Warm on a medium heat. Sprinkle in the gelatin and stir until melted, without boiling. Take the pan from the heat and leave the jelly to cool completely, but not set.

Joint the duckling, and arrange the joints on a flat serving dish. Stone the cherries and cut each one crossways into about 3 slices. Spoon half the jelly over the duck and scatter the herbs over the top. Refrigerate for the jelly coating to set. Arrange the cherry slices on top of the herbs and spoon over the rest of the jelly, making sure that the cherries are at least thinly coated or they may start to go brown. Refrigerate again for the second coat of jelly to set.

Serves 4.

Cherry and mint sauce

8 oz (225 g) red cherries
1 teaspoon honey
3 tablespoons red wine vinegar
4 tablespoons chopped mint

When first made, this sauce is pink and frothy, but as it stands it gradually becomes a dark cherry-red. It is light in texture and ideal for cold summer meat salads and hot lamb dishes.

Stone the cherries and put them into a blender with the honey and wine vinegar. Blend until the mixture is pink and frothy. Stir in the mint.

Pour the sauce into a dish or sauce-boat and leave it to stand for 30 minutes.

Serves 4–6.

Cherry batter

4 oz (125 g) 85% flour (if unavailable, use a mixture of wholemeal and white)
2 eggs, separated
1/4 pint (150 ml) milk
8 oz (225 g) sweet black or red cherries
butter for greasing a 1 1/2-pint (850 ml) pudding basin

Sweet, plump cherries stay whole and firm in a light, steamed batter to make a traditional Kentish dish. It is semi-sweet, so you might like to serve it with melted honey or a sprinkling of brown sugar.

Put the flour into a bowl and make a well in the centre. Add the egg yolks and start gradually to beat in the flour from the edges of the well. Add the milk by degrees, beating it into the flour until you have a thick batter. Beat until the bubbles form on the surface and leave for 30 minutes.

Stone the cherries. Stiffly whip the egg whites and fold them into the batter. Quickly fold in the cherries. Pour the mixture into the prepared basin and cover the top with a layer of greaseproof paper and a layer of foil. Tie the covers down with string, making a handle for easy lifting.

Bring a saucepan of water to the boil, lower in the pudding and steam for 1 hour and 30 minutes, keeping the water boiling and topping up when necessary.

Serve hot, either spooned out of the basin or turned on to a plate.

Serves 4–6.

Cherry and almond cake

4 oz (125 g) wholemeal flour
4 oz (125 g) self-raising flour
pinch fine sea salt
8 oz (225 g) glacé cherries
6 oz (175 g) butter, softened
6 oz (175 g) golden caster sugar
3 eggs, lightly beaten
3 oz (75 g) ground almonds
3 fl oz (90 ml) Madeira or sweet sherry
butter for greasing a 7-inch (18 cm) diameter cake tin

Glacé cherries are best of all in cakes. This one is moist and rich, with the flavour of almonds.

Heat the oven to 350F/180C/gas 4. Mix the two flours with the salt. Halve the cherries and toss them in 3 tablespoons of the flour.

Cream the butter with the sugar so the mixture becomes light and fluffy. Gradually add the eggs, beating well. Using a metal spoon, fold in the flour and then the almonds. Mix in the Madeira or sherry and fold in the cherries.

Put the mixture into the prepared tin and bake for 1 hour 40 minutes, or until it has shrunk slightly from the sides of the tin and a skewer in the centre comes out clean. Leave for 15 minutes and turn it on to a wire rack to cool.

CITRUS FRUITS

CITRUS SPECIES

Orange, Lemon, Lime, Citron, Kumquat, Pomelo, Grapefruit, Sweetie, Ugli-fruit

CITRUS FRUITS ARE all fresh-flavoured, juicy and packed full of Vitamin C. They have translucent, segmented flesh and thick pithy skins coated with a bitter-sharp, coloured zest. Many can be squeezed for their juice, some are sharp and fresh to wake you up in the morning, others are best after dinner at night. Most can be used in countless dishes throughout the day, both sweet and savoury.

ORANGE

Next to apples and pears, oranges must be the fruit most commonly available in the Western world. Large, small and middle-sized, they are available all year round from a number of different countries. They have sweet juice which can be squeezed for drinking, luscious flesh with a sweet-sharp flavour to eat just as it is or use in sweet and savoury dishes, zest to enliven the flavour of anything from stuffings to syllabubs, and a thick skin that can be made into marmalade.

There are two types of orange, bitter and sweet. They came originally from Asia, the sweet in particular from China. Arab traders introduced oranges to the Romans, and soon there were orange groves around the Mediterranean. The first Britons to taste them were Crusaders camped around Jaffa in the late twelfth century. Very gradually, oranges and lemons began to arrive in England, in small amounts and at exceptionally high prices. Some of the first were a consignment of seven oranges and fifteen lemons brought into Portsmouth in 1289 for Queen Eleanor, a former princess of Castile. Consignments gradually increased throughout the Middle Ages, arriving on Spanish, Portuguese and Italian spice ships.

All these early oranges were of the Seville type now used for marmalade. They were served baked whole, made into fritters, and given by rich husbands to their pregnant wives as an appetite stimulant. Very often they were candied and used as we would use candied peel. Even when sweet oranges finally made their appearance, many recipes calling for 'orange' referred to the Seville type.

The first sweet oranges came to Britain in the middle of the seventeenth century and in the 1660s were a popular refreshment at London theatres, sold by orange girls like Nell Gwynne. In 1669, Samuel Pepys took his first glass of freshly squeezed orange juice at his cousin's house: '. . . and here they drink the juice as wine, with sugar, and it is a very fine drink; but, it being new, I was doubtful whether it might not do me hurt.' Little did he know how popular it would become.

Today our markets are always well stocked with oranges, from Spain, Israel, Morocco, Cyprus, Greece, Turkey, Florida, California and South America. They are also grown in Australia.

Navel oranges are probably the best known of the sweet varieties. They have a miniature orange in the top, looking rather like a navel, and were first grown in Washington, USA. Now they come from Florida, California and Spain. **Shamouti** oranges are large and seedless and come from Israel and Cyprus. **Valencia lates** were first grown in Portugal, taken to California, and are now grown mainly in Spain. They are the last of the Spanish oranges to arrive in the winter as they have a long season.

The delicious, thin-skinned, red-fleshed, raspberry-flavoured **blood** oranges, available from December to March, are a mutant of the sweet types. The colour changes permanently from orange to red as soon as the night temperature drops below 40F (5C).

When sweet oranges are picked they are more green than orange in colour. The orange is increased by a treatment with ethylene gas. They are then given a light coating of wax to improve their shine.

Spain is the sole grower of **Seville** oranges and Britain takes ninety per cent of the crop for making marmalade. The rest go for making bitters. Seville oranges are usually on the small side with a rougher, more knobbly skin than sweet oranges. They have a greater number of pips and, even though their flesh seems very loosely packed, yield a great deal of juice. The flavour of Seville oranges is as sharp as that of lemons, but they have an underlying, mellow, bitter quality that comes through in the flavour of marmalade.

Nutrition

Oranges are renowned for their high Vitamin C content and supply 11 per cent of the national intake, even though the average weekly consumption per person is only one medium orange. Potassium and calcium counts are also high.

Buying and storing oranges

Oranges should look bright and glossy and should have a fresh smell. Dull, wrinkled oranges may well have a mouldy flavour. Store in a cool, dark larder for up to two weeks.

As they are so readily available there is no point in freezing sweet oranges, but conveniently Seville oranges to be used later for marmalade can be frozen whole.

Oranges in the kitchen

Before use, oranges should be peeled. If the slices are to be used as a garnish, cut all the peel and pith away with a sharp knife. If you are going to use the zest, scrub the orange first to rid it of its wax coating.

The juice of sweet oranges can be used as a drink, either diluted, plain, or mixed with champagne to make Buck's Fizz. Add it to cake mixtures and sweet sauces and use it for jellies, mousses, soufflés and cheesecakes. Add it also to marinades for beef, to savoury sauces, casseroles and sauté dishes.

Add sliced sweet oranges to all kinds of side salads and fruit salads. Poach them in syrup to use as a garnish for desserts, or make them into twists, complete with their peel, to decorate savoury dishes.

Orange zest, the outer part of the peel, can be grated and added to baked goods, puddings and whipped cream syllabubs, to marinades and to sweet and savoury sauces. Pared very thinly, it can be blanched and cut into matchstick pieces to garnish casseroles and sauté dishes, besides fruit compotes and creams.

As well as being made into marmalade, Seville oranges can be used in many sweet and savoury dishes in a simlar way to lemons. The squeezed juice can be added to casseroles and sauté dishes of meat, used instead of vinegar in salad dressings, and squeezed over fish either before or after cooking. In any creamy desserts or cheesecakes using sweet oranges, try a Seville orange for a bitter-sweet, marmalade flavour.

LEMON

CITRUS LIMON, SYN. C. LIMONIUM

Wherever there is a serious cook, you will find lemons in the kitchen. A squeeze of lemon juice enhances the flavour of many dishes, both sweet and savoury. It helps to tenderize meats and keep the colour of cut vegetables and fruits, make a refreshing drink and will even help to clean your copper pans.

It is not exactly certain where lemons first came from, but it was probably an area taking in the Himalayas, east India, Burma and south China. The Arabs took them along the trading routes to Iran and introduced them to the Romans who cultivated them under the name of Median apples. After the fall of the Roman Empire, lemons were forgotten until the Arabs rediscovered them in about the tenth century and established irrigated lemon groves all around the Mediterranean. It was here that the Crusaders found lemons in 1191.

Like oranges, lemons came to Britain very gradually. Queen Eleanor had a liking for them and paid the then staggering sum of twenty shillings (£1) for thirty-nine lemons at the time of her last illness in 1290. By the fifteenth century, lemons were being grown on some British manors, but only as a novelty. Most were imported from southern Europe.

The anti-scorbutic property of lemons was discovered in the seventeenth century and they were very soon taken on long sea voyages. The British fleet, although known in the eighteenth century as Limeys, actually used more lemons than limes on board ship. The squeezed juice was mixed with rum in order to preserve it and measured out to the ratings every ten days. The regular lemon ration enabled British ships to stay at sea for longer without having to take on fresh supplies and thus, it is said, helped to defeat Napoleon.

From Europe, lemons travelled all over the world and besides the Mediterranean area they are now grown in Turkey, Florida, Texas and California, Brazil, China, Japan, Australia and South Africa.

Lemons are seldom sold by named varieties, but very many different types are grown. Some are small with thin skins but exceptionally juicy flesh, whereas other, thick skinned ones may look lush, but when cut, reveal only a small amount of flesh that yields little juice.

European fruits come in from November to April. The first are the fruits from the first flowers, called *prima fiori*. They are picked green in Italy and may still have a green tinge when bought. The biggest Spanish variety is the Berna or Verna which has a knobbly skin. Turkish lemons, available in the late summer, are individually wrapped and stored in limestone caves from December to July. They are stamped or labelled *yatk*, which means bed. Californian lemons are stored for four months before washing and shipping. They have soft skins and a high juice and Vitamin C content. From South Africa in the summer come Eureka lemons, oval-shaped with smooth, bright yellow skins and a high juice content.

Most lemons are coated in wax in order to preserve them and enhance their appearance. Safeways, the supermarket chain, are now selling unwaxed lemons in response to public demand.

Nutrition

Old English sailors were right. Lemons are a rich source of Vitamin C, although they do not contain quite as much as oranges. They also contain significant amounts of potassium and calcium.

Buying and storing lemons

Always buy fresh lemons. Avoid squeezy plastic ones full of juice which has been reconstituted from frozen concentrate with sulphur dioxide and/or sodium benzoate added, and has a lowered Vitamin C content due to processing and long storage.

Fresh lemons should be firm, bright and shiny, with a fresh scent. Don't buy any that have very soft skins or those with skins becoming dull and hard. They will keep for up to two weeks in a cool, dark larder.

Lemons in the kitchen

As with oranges, both the juice and the zest can be used. If you need the zest, scrub the lemon first, unless the fruit is unwaxed. A fine cheese or multi-purpose grater will do the job but does tend to squash the zest and spoil its flavour. A lemon zester, therefore, is not an extravagance in a busy kitchen. With it, you can take off long, thin squiggles of zest which you can chop to the size you need. Add the zest to biscuit, pudding and cake mixtures, to stewed fruits and creamy desserts and also to marinades for meat and fish. Thin strips pared off with a potato peeler can be cooked with fruits or tied into a bouquet garni for adding to stocks or poaching fish or meat.

The juice of a lemon makes up 45 per cent of its weight. To extract as much as possible, hold the lemon under running warm water for a few minutes and knead it gently with your fingers before cutting. Do not press too hard when you squeeze a lemon, as this may affect the flavour and destroy Vitamin C. Always use the juice as soon as possible. After several hours it will start to become bitter. Use in marinades for fish and meat and as a substitute for vinegar in salads. Add to fruits and vegetables as they cook, and use as an anti-oxidizing 'paint' for apples or avocados, which turn brown when cut. Lemon juice forms the base for many desserts, including jellies, mousses, soufflés and, of course, lemon meringue and lemon chiffon pies. Lemon curd, made by stirring the juice with butter and eggs, is one of the quickest preserves that you can make.

Lemon flesh is delicious in leafy summer salads and lifts the flavour of salads made from beans such as chickpeas and haricot beans. Cut away all the rind and pith and chop the rest, removing the seeds.

The flesh is also essential when you are making lemonade. Grate the zest from two lemons and put it into a large jug. Cut away and discard all the pith, thinly slice the flesh and add to the jug with the zest. Add 4 tablespoons honey and pour in 2½ pints (1.4 litres) boiling water. Stir well and leave until quite cool. On a summer's day it is the most refreshing drink that you can imagine.

Lemons, diced or sliced, complete with their rinds, can be made into chutneys and pickles.

LIME

CITRUS AURANTIFOLIA; C. LIMETTA

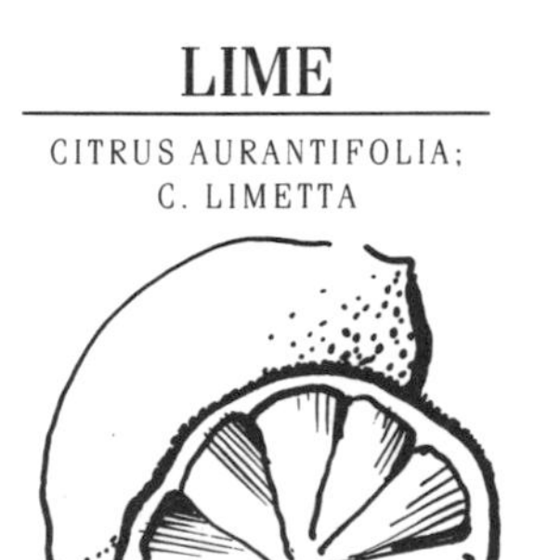

Limes are essentially a fruit of the tropics, similar to lemons in shape and slightly smaller, with a sharp, spicy, flavour, more complex and flowery than that of a lemon. Lime skins are thin, and so the fruits yield large amounts of juice for their size.

Limes came originally from the East Indies and, like oranges and lemons, were taken along the old trading routes by the Arabs to India, Persia and the Mediterranean. Spaniards took them to the West Indies where they quickly became naturalized, but they never really became popular in Britain until the seventeenth century, when their anti-scorbutic properties were recognized.

By the 1680s limes were being grown in profusion in Jamaica. At the ports, presses extracted their juice which was put into barrels and exported to Europe. Some was mixed with the local rum and used by the British Navy. A mixture of rum, hot water and lime or lemon came to be known as 'grog' from the nickname of Old Grog given to Admiral Edward Vernon because he always wore a coat of grogram, a coarse mixture of silk and wool.

The drinking of sweet lime cordial is peculiar to Britain. It is made from a variety of lime about the size of a pigeon's egg with numerous seeds. The fruits are crushed whole and fermented in barrels for thirty days until the mixture separates into three layers, oil and pulp on the top, juice in the centre and sludge at the bottom. The top layer is removed and the juice strained off, having developed a characteristic musty flavour.

Fresh limes are available in Britain all the year and come mainly from Israel, Brazil, Mexico, Kenya and Jamaica. They are also grown in Egypt, Florida and India and many other areas of the tropics and sub-tropics.

There are many different types of lime, although they are rarely named in the shops. They vary in size and colour, ranging from green to yellow, the green being sharper and fuller flavoured. Some varieties are seedless. West Indian limes are the best. They are bright green and larger than most other types, being about 2 inches (5 cm) in length, with juicy, fragrant flesh. Key limes are grown in Florida along the Gulf Coast. They are semi-wild, small and acid and known as Florida Keys. Indian limes are small and yellow and those grown in Tahiti are exceptionally fragrant.

Nutrition

Limes are high in Vitamin C, although they do not contain as much as lemons or oranges. They also have significant amounts of Vitamin A, potassium, calcium and phosphorus.

Buying and storing limes

Lime skins should look oily and fresh. As the fruits age, the skins become dry and hard, and the fragrant scent and flavour of the juice begins to diminish.

Limes can be stored in a cool, dark larder for up to two weeks and in a refrigerator for up to eight weeks.

Limes in the kitchen

The zest and juice of limes can be used in a similar way to those of lemons, but do not use them indiscriminately, as the flavour can be very different.

Lime juice has the ability to draw out the flavour of blander tropical fruits such as the paw paw or custard apple. Whether the fruits are to be served diced or puréed, a squeeze of lime juice will work magic, bringing them to life and restoring a freshly-picked flavour. By itself, the juice can be used as a flavouring for desserts such as jellies, soufflés, cream desserts and pies such as the American chiffon pies and key lime pie.

As a marinade for meats and fish, lime juice acts as both tenderizer and flavourer and can be used to raw cook white fish. For the Latin American dish known as ceviche, fish must be very fresh, cut into strips and covered in lime juice for at least four hours, after which it can be served with chillies and salad vegetables.

There are lime pickles, chutneys and yoghurt-based relishes known as sambals, besides lime or mixed fruit marmalade.

The sharp, fragrant flavour of lime juice makes it ideal for cocktails and other mixed drinks such as lime julep with mint and brandy and Margarita with Cointreau. In Mexico, sucking a lime wedge and licking salt are essential rituals before drinking a sip of the fiery cactus spirit known as tequila.

CITRON

CITRUS MEDICA

Citrons are never used fresh in Britain. They are lemon-like in appearance, but slightly larger and more knobbly, pale yellow, with a sweet, rich, perfumed scent, thick skin and a small amount of flesh.

The citron originated in the Himalayas, where it grows wild but is seldom used. It was one of the first citrus fruits to reach Europe and, like the lemon and oranges, was taken there first by Arab traders. The chief use of the citron has always been for candying, although it was occasionally made into a fruit syrup in the eighteenth century and can be made into marmalade.

Citrons are grown in the West Indies and around the Mediterranean and are sold fresh in Italian, and sometimes French and Spanish, shops and markets, although the main part of the crop is sent to the United States.

Citron in the kitchen

Citron peel is candied and sold either in whole pieces or in mixtures of chopped candied peel. The whole pieces keep well and are generally of better quality and add flavour, without extra sweetness, to cakes and other baked goods. The syrup from the chopped kinds adds extra sweetness, so cut down slightly on the amount of sugar in the recipe.

KUMQUAT

FORTUNELLA SPECIES

Kumquats, like beautiful baby oranges, appear regularly in greengrocers and supermarkets in winter. Although expensive, they are popular, as they can be bought in small quantities to add a special, colourful touch to winter meals.

Kumquats are not really citrus fruits at all, but a species of *Fortunella*, named after plant collector Robert Fortune who introduced them to Europe from their native Far East in 1846. They have so many citrus-like features, however, that they deserve to feature in this section. In appearance they are oval, about 1 inch (2.5 cm) long and ½ inch (1.3 cm) wide, bright orange and with a citrus-like rind. This rind, however, is far softer than that of citrus fruits and has a sweet, tangy flavour without a hint of bitter pithiness. Unlike the rind of citrus fruits, it is completely edible, both raw and cooked. The flavour of the flesh, which also looks like that of an orange, is sharp and sherbet-like.

Kumquats have long been cultivated in China, Japan and Malaysia and are now also grown in Australia, Japan, Israel, East Africa and California and Florida in the United States. All parts of the plant are sweetly scented and they are often grown as pot plants.

Nutrition

Kumquats are high in potassium and also have significant amounts of calcium, phosphorus and Vitamins C and A.

Buying and storing kumquats

Kumquats should look firm and fresh and when ripe they are bright orange. Do not buy them if they look soft and shrivelled. They will keep for about four days at room temperature and for about nine days refrigerated in a polythene or paper bag.

Kumquats in the kitchen

To appreciate kumquats to the full, eat them raw. Sliced thinly crossways, they are wonderful in winter salads and go well with curly endive, lolla rossa or iceberg lettuces, chicory, red and white cabbages, celery, celeriac and watercress. You can also add them to salads of meat, poultry and cooked dried beans, either as a mixed-in ingredient or a garnish. Sliced or cut into tiny wedges they make a perfect garnish for sea food and meat, fish and vegetable pâtés. Add them to stir-fried meat dishes and to sautées of chicken or pork or set them in the top of pâtés before cooking.

Chopped kumquats can be made into relishes and they can also be preserved in syrup. Some specialist shops sell kumquats tinned or bottled in syrup.

POMELO

CITRUS MAXIMA

Pomelos are a wonderfully generous fruit, large, glossy, yellow-green and pear-shaped with luscious sweet-sour, pale yellow flesh. Originating in the Far East, they have been known in Europe for many years, although it is only recently that they have been commonly available.

The history of the pomelo is somewhat tangled. It was taken to the West Indies by Columbus on his second voyage, where it became quickly established as a food for the native Indians. Much later, in the seventeenth century it was discovered growing in Polynesia by Captain Shaddock, an English sea-captain, who left some of its seeds in Barbados, took some of the fruits home (this was the first time they had been seen in Britain) and gave it its second name of Shaddock.

Perhaps the most important fact about the pomelo is that one tree threw up a mutant that became the grapefruit. With their wonderful shape and abundance of flesh it is small wonder that pomelos were once so much prized. They have been neglected in more recent years, probably because they were grown more for candied peel than as a dessert fruit, but are finding popularity at last, thanks to the Israelis, who are growing them commercially on an increasing scale.

Nutrition

Pomelos are high in Vitamin C and potassium.

Buying and storing pomelos

Pomelos should look shiny, firm and fresh. They will keep for up to three weeks in a cool dark larder.

Pomelos in the kitchen

Pomelos have a very thick skin. To peel one efficiently, slit this skin into eight sections from the top, using a sharp knife and being careful not to go through to the flesh, and then peel each piece off whole. This skin makes excellent candied peel.

Each segment of pomelo is covered with a tough skin which, if left on, makes for rather unpleasant eating. However, once it is removed, you can really appreciate the flesh, which is pale yellow, firm yet juicy and can be peeled off in lush segments. Its flavour is sweet and slightly sour, with none of the sharpness of grapefuit. Appreciate it on its own at first, either as a dessert or before a meal. Put it into leafy salads or serve it as a garnish for seafood and cold poached fish such as salmon and trout. It also goes well with cold turkey and chicken, either in salads or as a garnish.

GRAPEFRUIT

CITRUS PARADISI

The grapefruit, although now well known and widespread, is a latecomer to the fruit world. The first tree appeared in the West Indies as a mutant of the pomelo sometime during the eighteenth century and soon became established throughout the islands, where it was called the 'forbidden fruit' by Western traders. The first person to realize the grapefruit's potential was a chief surgeon in Napoleon's army who had been captured at Trafalgar and sent to the Bahamas as a prisoner. He so much enjoyed the citrus fruits he found there, that when he was freed in 1807 and went to South Carolina to practise medicine, his one dream was to establish a citrus plantation. This he achieved in Florida, in 1823. He sent to the Bahamas for grapefruit seeds, succeeded in propagating them, and in seven years the fruit became established and recognized.

This first grapefruit plantation was small and it was not for another fifty years that large scale growing was taken up in Florida and later

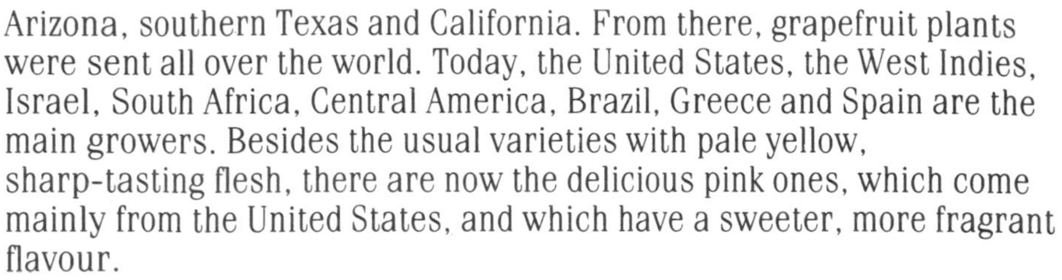

Arizona, southern Texas and California. From there, grapefruit plants were sent all over the world. Today, the United States, the West Indies, Israel, South Africa, Central America, Brazil, Greece and Spain are the main growers. Besides the usual varieties with pale yellow, sharp-tasting flesh, there are now the delicious pink ones, which come mainly from the United States, and which have a sweeter, more fragrant flavour.

Why was the grapefruit such a success when the older pomelo remained in obscurity? There are several reasons. The fruit is smaller and of a more manageable shape. It can be conveniently cut in half and each half placed in a normal-sized bowl. The flesh is softer and juicier, and the skin softer and less obtrusive than that of the pomelo. The abundant juice can also be squeezed out and used as a drink. Also, the Americans realized that they had a marketable success on their hands and successfully set about achieving its promotion.

Grapefruit was promoted as a healthy start to the day and for many years, before other ingredients and recipes were readily available, seemed to be the world's favourite first course.

Nutrition

Grapefruit is high in Vitamin C, and has significant amounts of potassium.

Buying and storing grapefruit

As for pomelos, page 61.

Grapefruit in the kitchen

Cut the segments away from the skin and mix them with tomatoes and a mayonnaise dressing; watercress and diced feta cheese with a lemon vinaigrette; or seafood such as prawns or even cockles in a dressing flavoured with tomato purée and paprika, pile the mixture back into the shells, and you are on your way to an interesting first course.

Diced grapefruit flesh can also be added to side salads. It goes well with watercress, mustard and cress, and various types of lettuce.

The sharp flesh complements chicken and turkey, either in sauté dishes, as a garnish for sliced cold meats, or mixed into salads with a creamy dressing.

Grapefruit are rarely used in desserts because their flavour tends to be too bitter. It is a refresher, rather than a fruit with which to end a meal.

The sweeter, pink grapefruit can be used in the same ways and can also be added to fruit salads and used as a decoration on desserts.

SWEETIE

The sweetie is grown in Israel and looks like a large, yellow-green grapefruit with deeply pitted, shiny skin. Its pale yellow flesh looks like that of a grapefruit and it has the same bitter quality without the sharpness. It can be treated as a grapefruit or eaten quite plainly as a dessert fruit. The growers recommend that you slice off the top and bottom and cut the fruit, still with its rind attached, into lengthways sections which can be sucked or chewed like an apple.

UGLI-FRUIT

In the late nineteenth century a blight in the Florida citrus plantations caused many more citrus fruits to be planted in Jamaica and new varieties to be developed. The ugli-fruit, a hybrid of a grapefruit and an orange, was one of these varieties and, in its country of origin is called a 'hoogli'. It is about the size of a grapefruit with a rough, knarled, dull yellow-brown skin tinged with orange. This skin is very loose and easy to peel away. The firm, juicy flesh has the sweetness of an orange with an underlying flavour of grapefruit without the sharpness. It is most often used as a dessert fruit and is generally available from January to April.

Beef braised with orange

Oranges are one of the few fruits that go well with beef.

2½ lb (1.1 kg) lean topside of beef
grated rind of 1 small orange and juice of 2
1 black olive, stoned and finely chopped
1 clove garlic, finely chopped
4 sprigs thyme

RELISH

4 tablespoons preserved grated horseradish
1 small orange
5 black olives
2 medium tomatoes
1 teaspoon chopped thyme

Heat the oven to 350F/180C/gas 4. Put the meat into a casserole. Grate the orange rind over the top and add the orange juice, chopped olive, garlic and thyme. Cover the casserole and put it into the oven for 1 hour 40 minutes.

For the relish, put the horseradish into a bowl. Cut the rind and pith from the orange and finely chop the flesh. Stone and finely chop the olives. Add the orange and olives to the horseradish. Scald, skin and seed the tomatoes and purée them in a blender. Mix the purée and thyme into the horseradish.

To serve, carve the meat and serve it quite plainly. Serve the relish in a separate dish.

Serves 4.

Cod baked in a Seville orange marinade

2 lb (900 g) cod fillet (thick end if possible)
1 medium Seville orange
1 small Seville orange
3 tablespoons olive oil
2 teaspoons spiced granular mustard
1 small onion, finely chopped
2 tablespoons chopped parsley

Marinade the fish before cooking to give it the maximum flavour.

Skin the fish and cut it into 8 even pieces. Grate the rind and squeeze the juice from the medium orange. In a flat, ovenproof dish mix with the oil, mustard, onion and parsley. Turn the pieces of cod in the mixture and leave them, skinned side up, for 2 hours at room temperature. Turn them back over.

Heat the oven to 350F/180C/gas 4. Thinly slice the remaining orange and lay one slice on top of each piece of fish. Bake the fish for 20 minutes and serve straight from the dish.

Serves 4.

Brown beans with orange

8 oz (225 g) brown kidney beans or pinto beans
2 large oranges
8 green olives
4 tablespoons olive oil
2 medium onions, thinly sliced
1 garlic clove, finely chopped
1 tablespoon tomato purée
1 tablespoon chopped thyme
4 tablespoons chopped parsley

This is the vegetarian equivalent of the beef recipe on page 63. Serve the beans with rice or pasta.

Soak the beans for 6 hours. Cook them until tender, about 1½ hours, and drain. Squeeze the juice from one of the oranges. Cut the rind and pith from the remaining orange. Cut the flesh into lengthways quarters and thinly slice them. Stone and chop the olives.

Heat the oil in a saucepan on a low heat. Stir in the onions and garlic and soften them. Mix in the tomato purée and then the beans, olives, thyme, parsley and orange juice. Cover and simmer for 5 minutes. Mix in the sliced orange and let it heat through.

Serves 4.

Seville zabaglione

2 egg yolks
2 tablespoons clear honey
grated rind of 1 Seville orange and juice of 2
4 fl oz (125 ml) Marsala
½ oz (15 g) gelatin
6 fl oz (175 ml) hot water

Seville orange juice gives a pleasant tang to this rich, Italian dessert.

Put the egg yolks and honey into a bowl. Using an electric beater, whisk in the orange juice and Marsala. In a medium-sized saucepan, soak the gelatin in 2 tablespoons of the hot water. Add the rest of the hot water to the egg yolk mixture a little at a time, beating all the while with the electric beater. Melt the soaked gelatin on a low heat, without boiling. Remove it from the heat and stir in the mixture. Set the pan back on a very low heat and stir the mixture, without boiling, until it becomes thick and coats the back of a wooden spoon. Remove the pan from the heat and stir in the grated orange rind.

Pour the zabaglione into four small dishes and leave in a cool place to set.

Serves 4.

Lamb, lemon and honey

1½ lb (675 g) fillet of lamb, or 8 small, boneless lamb chops
2 lemons
4 tablespoons olive oil
2 teaspoons clear honey
1 small onion, finely chopped
1 garlic clove, crushed with a pinch sea salt
1 tablespoon chopped lemon thyme
¼ teaspoon cayenne pepper

The honey and lemon used in this marinade make the lamb rich and succulent, while the cayenne pepper and herbs add the savoury flavours.

Cut the fillet of lamb in half lengthways and then into 8 flat pieces. If you are using chops, trim them of any excess fat. In a large, flat dish, mix the grated rind and juice of one of the lemons with the oil, honey, onion, garlic, lemon thyme and cayenne pepper. Turn the lamb in the mixture and leave it standing for at least 2 hours at room temperature, turning it several times.

Heat the grill to high. Lay the pieces of lamb on the hot grill rack, and spoon half the onion from the marinade over the top. Grill until a good brown on one side. Turn over, and spoon over the rest of the onion together with the marinade. Brown the second side and then continue cooking until the lamb is cooked through, turning several times. Cut the remaining lemon into 8 thin slices. Lay a slice on each piece of lamb and return the lamb to the grill for the lemon to heat through.

Serve the lamb with any juices from the pan spooned around it.

Serves 4.

Lemon pudding

4 oz (125 g) wholemeal flour
4 oz (125 g) self-raising flour
pinch fine sea salt
4 oz (125 g) suet
4 oz (125 g) currants
4 fl oz (125 ml) cold water
3 oz (75 g) butter
3 oz (75 g) demerara sugar
1 lemon

This is a traditional English pudding, a version of the Kentish Well and Sussex Pond puddings. The lemon steamed inside the suet crust gives a delicious, bitter, marmalade flavour, contrasting well with the sweet buttery sauce and rich dough.

You can use vegetable suet if you like, but do not replace the butter with margarine, as the flavour will not be nearly as good.

Mix the flours, salt, suet and currants in a bowl. Make a well in the centre, pour in the water and mix everything to a stiff dough. Roll out about two thirds of the dough and line a 2 pint (1.5 litre) pudding basin.

Cut the butter into small pieces and mix with the sugar. Put about one-quarter of the mixture into the lined basin. Scrub the lemon but leave it completely whole. Set it, end up, inside the basin and surround it with the remaining butter and sugar. Cover with the remaining dough and seal the edges.

Cover the basin with greaseproof paper and foil and tie them down, making a handle with the string for easy lifting. Bring a large pan of water to the boil. Lower in the pudding and steam it for 3 hours, topping up the water as and when necessary.

Invert the basin on to a plate and turn out the pudding. Cut it open with a sharp, pointed knife. As soon as the knife pierces the lemon, the delicious juice and softened flesh will moisten and flavour the inside of the pudding. Scrape a little of the flesh from the lemon shell on to each portion of pudding that you serve.

Serves 6.

Whiting and limes

2 medium whiting
juice 2 limes, plus ½ lime for optional garnish
4 tablespoons olive oil
sea salt and freshly ground black pepper

Serve this as a first course or light snack. The flavour is light and delicious and almost pickled.

Fillet the whiting and cut each fillet in half crossways. Lay the fillets on a large, flat dish, overlapping as little as possible. Beat the juice from 1 lime with 2 tablespoons of the oil and spoon over the fish. Sprinkle the fish with salt and pepper and refrigerate for 24 hours. Cut into ½-inch (1.3 cm) strips.

Heat the remaining oil in a frying pan on a high heat. Put in the pieces of fish and stir-fry until they are cooked through and on the point of breaking up. Pour in the juice from the remaining lime and let it bubble. Season with more black pepper. Take the pan from the heat immediately and transfer the whiting to four small dishes. Each can be garnished with a twist of lime, if wished.

Wholemeal bread and butter is the best accompaniment.

Serves 4.

Lime pie

shortcrust pastry made with 4 oz (125 g) wholemeal flour
½ pint (275 ml) Greek style natural yoghurt
6 oz (175 g) dark Muscovado sugar
3 eggs, beaten
juice 3 limes

The original key lime pie had a similar filling to this, only it was made with condensed milk. This is a rich, sweet, creamy textured pie with the sharp overtones of lime.

Heat the oven to 375F/190C/gas 5. Line an 8 inch (20 cm) diameter tart tin with the pastry. Beat all the remaining ingredients together until you have a smooth, brown mixture. Pour it into the pastry case.

Bake for 40 minutes, or until the filling is set.

Serves 4–6.

Kumquat and avocado salad

1 lolla rossa (red-edged) lettuce
2 small heads chicory
2 ripe avocados
16 kumquats
4 tablespoons olive oil
juice ½ lemon
1 garlic clove, crushed
1 teaspoon honey
1 teaspoon spiced granular mustard

Kumquats transform any simple salad into something special. These small salads can either be served as a first course, or as an accompaniment to a main meal.

Separate and wash the lettuce leaves. Chop the chicory. Peel and stone the avocados and cut them into long, thin strips. Thinly slice the kumquats.

Arrange the lettuce leaves on each of four plates. Pile the chicory in the centre and arrange the avocado strips on the chicory. Put the sliced kumquats around the edge.

Beat the remaining ingredients together to make a dressing and spoon it over the salads.

Serves 4.

Upside-down kumquat and honey cake

4 oz (125 g) butter, plus extra for greasing
4 oz (125 g) clear honey, plus 2 extra tablespoons
4 oz (125 g) wholemeal flour
½ teaspoon ground cinnamon
⅛ nutmeg, freshly grated
1 teaspoon baking powder
2 eggs, beaten
16 kumquats

Baked under a cake mixture, kumquats soften and sink slightly into the cake and provide a sharp contrast to the rich honey flavour.

Heat the oven to 350F/180C/gas 4. Grease a 7 by 11 inch (18 by 26 cm), 2-inch (5 cm) deep cake tin and spoon in the 2 tablespoons of honey.

Cream the butter with the 4 oz (125 g) honey. Toss the flour with the spices and baking powder and beat it into the butter alternately with the eggs. Cut the kumquats in half crossways and put them, cut side down, on the honey in the tin. Carefully spoon in the cake mixture, keeping the kumquats evenly spaced.

Bake the cake for 20 minutes or until it is firm. Cool it in the tin for 2 minutes. Loosen the edges of the cake and turn it on to a board or large serving plate. Eat it warm, with yoghurt or cream, as a dessert, or cold for tea.

Serves 6.

Pomelo and prawn salad

2 pomelos
6 oz (175 g) shelled prawns
4 tablespoons olive oil
2 tablespoons tomato purée
1 teaspoon paprika
1 head chicory or 1 box mustard and cress, or both

Pomelos go superbly with seafood and need little else to complement the flavours. Other salad vegetables, such as very finely shredded lettuce, can be used instead of the chicory or mustard and cress.

No vinegar or lemon juice is needed in the dressing as the pomelo itself provides all the freshness and acidity that is needed.

Segment and skin the pomelos. Chop each segment into four pieces. Mix with the prawns. Beat together the oil, tomato purée and paprika. Fold this dressing into the salad.

Put a portion of the salad into the centre of each of four small plates. Surround it with chopped chicory and/or a scattering of mustard and cress.

Serves 4.

Candied peel

peel of four pomelos
12 oz (350 g) granulated sugar
3 tablespoons honey or golden syrup
1 pint (575 ml) water

Pomelo peel is best for candying as it is very thick. Use this peel in cakes, breads and buns.

Put the pomelo peel into a large saucepan and cover with cold water. Bring to the boil and drain. Repeat this twice more. Return the peel to the saucepan and cover it with fresh water again. Bring to the boil. Cover, and simmer for 3 hours or until the peel is soft. Drain.

Put the sugar, honey and water into the cleaned pan and stir on a low heat until dissolved. Bring the syrup to the boil. Add the peel and boil until the syrup has evaporated and the peel looks transparent.

Lift the peel on to greaseproof paper and leave to dry.

Grapefruit and cockles

2 yellow grapefruit
4 oz (125 g) cockles
¼ pint (150 ml) natural yoghurt
1 tablespoon tomato purée
½ teaspoon Tabasco sauce
parsley sprigs for garnish

The combinations in this recipe may seem a little surprising, but grapefruit marry well with seafood and the robust flavour of cockles is complemented by the sharpness of the fruit.

Peel the grapefruit and cut each one crossways into 6 slices. Arrange 3 overlapping slices on each of 4 serving plates and put the cockles on top.

Mix together the yoghurt, tomato purée and Tabasco sauce and spoon over the cockles. Garnish with parsley sprigs.

Serves 4.

Pink grapefruit salads

Pink grapefruit have a sweeter, less bitter flavour than the yellow kinds, and go best with cream cheese, creamy yoghurt and dressings made with tahini (page 247). Slice and arrange them as in grapefruit and cockles recipe. Put portions of cream cheese or low fat cheese on top of the grapefruit slices, and garnish with hazelnuts, walnut halves or small pieces of kiwi fruit. Or mix 2 tablespoons tahini with ¼ pint thick yoghurt and spoon it over the slices. Garnish with a sprinkling of sesame or sunflower seeds.

Using the same toppings, the slices of grapefruit can also be cut into quarters and placed on beds of chicory or lettuce.

Chicken with grapefruit

one 3 lb (1.35 kg) roasting chicken
4 tablespoons olive oil
1 large onion, quartered and thinly sliced
1 garlic clove, finely chopped
1 teaspoon ground cumin
1 teaspoon ground coriander
¼ pint (150 ml) stock
1 large yellow grapefruit
¼ pint (150 ml) natural yoghurt
1 box mustard and cress

This lightly spiced and creamy coloured chicken dish has a gentle hint of citrus. It goes well with long grain brown rice.

Cut the chicken into 8 pieces. Heat the oil in a large flameproof casserole on a medium heat. Cook the chicken pieces, in 2 batches if necessary, until golden brown all over and the meat is just beginning to shrink from the bone. Remove from pan and lower the heat.

Stir in the onion and garlic, and cook them until the onion is soft. Sprinkle in the spices. Pour in the stock, bring to the boil and grate in the grapefruit rind. Cover the casserole and cook on a very low heat for 1 hour.

Peel the grapefruit, cut into lengthways quarters, and thinly slice the quarters. Take the casserole from the heat and let the juices come off the boil. Fold in the yoghurt, grapefruit pieces and mustard and cress. Warm the dish for 5 minutes before serving, but do not let it boil or the yoghurt will curdle.

Serves 4.

SOFT CITRUS FRUITS

Satsuma, Kara, Clementine, Wilking, Yafit, Ortanique, Topaz and Tangor, Dancy Tangerine, Ellendale, Tangelo

Soft citrus fruits are usually small and sweet, with easily peelable skin and softer flesh than that of an orange or grapefruit. There are numerous varieties, many of which are pipless, and all have similar uses.

Most soft citrus fruits are available during winter, and all will keep for up to two weeks in a cool larder. They are used mainly in desserts, but make excellent additions to winter salads and are ideal garnishes. Like other citrus fruits, they are a rich source of Vitamin C.

All soft citrus come either under the heading of mandarin or tangerine, two words for the same type of fruit. There are many different varieties and the fruit has also been crossed with other citrus fruits to produce a large number of hybrids.

SATSUMA

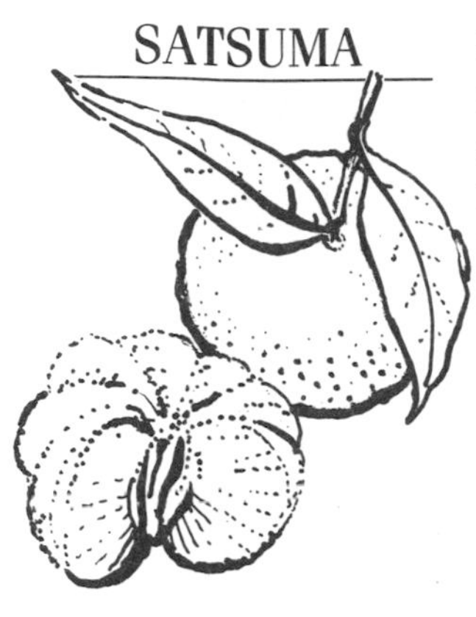

Satsumas are one of the older hybrids and also one of the most popular. They are a cross between a mandarin orange and a sweet orange, and were raised originally in Japan. They came to Europe in the nineteenth century and were established in hot-houses in Kew Gardens before being taken to Spain. Satsumas are small and squat, slightly flattened from top to bottom, with a pale orange skin that peels off extremely easily. All those reaching northern European countries come from Spain as, although the Japanese are large growers of citrus fruits, they eat them all themselves.

KARA

A cross between a king mandarin and a satsuma, available from Spain in spring.

CLEMENTINE

Called 'O My Darlings' in London markets, clementines are a cross between a mandarin orange and a Seville orange, first raised in Algeria around 1900 by a monk named Père Clement, who gave the variety its name. Clementines are almost perfectly round with deep orange, shiny, tight fitting skins, few or no pips and a very sweet flavour with a hint of sharpness. Winter types are imported from Spain, Morocco and Corsica, and in summer small quantities come from South Africa.

WILKING

A cross between king and common mandarins. They were quite popular a few years ago, but are now mainly used for breeding other varieties as they are extremely pippy.

Murcots, **Temples** and **Michals** are also mandarin crosses.

YAFIT

A cross between a Wilking and a mandarin.

ORTANIQUE

A cross between a mandarin and a sweet orange, raised originally in the West Indies. It is larger than most mandarins and very sweet.

TOPAZ AND TANGOR

The Topaz and the Tangor have been raised in recent years in Israel from a sweet orange and mandarin cross. The Tangor is large, with a rough skin and will probably be phased out in the near future as the Topaz is developed. The Topaz is larger, with a smooth, bright orange, loose skin and sweet, juicy flesh. Both are available in early spring and are occasionally sold under the name of **Jaffarines**.

DANCY TANGERINE

This is a cross between a sweet orange and a mandarin developed in Florida. The flesh is sweet and aromatic, but it does have pips.

ELLENDALE

Similar to a Dancy tangerine, but without pips.

TANGELO

There are several varieties of Tangelo, all crosses between a mandarin and a grapefruit. **Minneolas** are a cross between a Dancy tangerine and a grapefruit, originally developed in California. Supplies also come from Israel, Cyprus and South Africa. Minneolas are about the size of a small orange, a very deep orange colour with a pronounced bump on the top. If the peel is broken at the top it comes away easily. The flesh has an aromatic, sharp flavour.

Orlandos are one of the newest Israeli fruits, also of the tangelo type, but are only occasionally available in Britain.

Ortanique, almond and parsley salad

4 ortaniques
3 oz (75 g) almonds
6 tablespoons chopped parsley
juice 1 lemon
4 tablespoons olive oil
1 garlic clove, crushed
freshly ground black pepper

A bright, glossy salad to refresh the palate before a meal.

Cut the rind and pith from the ortaniques. Cut the segments from the skin and chop them. Blanch and split the almonds and put them into a bowl with the ortaniques and parsley. Beat the lemon juice, oil, garlic and pepper together and fold into the salad. Serve in small bowls.

Serves 4.

Temple or minneola salad

2 ripe, firm avocados
4 temples or minneolas
4 fl oz (120 ml) natural yoghurt
2 tablespoons sunflower oil
1 garlic clove, crushed
2 oz (50 g) sunflower seeds

Citrus fruit goes well with the rich creaminess of avocado.

Peel, halve and stone the avocados. Cut each half into 6 crossways slices. Peel the temples or minneolas and pull them into segments. Arrange the avocado slices, cut side down, putting 3 fruit segments between the largest slices of avocado on each plate, and the rest round the edge.

Beat the yoghurt with the oil and garlic and spoon over the avocados. Scatter the sunflower seeds over the top.

Serves 4.

Duck with clementines and caper sauce

one 3½ lb (1.6 kg) duck
2 teaspoons fine sea salt
1 large orange
freshly ground black pepper
1 sprig each thyme, marjoram and sage
¾ pint (425 ml) stock, preferably made from the giblets
4 tablespoons chopped capers
3 clementines

Duck with orange is a classic and wonderful combination. Any small, soft citrus fruits can be used instead of clementines in this recipe.

Heat the oven to 375F/190C/gas 5. Prick the skin of the duck all over with a fork and rub it with salt. Grate over the rind of half the orange and squeeze and reserve the juice. Season the inside of the duck with pepper. Thinly slice the other half of the orange and put it inside the duck, together with the herbs. Put the duck on a rack in a roasting tin and cover with foil. Put it into the oven for 1 hour 15 minutes. Remove foil and continue cooking for up to 30 minutes until the skin is brown. Remove the duck, carve the meat into slices and keep warm.

Pour all the fat from the roasting tin and put the tin on top of the stove on a high heat. Pour in the stock and bring to the boil, scraping in the sticky residue from the bottom of the tin. Add the orange juice and capers. Reheat the sauce and serve separately.

Just before serving, peel the clementines and pull them into segments. Scatter the segments among the slices of duck.

Serves 4.

Orange dessert cake with satsumas

CAKE

4 oz (125 g) wholemeal flour
1 teaspoon bicarbonate of soda
4 oz (125 g) dark Muscovado sugar
grated rind and juice of 1 large orange
4 tablespoons corn oil, plus extra for greasing
2 eggs, beaten

TOPPING

7 fl oz (200 ml) double cream
grated rind of 1 large orange
3 tablespoons Drambuie or orange liqueur (optional)
at least 2 satsumas

Use as many satsumas as you like for decorating this cake, placed either around the edge or all over the top. Their fresh, sweet flavour contrasts well with the rich cake and cream.

Heat the oven to 350F/180C/gas 4. For the cake, mix the flour, bicarbonate of soda, sugar and orange rind in a bowl. Make a well in the centre, pour in the orange juice, oil and eggs and gradually beat in flour from the sides of the well until you have a smooth, thick batter.

Line an 8 inch (20 cm) diameter tart tin with oiled greaseproof paper. Pour in the batter and bake for 20 minutes or until firm. Turn on to a wire rack to cool.

Whip the cream with the orange rind. Whip in the liqueur. Spread the cream over the cake base. Pull the satsumas into segments and use them as a garnish.

Serves 6–8.

CRANBERRY, LINGONBERRY AND WINEBERRY

CRANBERRY

VACCINIUM MACROCARPUM

CRANBERRIES ARE LIKE small, shiny, deep red marbles, with a thick skin that enables them to be stored for long periods. There are several varieties, all members of the heather family. They are essentially an American fruit. British cranberries were never cultivated, but grew wild in the East Anglian fens and in parts of northern England, Wales and Scotland. Although picked and enjoyed locally, they were never taken to other areas. No cookery book ever contained a cranberry recipe although there were certainly local ones for sauces, tarts and puddings. William Cobbett described the cranberry as 'the finest fruit for tarts that ever grew.' When the fens were drained, cranberries all but disappeared from the more southern parts of England but can still occasionally be found in Cumbria and parts of Scotland and Wales.

When the Pilgrim Fathers arrived in New England, they found the American cranberry, which is larger than the British variety, being harvested by the American Indians who, among other things, used them in the winter preservation of meat. The settlers soon realized how important this fruit could be to them.

The American cranberry grew wild from Newfoundland to South Carolina, and westwards to Saskatchewan. It was so prolific that at first, cultivation was not necessary. The wild berries ripened in autumn and were picked all through winter, softening and mellowing in the colder weather. In the eighteenth century some were sent back to Britain, packed for the journey in barrels of water.

Cranberry cultivation began in the early nineteenth century in Cape Cod, Massachusetts, where the fruit was first found. This area still produces 70 per cent of the total American cranberry crop.

The water level in the cranberry bogs is artificially controlled, lowered during the main growing time in the summer and raised from

December to April for the harvest. After mechanical cutting, the fruit floats, to the top of the water and is swept together to form separate 'islands', showing deep red against the water. In the early days rotten berries were sorted out by bouncing the cranberries down steps, removing any that didn't bounce and were less sound. As a result, cranberries were often referred to as 'bounce berries'. Modern grading machines work on the same principle, bouncing the berries over 4-inch (10 cm) barriers.

Cranberries for export are packed in plastic containers or vacuum packs. They are available in British shops from November to January.

Nutrition

Cranberries are rich in potassium, calcium and Vitamins C and A.

Buying and storing cranberries

Cranberries keep exceptionally well as they contain their own natural preservative, and are usually sound when bought. Still in their plastic packs, they will keep for up to two months in the refrigerator, and kept in jars, covered with cold water, they will keep in the refrigerator for up to four months. Put directly into the freezer in their wrapping, they will keep for up to a year.

Cranberries in the kitchen

Cranberries have a hard skin and a sharp flavour which makes it impossible to eat them raw. However, as they cook, the skin softens and bursts with a pop, and the addition of sugar or honey draws out their true flavour. To cook them, you will need ¼ pint (150 ml) liquid (either water or orange juice) and 4–8 oz (125–225 g) sugar or honey, depending on the recipe, per 1 lb (450 g) cranberries. Put the water and cranberries into a saucepan, cover, and set on a low heat until the skins pop. You will hear this happening and should take care when lifting the lid in case they pop out. After they have burst, stir in the sweetener and let it dissolve.

One of the most popular uses of cranberries is for sauces and relishes to go with poultry, meat and game. Once cooked, they can be put into puddings, pies and tarts or puréed and made into ice-creams, jellies, mousses and cheesecakes.

Bottled cranberry juice is available and can be used as a drink or cooking liquid when cooking cranberries or other fruits.

LINGONBERRY

Lingonberries grow wild in Scandinavian swamps and are harvested after the winter frosts and snows have softened and sweetened them. They are dark red, about a quarter the size of cranberries, and have a resinous flavour. Like cranberries, they keep exceptionally well in tubs of cold water. Lingonberries can be made into sauces for meat and game, piled on to pancakes, baked in puddings and made into cream desserts.

WINEBERRY

Wineberries, sometimes called checkerberries, grow wild in the United States, and are the fruit of an evergreen herb. They are used like cranberries.

Galantine of turkey with cranberries and walnuts

A superb way of preparing cold turkey for a special buffet party or cold sit-down meal. When sliced you can see the rich, red stuffing in the centre of each slice. The texture of the stuffing is light and it has a fresh, fruity flavour.

one 12 lb (5.5 kg) turkey
1½ oz (40 g) butter, softened

STUFFING

4 oz (125 g) walnuts
1½ oz (40 g) butter
1 large onion, quartered and thinly sliced
12 oz (350 g) cranberries
4 oz (125 g) wholemeal breadcrumbs
4 tablespoons dry red wine
2 tablespoons chopped parsley
1 tablespoon chopped thyme
1 tablespoon chopped marjoram
sea salt and freshly ground black pepper

Bone out the turkey by first slitting it down the back bone. Remove the rib cage and finally the leg and wing bones. Alternatively, ask the butcher to do this for you.

Finely chop the walnuts. Melt the butter in a large frying pan on a low heat and cook the onion and cranberries until the onion is soft and all the cranberries have burst. Take the pan from the heat and mix in the walnuts, breadcrumbs, wine, herbs and seasonings.

Heat the oven to 400F/200C/gas 6. Lay the boned turkey out flat, skin side down. Lay the stuffing down the centre. Reshape the turkey and sew it up. Put it on a rack in a roasting tin and spread with the butter. Cover completely with foil and roast for 2 hours. Remove foil and continue cooking for another 30 minutes, so the skin becomes well browned. Cool the turkey on the rack and transfer to a large serving dish. Cover and leave for 12 hours in a cool place before slicing and serving.

Serves 10.

Cranberries on walnut shortcake

SHORTCAKE

6 oz (125 g) wholemeal flour
3 oz (75 g) chopped walnuts
2 oz (50 g) dark Muscovado sugar
4 oz (125 g) butter, softened

TOPPING

4 oz (125 g) cranberries
4 oz (125 g) honey
juice of 2 large oranges
½ oz (15 g) gelatin
½ pint (275 ml) Greek-style natural yoghurt

Cranberries mashed into a rough purée for this mousse-like topping, give an interesting, dappled texture.

Heat the oven to 400F/200C/gas 6. For the shortcake, put the flour, walnuts and sugar into a bowl. Rub in the butter and bring the mixture together to make a crumbly dough. Press into a greased, 10-inch (25 cm) diameter tart tin with a removable base. Bake for 15 minutes, or until firm, but not coloured. Cool completely in the tin.

Put the cranberries, honey and orange juice into a saucepan. Cover, and bring to the boil on a low heat. Simmer until the cranberries can be mashed to a thick purée.

Off the heat, sprinkle in the gelatin and stir well until dissolved. Leave the cranberries until cool and on the point of setting. Stir in the yoghurt. Spoon the mixture on top of the walnut shortcake, still in the tin, and leave in a cool place to set completely.

Serves 6–8.

CURRANTS, BLACK, RED AND WHITE

RIBES SPECIES

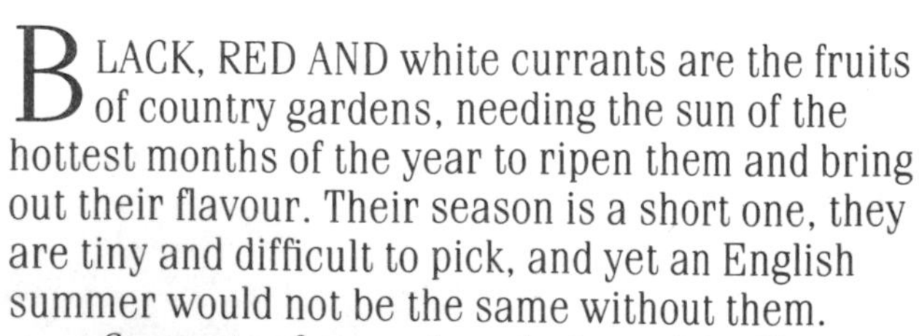

BLACK, RED AND white currants are the fruits of country gardens, needing the sun of the hottest months of the year to ripen them and bring out their flavour. Their season is a short one, they are tiny and difficult to pick, and yet an English summer would not be the same without them.

Currants of some description originally grew wild across the whole of northern Europe, as far as Siberia, Asia and the Himalayas and also in north Africa. They were brought into gardens in the fifteenth century and the varieties were gradually developed and improved. In the nineteenth century, types of currants became more distinct, more named varieties were developed, and they were taken to many temperate countries across the world.

In Britain, they are a popular garden fruit as they are low growing and take up little room. A large majority of the commercially grown fruits go for processing but, with the development of the Pick-Your-Own system, more people are able to enjoy the delights of the fresh fruits.

BLACK-CURRANTS

RIBES NIGRUM

Blackcurrants are the largest of the currants, and the plumpest can be up to ½ inch (1.3 cm) in diameter. Black or dark purple in colour, they have a mellow flavour with a distinct sharpness.

Nutrition

Blackcurrants have a higher Vitamin C content than any other fruit. They are also high in potassium and contain significant amounts of calcium, phosphorus and Vitamin A.

Buying, picking and storing blackcurrants

Pick your own blackcurrants on a hot, sunny day, as the sun draws out their flavour. They are ripe as soon as they are black all over, and should be picked as soon after this as possible. They should not be stored for too long at this stage, however, especially if the weather is hot, or they will become squashy. When buying blackcurrants, make sure that they are ripe, but not over-ripe.

Blackcurrants should not be kept for more than one day after picking, in the refrigerator.

Freeze them on trays before packing into polythene bags. They will keep for up to four months.

Blackcurrants in the kitchen

Before using blackcurrants, wash them, remove them from their thin stems and pick out any that are under- or over-ripe. There is no need to remove the brown remains of the flower on the top of each fruit, as these soften and disappear in cooking and are not noticeable when the fruit is eaten raw. Use blackcurrants sparingly in mixtures of raw fruits. There is no need to cook them for pies, crumbles and other pastries, as the time that it takes to cook the topping will be sufficient to soften them.

When cooking blackcurrants, you will generally need no more than four tablespoons of liquid per 1 lb (450 g) fruit, plus 4–6 oz (125–175 g) sugar or honey. Put them into a saucepan with the water and sweetener, cover, and set on a low heat for 10–15 minutes, by which time they will have softened and become very juicy. A sprig of mint gives a fresh flavour, and a few lemon balm leaves a hint of lemon and honey. Cooked blackcurrants, on their own or with other soft fruits, can be sieved and used for summer puddings, ice-creams, jellies, cheesecakes and other cream desserts. They make excellent jams and jellies and also fruit syrups and country wines. In France they are made into the liqueur known as cassis which can be drunk alone or mixed with dry white wine.

RED AND WHITE CURRANTS

Red and white currants are smaller than blackcurrants and hang on the bushes in long, delicate strings. Their flavour is sharper, too, the red probably more so than the white, so they can be used in savoury as well as sweet dishes. Although white currants look like unripened red currants they are, in fact, a separate species, beginning green like the red currants, and turning very pale and transparent as they ripen. They are popular in the north of England. Both can tolerate drought and poorer soil conditions than the blackcurrants.

Nutrition

Both fruits are high in potassium. Their Vitamin C content is significant, but nowhere near that of blackcurrants.

Picking, buying and storing red and white currants

If you pick your own, make sure that they are fully ripe and not green, but not too soft. Once ripe, they stay in good condition for longer than do blackcurrants.

When buying red and white currants, make sure that they are fully ripe and not soft. They should look very shiny.

Red and white currants will keep in the refrigerator for up to three days. To freeze them, remove them from the strings and freeze them on trays before packing into polythene bags. They will keep for up to four months.

Red and white currants in the kitchen

Red currants can be made into both sweet and savoury dishes. White currants are nearly always used in desserts. Both can be stewed gently together, or with blackcurrants and other soft fruits to make a summer pudding.

Put them raw into pies, tarts and crumbles as for blackcurrants. They are rarely made into cream-based desserts, more often into lighter sherbets and water ices.

Red currants can be added raw, with chopped mint, to summer salads, where they glisten amongst the green leaves. They can also be scattered raw over meat dishes as a garnish. Add them to sauté dishes and stuffings, and use them to make savoury sauces and relishes.

Red currant jam tends to be very pippy, but every cook needs red currant jelly in the larder to serve as an accompaniment to meat and game; to add to sauces, both sweet and savoury; to add to braised red cabbage; and to use as a glaze for fruit tarts.

Gigot of lamb with red currants

1 oz (25 g) butter
4 small gigot cutlets of lamb, about 1¼ lb (575 g) altogether
1 small onion, finely chopped
1 celery stick, finely chopped
¾ pint (425 ml) stock
4 oz (125 g) red currants
2 tablespoons chopped mint

If you need to prepare a summer dinner party in a hurry, this dish is perfect. It is quick and easy to prepare, and looks wonderful with its garnish of glossy red currants and bright green mint.

Melt the butter in a frying pan on a high heat. Brown the cutlets on both sides. Continue cooking until they are tender, but still pink in the middle, about 10 minutes altogether. Remove, and keep warm.

Lower the heat and soften the onion and celery. Pour in the stock, and bring to the boil. Add 2 oz (50 g) of the red currants. Boil the stock until reduced by half, then strain it through a sieve. Return to the cleaned pan and reheat it.

Slice the cutlets thinly. Divide the sauce between four dinner plates and arrange the slices of lamb on top. Scatter the remaining red currants over the lamb and sprinkle the chopped mint on to the sauce.

Serves 4.

Blackcurrant cake

8 oz (225 g) blackcurrants
7 oz (200 g) light Muscovado sugar
2 tablespoons water
8 oz (225 g) wholemeal flour
2 teaspoons baking powder
pinch fine sea salt
6 oz (175 g) butter, plus extra for greasing
3 eggs, beaten
4 oz (125 g) almonds, blanched and ground (see page 208)
4 tablespoons milk
6 oz (175 g) sweet cream cheese or low fat soft cheese
4 tablespoons soured cream
2 tablespoons honey

A deliciously moist cake, with the full flavour of blackcurrants.

Put the blackcurrants into a saucepan with 1 oz of the sugar and the water. Cover, and set on a low heat until the juice is just beginning to run, about 10 minutes.

Heat the oven to 350F/180C/gas 4. Mix the flour with the baking powder and salt. Cream the butter with the remaining sugar, and beat in the flour, alternately with the eggs. Mix in the almonds, milk and blackcurrants together with their juice. Mix well. Put the mixture into a buttered 7-inch (18 cm) diameter cake tin and bake for 1 hour 15 minutes, or until a skewer inserted into the centre comes out clean. Turn the cake on to a wire rack to cool completely.

To make the frosting, beat the soured cream and honey into the cream cheese. Cut the cake in half horizontally, and sandwich it together with one-third of the frosting. Spread the remainder over the top and sides of the cake.

Serves 4.

Blackcurrant sherbet

1 lb (450 g) blackcurrants
1 mint sprig
½ pint (275 ml) diluted Ribena or other blackcurrant drink
4 oz (125 g) honey
½ pint (275 ml) water
¼ pint (150 ml) yoghurt
mint leaves for garnish

A beautiful, dark purple ice with a really refreshing flavour.

String the blackcurrants and put them into a saucepan with the mint sprig, 6 tablespoons (90 ml) of the blackcurrant drink and the honey. Cover, and set on a low heat. Cook for about 12 minutes, or until soft. Remove the mint sprig and rub the blackcurrants through a sieve. Set aside half the purée to be used as a sauce and mix the rest with the remaining blackcurrant drink and water. Chill for 1 hour.

If you are using an ice-cream machine, stir in the yoghurt after chilling, and freeze according to the manufacturer's instructions.

Otherwise, put the chilled mixture into a freezing tray and place in the coldest part of the freezer, or into the freezing compartment of the refrigerator set at its coldest temperature. Chill for about 2 hours, or until the mixture has become a slush. Turn the slush, into a bowl and beat it well. Beat in the yoghurt. Return the mixture to the freezing tray and freeze completely.

Once the sherbet is frozen, scoop it out with an ice-cream scoop and put each portion on to a freezing tray. Freeze solid once more.

Serve the sherbets straight from the freezer, with a little of the reserved blackcurrant purée spooned over and garnished with mint leaves.

The sherbets can be packed in polythene bags and stored in the freezer for up to three months.

Makes 12 scoops.

Red and white currant tart

A pretty summer tart with fresh, slightly sharp fruits combined with rich, sweet pastry. If you cannot get white currants, substitute black.

14 oz (400 g) wholemeal flour
pinch fine sea salt
2 eggs, separated
9 oz (250 g) butter, softened
2 tablespoons honey
8 oz (225 g) red currants
8 oz (225 g) white currants
3 oz (75 g) golden caster sugar

Heat the oven to 400F/200C/gas 6. Put the flour on to a work top, scatter on the salt and make a well in the centre. Put in the egg yolks, butter and honey and pound the mixture with your fingertips, gradually bringing in flour from the sides. Work until you have a smooth dough. Gather it into a ball, cover with a cloth and leave for 15 minutes.

String the red and white currants, keeping them separate. Mix each type with half the sugar.

Roll out just over half the pastry and use it to line a 10-inch (25 cm) diameter tart tin. Cut the remaining pastry into strips the depth of the tin and arrange on edge to separate the tart into 12 sections. Fill the sections alternately, with red and white currants. With the pastry trimmings, make a rose for the centre. Brush the pastry with egg white.

Bake the tart for 25 minutes and serve warm with single cream, or cold with whipped double cream.

Serves 6–8.

Red currant triple-decker pie

shortcrust pastry made with 8 oz (225 g) wholemeal flour
1 lb (450 g) red currants
4 oz (125 g) light Muscovado sugar
2 lemon balm leaves, finely chopped (optional, but very good if you have them)
1 egg, beaten

A traditional pie from the north of England.

Heat the oven to 350F/180C/gas 4. Divide the pastry into 3 equal portions. Roll each piece into a round that will fit into a straight-sided, 6-inch (15 cm) diameter, ovenproof dish. String the red currants and mix with the sugar and lemon balm leaves.

Put one pastry round in the bottom of the dish, pile in half the red currants, add another pastry round and then the remaining red currants. Top with the remaining pastry. Brush the top with the beaten egg.

Bake for 45 minutes, or until golden brown on top.

Serves 4–6.

CUSTARD APPLE AND CHERIMOYA

ANNONA SPECIES

CUSTARD APPLE, CHERIMOYA, sugar apple, atemoya, ilama and sour sop are interchangeable names for members of the *Annona* family. They are all conical or heart-shaped and of varying sizes, with a thick skin ranging from dull yellow to grey-green, patterned in scale shapes making the fruit look reptilian. Inside is a soft, white, sweetly fragrant flesh containing hard black seeds with the feel of pebbles.

The fruits are native to tropical America, Ecuador and the Peruvian Andes, where they were first taken into cultivation by the Incas. European explorers took them to the West Indies, where they quickly became established. Some were grown in European hot houses in the sixteenth and seventeenth centuries, but it took the British West Indian population in more recent years to ensure their continued shipment to this country.

They are also grown in Israel, Australia, Florida and South Africa.

The **cherimoya** is the most readily available, and is being grown on a large scale in Israel. The fruits vary in size, but are usually about 6 inches (15 cm) long and 5 inches (12.5 cm) in diameter at the base, tapering to a rounded point. The skin is grey-green with large, V-shaped indentations. The flesh of the cherimoya is just off-white, very sweet and almost perfumed, and it is considered the best of all the *Annona* fruits. Very similar to the cherimoya is the **atemoya**, which crops more heavily and contains fewer seeds.

The **custard apple** is probably the best known variety, and its name has often been used for all the rest. It is rounder than the cherimoya, with a smooth, yellow-brown skin, and can weigh up to 4½ lb (2 kg). Its flesh is a pale yellow, with a slight granular texture.

The **sugar apple** is grown in gardens in Central America and is also popular in India. It is yellow-brown and scaly in appearance with a sweet, firm, pale yellow flesh.

The **ilama** can be conical, oval or round and its colour varies from pale pink to green. The colour of the flesh varies with that of the skin. Those with a green skin are sweet, and those with pink are slightly acid.

The **sour sop** is also acid, more so than any of the others, with rather pithy flesh. It is the largest of the *Annona* fruits and can weigh up to 8 lb (3.5 kg).

Nutrition

The nutritional properties of these fruits vary. The custard apple is high in Vitamin C, the cherimoya and the sour sop in Vitamin A. There is also a significant amount of potassium in the sour sop.

Buying and storing custard apples and cherimoya

When ripe, the fruits should yield slightly if pressed. They are often sold under-ripe, and can be ripened off in a day or so in a warm room. Over-ripe fruits are either browned, too soft, or both.

Once the fruits are soft, they should be eaten as soon as possible, although they will keep for up to two days in the refrigerator.

Freezing them is not a good idea, as they are best fresh and raw.

Custard apples and cherimoya in the kitchen

For many years, custard apples have been the instant young childrens' food for West Indian mothers. The soft, sweet and creamy flesh can be spooned out and eaten just as it is needing no preparation and no sugar. It can be eaten on its own, mashed with bananas or yoghurt, or as a creamy sauce on top of other fruits. Mix it into yoghurt or whipped cream to make a fool. Mixed with water and fruit juice, it makes a delicious drink. A squeeze of lime juice will help to bring out its flavour for adults and, like this, it can be a base for cream desserts, ice-creams and trifles.

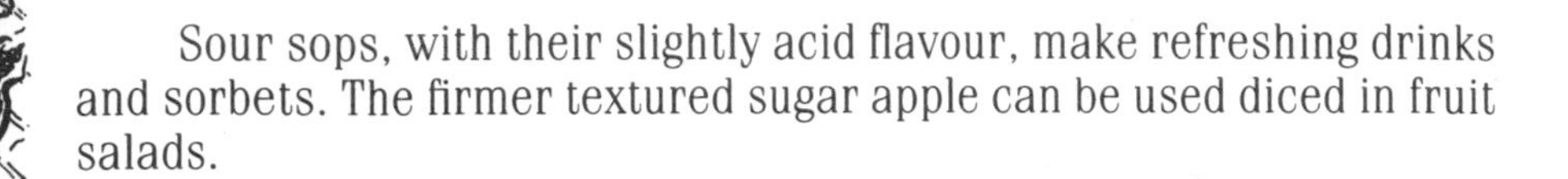

Sour sops, with their slightly acid flavour, make refreshing drinks and sorbets. The firmer textured sugar apple can be used diced in fruit salads.

Sliced and spiced custard apple

2 custard apples, slightly under-ripe
½ teaspoon ground cinnamon
½ teaspoon ground allspice
4 tablespoons dark Muscovado sugar
4 tablespoons rum

This is so simple it is hardly a recipe at all, but even so it makes a rich and unusual dessert, tasting rather like vanilla ice-cream with a spiced rum sauce.

Peel the custard apples and cut into thin, lengthways slices, removing as many seeds as you can. Put them into a bowl and sprinkle with the spices, sugar and rum. Cover, and leave at room temperature so the sugar, spices and rum combine to make a rich, dark sauce.

Serve just as it is, or sprinkled with finely chopped candied peel.

Serves 4.

Custard apple whip

2 ripe custard apples, each about 12 oz (350 g)
¼ pint (150 ml) double cream
4 oz (125 g) fromage frais
½ teaspoon ground cinnamon
juice ¼ lime, plus extra to taste
coconut flakes or mixed chopped nuts for decoration

Serve this plain as a dessert, or as a topping for a tropical fruit salad, cake or trifle.

Peel the custard apples and rub the flesh through a sieve. Stiffly whip the cream. Whip in the fromage frais and the custard apple purée, cinnamon and lime juice. Taste, and add extra lime juice if wished.

Put the whip into individual glasses and chill for 30 minutes. Serve scattered with coconut flakes or chopped nuts.

Serves 4.

Custard apple and yoghurt drink

1 ripe custard apple, about 12 oz (350 g)
½ pint (275 ml) natural yoghurt
½ teaspoon ground cinnamon
½ pint (275 ml) natural spring water (not essential, but tastes better than tap water)
crushed ice (optional)

A refreshing concoction to serve plain or poured over crushed ice as a cooling summer cocktail.

Slice the custard apple into 8. Pick out the seeds and cut away the skin. Roughly chop the flesh, and purée it in a blender. Add the yoghurt and cinnamon and blend again until the mixture is smooth. Add the water and blend until the drink is evenly mixed. Pour into glasses straightaway, or half-fill four tall glasses with crushed ice and pour the drink over the top.

Scrves 4.

DATE

PHOENIX DACTYLIFERA

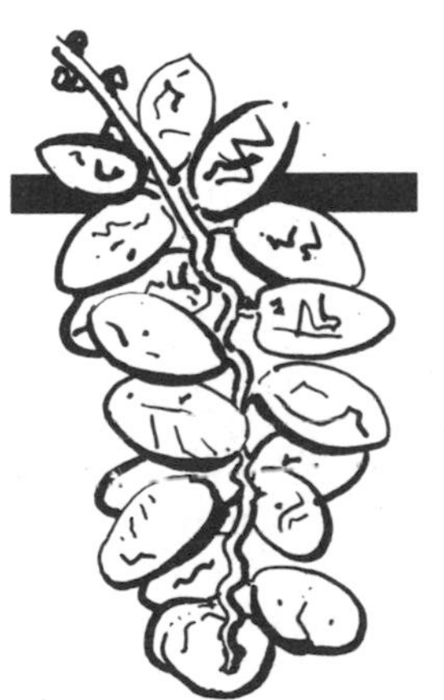

THE DATE PALM is the most bountiful of trees, producing an average of 100 lb (45 kg) of highly nutritious fruits every year, for at least sixty years. It is also one of the most ancient. Its exact origins are unknown, but many thousands of years ago wild trees were growing in western India and around the Persian Gulf, and dates were cultivated in the Indus Valley in at least 3,000 BC. At this time they were cheaper than grain and, both fresh, or dried and ground into flour, were a staple diet of the poor.

Because of their high calorific value and great sustaining properties, dates have always been highly valued, especially in the Arab world. In medieval times dates were carried to Britain on the spice ships from southern Europe, and were prized as a sweetener not only in desserts, but also in fish and meat dishes, at a time when sugar was scarce and expensive.

Today, date palms grow in all dry, tropical countries and are mostly exported from California and Arizona in the United States, and from Israel, Iraq, Iran, Saudi Arabia, Tunisia and Algeria.

Dates are dried for dessert or cooking purposes and are also sold fresh. Due to the efforts of the Israelis, fresh dates come into the country all year round. Most have been stripped from their thin stems, known as strands, and frozen. They are dark brown and plump, with a thin, shiny skin. The flesh is dark brown, firm and succulent.

In the autumn a very few fresh, unfrozen dates come into the country, still on their strands. These are a real treat and to cook with them would be a crime, so eat them as sweets and relish them. They are yellow-brown in colour, both outside and in, with sweet, honeyed and melting flesh.

The dessert dates that are sold in wooden boxes are of a similar type to those that are sold fresh. They are grown mainly in Algeria, Tunisia and California and the main varieties are Deglet Nour and Deglet Ennour. Dessert dates are harvested mechanically, washed and graded, and left unstoned. A very few are sun-dried, but most are spread on wire trays in dehydration rooms, where they stay for up to eight days. From Algeria and Tunisia the loose dates are shipped to be packed, herring-bone fashion, into wooden boxes.

Most cooking dates are of a different variety, shorter and fatter than the dessert types, and are grown in Iraq and Iran. They are cheaper to produce, have a coarser, more fibrous texture and all are sold completely dried. They are nearly always stoned.

Nutrition

Dates have a high sugar content, are remarkably high in potassium and also have significant amounts of calcium and phosphorus, plus Vitamins A, B1, B2, C and D.

Buying and storing dates

Fresh dates still on the strand should be firm and have shiny, yellow-brown skins. Signs of ageing are dull or slightly wrinkled skin. They will keep for about three days in the refrigerator. Fresh, previously frozen dates should be dark brown, shiny and slightly sticky looking. Do not buy them if they look dull or have a whitish bloom on the skin. They will keep for up to a week in the refrigerator.

Dessert dates in wooden boxes should be light brown, smooth-skinned and shiny. They will keep in their box in a cool place for up to two months, and although still edible after this, will probably harden.

Cooking dates should look soft and sticky, not hard and dry. They will keep for up to three months in an airtight container in a cool place.

Dates in the kitchen

Fresh dates can be eaten as sweet treats or used in cooking. Their skins are thin and papery and quite edible, but can be slipped off very easily. Simply remove the short piece of stalk from one end and then gently squeeze at the other end so the date slips out. To stone dates, loosen the stone around the stalk end with a hair pin or a small pointed knife, and winkle it out, or push it straight through from one end to the other.

Fresh dates are often stuffed with sweet or savoury fillings. They go exceptionally well with cheese, so try mixtures of cream or curd cheese, herbs and garlic to serve them before a meal, or marzipan and other sweetened, ground nut mixtures to serve as sweetmeats. Leave the skins on, and remove the stones by slitting all down one side. The slit can then be filled with the stuffing.

Chopped, fresh dates are delicious, added sparingly to side salads and salads for main courses. They are excellent with the more bitter salad vegetables such as curly endive, and in a main course salad, go well with cheese. Chopped and mixed with cream cheese, either sweetened or with savoury ingredients added, they make a nourishing sandwich filling. Mixed into natural yoghurt, they add both sweetness and flavour.

Where you need a moist texture, such as in Fresh Date Cheesecake (page 91), fresh dates can be chopped and used in cooking. They will give the same rich sweetness as dried dates, but a much lighter feel to the whole dish.

Whole and stoned, they can be set into sharp jellies to give a contrast in flavour and texture, and can also be used as a garnish for cakes and other desserts.

Dried dates are mainly used in cooking, although they are also good in salads and sandwich fillings with the same ingredients as fresh dates. They do not need to be skinned, and both whole and pressed dates can be chopped with a sharp, heavy knife. Look out for stray stones hidden among the dates. If you need a softer date and frozen ones are not available, whole dried dates can be steeped in fruit juice or black tea for about an hour, or can be steamed for 10 minutes to soften them.

Chopped dried dates can be added to tea breads, cakes, scones, puddings and biscuits and, because they are so sweet, you will probably have to cut down on the amount of sugar. Simmered and liquidized in the simmering liquid, dates can be a complete substitute for sugar, as in the recipe for date and orange cake (page 91). Some makers of wholemeal biscuits are now using date paste as a substitute for sugar, giving a sweet flavour and crumbly texture.

JUBEJUBE OR CHINESE DATE

ZIZIPHUS JUBUBA

Jubejubes or Chinese dates have been cultivated in China since the third century BC. They grow wild around the Mediterranean and also in India. There are many different varieties, but the dried ones available in Britain are small and round, with a wrinkled red skin, a round stone and sweet, fondant-like flesh. They can usually be found in shops specializing in Chinese ingredients. In China, the dates are used in a number of sweet dishes including deep fried, batter coated balls of mixed dried fruits, and also in fillings for the steamed buns known as dim sum.

Fresh date and cheese salad

4 oz (125 g) fresh dates
6 oz (175 g) Cheddar cheese
4 oz (125 g) shelled walnuts
½ curly endive, or more
4 tablespoons olive oil
juice ½ lemon
1 garlic clove, crushed
pinch cayenne pepper
1 small onion, halved and very thinly sliced

A simple salad that shows just how well dates go with savoury flavours. If fresh dates are not available, you can use boxed dates, but the curly endive is essential for its robust flavour. Lettuce would simply disappear beneath the strength of the other flavours.

Serve the salad as a light main course.

Stone the dates, leaving them whole. Skin them if wished. Thinly slice them crossways. Coarsely grate the cheese. Chop the walnuts.

Break the endive into pieces and divide it between four individual plates. Scatter the dates and walnuts over the top. Beat together the oil, lemon juice, garlic and pepper. Spoon the dressing over the salad. Put a portion of cheese in the centre of each salad and top with pieces of onion.

Serves 4.

Peaches stuffed with dates

4 medium peaches
4 oz (125 g) dried dates
4 oz (125 g) ground almonds
¼ pint (150 ml) natural orange juice
8 glacé cherries

Heat the oven to 350F/180C/gas 4. Halve and stone the peaches and place in an ovenproof dish, cut side up. Finely chop the dates and mix with the almonds and 4 tablespoons of the orange juice. Fill the peach halves with the mixture and top each one with half a glacé cherry. Pour the remaining orange juice round the peach halves.

Bake the peaches for 10 minutes. Serve either warm or cool.

Serves 4.

Fresh date cheesecake

8 oz (225 g) fresh dates
1 lb (450 g) ricotta cheese
3 eggs, beaten
1 oz (25 g) wholemeal flour
2 tablespoons clear honey
butter for greasing

A firm, moist cheesecake without a pastry base. The fresh dates are essential, as they add to the moistness as well as to sweetness in the semi-sweet base. If ricotta cheese is not available, use cottage cheese instead.

Heat the oven to 375F/190C/gas 5. Skin, stone and chop the dates. Sieve the cheese into a bowl. Beat in the eggs, flour and honey and fold in the dates. Pour the mixture into a greased, 8 by 10 inch (20 by 25 cm) shallow baking tin, preferably non-stick. Bake for 35 minutes or until set and golden brown on top. Turn on to a wire rack to cool. Cut into squares or fingers to serve.

Serves 4.

Date and orange cake

8 oz (225 g) dried dates
¼ pint (150 ml) natural orange juice
6 oz (175 g) butter, softened, plus extra for greasing
grated rind 1 large orange
1 medium carrot, finely grated
4 eggs, beaten
8 oz (225 g) wholemeal flour
1 teaspoon bicarbonate of soda

This recipe shows how dates can be used as a sweetener in baking. The cake is surprisingly light in texture, with a strong orange flavour. It is rich and tasty enough not to need any topping or decoration.

Heat the oven to 350F/180C/gas 4/. Butter an 8-inch (20 cm) diameter cake tin. Finely chop the dates and put into a saucepan with the orange juice. Set on a low heat and bring slowly to the boil. Simmer for 5 minutes. Take the pan from the heat and cool.

Cream the butter with the orange rind, and beat in the carrot. Add the bicarbonate of soda to the flour and beat in alternately with the eggs. Beat in the dates and orange juice.

Put the mixture into the prepared tin. Bake for 30 minutes, or until a skewer inserted into the centre comes out clean.

Serves 4.

ELDERBERRY

SAMBUCUS NIGRA

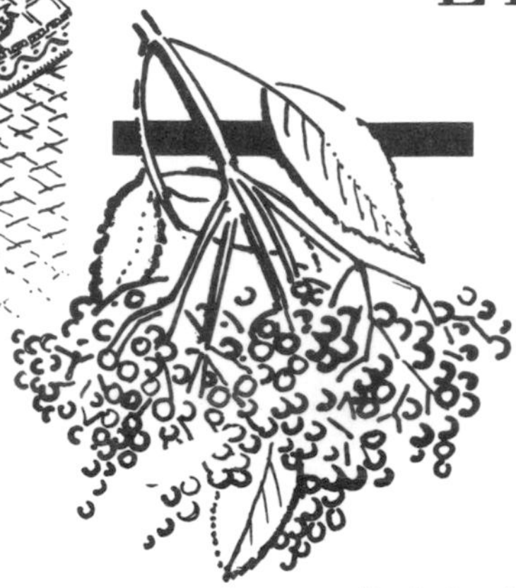

IT IS SAID that the English summer has not really arrived until the elder tree is fully in flower, and it ends when the berries are ripe. The elder has always been a wild tree and flourishes mainly in hedgerows and on waste land.

The elder is native to Britain, Europe and Scandinavia. In the United States there are the related species of sweet elder (*S. canadensis*), sometimes called the Elderblow, and the blue-berried elder (*S. glauca*) which has larger, juicier berries.

Elder trees in Britain have always been much revered by country people, who dared not cut one down or burn the wood for fear of the witch living in its heart. The flowers have been picked in summer to make into fritters, to flavour gooseberries, wine and beer and to make a sparkling country wine, and musical pipes have been made from its branches, so giving the tree its name, from *sambuca*, meaning a musical instrument. Leaves, bark and berries of the elder have always had great medicinal value.

Elder berries are small and black, and grow in huge, umbrella-like clusters which turn downwards as soon as the fruits are ripe. They have a rich flavour with a slightly crunchy texture, due to their tiny seeds.

Nutrition

Elderberries are rich in minerals, and are also a good source of Vitamin C.

Picking and storing elderberries

Elderberries are fully ripe when the heads hang down, the stems turn a deep, pinky red and all the berries are black. Ideally, they should always be picked at this stage but, if you want to beat the birds, you will have to pick them when a few berries on each cluster are still red. The whole sprigs should be broken off by hand.

Elderberries do not keep well, so use them as soon as possible.

Elderberries in the kitchen

To prepare elderberries, strip them from the sprigs with a fork, in the same way as you would black or red currants. Discard any that are very under-ripe.

Elderberries have mostly been used for making a rich, deep maroon country wine and a medicinal syrup known as elderberry rob. Mixed with apples, crab apples, blackberries, or a mixture they give a rich flavour to fruit jellies. A handful can also be added to apple pies, crumbles or pasties. They can also been used to make chutneys.

Elderberry turnovers

shortcrust pastry made with 8 oz (225 g) wholemeal flour
4 oz (125 g) elderberries, weighed on the stem
2 tablespoons clear honey
½ teaspoon ground cinnamon

Elderberries mixed with honey and spice make a filling that cooks down to a rich, purple jam.

Heat the oven to 400F/200C/gas 6. Take the elderberries off the sprigs and mix with the honey and cinnamon. Divide the pastry into six pieces and roll each one into triangle measuring 5–6 inch (12–15 cm) along the base. Put a small portion of the elderberries on one side of each triangle. Fold the opposite point across and seal the edges.

Put the turnovers on to a floured baking sheet and brush with the beaten egg or milk. Bake for 20 minutes or until golden brown. Serve hot with cream, or cold.

Serves 6.

Elderberry and malt wine

4 lb (1.8 kg) elderberries
3 lb (1.35 kg) sugar
1 lb (450 g) malt extract or black malt grains
1 gallon (4.6 litres) boiling water
all-purpose yeast (for amount see packet)
yeast nutrient
juice 4 lemons
1 tablespoon citric acid
1 Campden tablet

A rich, dark wine that is best drunk after a meal like port.

Strip the elderberries from the stalks. Put them into a container and crush them. Add 2 lb (900 g) of the sugar and all the malt. Pour on the boiling water and stir well. Cool to lukewarm. Add the yeast, yeast nutrient and lemon juice. Cover, and leave in a warm place for 3–4 days or until all the froth has sunk to the bottom, stirring every day.

Strain the liquid into a second container, and then siphon it into a demi-john (this makes sure that all the sediment is left behind). Fit a fermentation lock, and leave the wine for 3 weeks or until another thick sediment has formed at the bottom. Rack off into a second demi-john. Leave the wine for 2 weeks and rack again, letting the wine splash into the demi-john to aerate it.

Put the remaining 1 lb (450 g) sugar into a saucepan with 1 pint (575 ml) water and the citric acid. Bring to the boil, and simmer for 20 minutes. Cool the syrup completely. Add one-third of the resulting syrup to the wine. If there is still space at the top of the demi-john, top up the wine with cooled, boiled water. Fit a

fermentation lock, and leave the wine for 2 weeks.

Rack again and taste the wine. If it is a little on the dry side, the alcohol content may well be low, so add a further third of the syrup. Fit a fermentation lock and leave the wine for 3–4 months, or until it is completely clear. Taste again. If the wine is still too dry, add the remaining syrup and leave for a further 2 weeks. When the wine is ready, add the crushed Campden tablet and leave for a further week.

Siphon the wine into bottles, and leave for at least 6 months before opening.

FEIJOA

FEIJOA SELLOWIANA

THE FEIJOA IS a new fruit, only available at present for two months of the year. It came originally from South America, and was taken to Europe in 1890 and grown partly for its fruits, but mainly for its beautiful red and mauve, yellow-stamened flowers.

The feijoa reached California in 1900, where it has since been grown commercially, as it has in Florida, New Zealand, Australia and Israel. Those that reach Britain come from Israel in November and December. New Zealand fruits are available from March to May, and those from Florida from August to October but, at the time of writing, these have yet to reach our shores.

The feijoa fruit is about 3 inches (7.5) long, 1½ inches (4 cm) in diameter, and oval. It has a waxy, pitted, mid-green, thin skin with the stubble of a calyx at one end. The flesh of those available in Britain is creamy coloured, soft and granular, with one or two tiny black seeds in the centre. The flavour of a feijoa is fresh, lemon-like and sherbetty and very sweet in the centre, almost like a banana. There is also a hint of the exotic fruitiness of the guava.

Nutrition

Vitamin C and calcium are the feijoa's most important nutrients.

Buying and storing feijoa

Feijoa fruits are ready when they yield slightly to your thumb. They can be ripened at room temperature and, once ripe, should be used as soon as possible, although they can be stored in the refrigerator for about two days.

Feijoa in the kitchen

To taste a feijoa at its best, cut it in half lengthways, squeeze over a little lime or lemon juice, and put a spoonful of clear honey on top. Then simply spoon it out with a teaspoon. Thin slices of the raw fruit can be used as a decoration for ice-creams and cream desserts, where the pale colour and green skin can look extremely attractive. Coat them well in lemon juice before use, to prevent them from turning brown. Raw feijoa also goes exceptionally well with cold meats and smoked fish.

In New Zealand, where feijoa are popular and plentiful, they are made into jellies, preserves and marmalades. At present this would hardly be economical when the fruits are so scarce, but it is worth bearing in mind for the future. Sliced, complete with their skins, and poached gently in a sugar syrup, they make an aromatic compote which can be used as a base for a fruit salad. Cook them for about 3 minutes only and do not let them become over-soft and sloppy.

Feijoa fans

A simple and pretty first course.

2 feijoa
juice ½ lemon
4 large slices smoked salmon or smoked meat such as Prosciutto ham or smoked venison
28 very small, thin slices smoked salmon or smoked meat as above

Cut each feijoa in half lengthways. Then cut each half into 8 thin slices, keeping them joined at the top. Gently spread the slices out to make a fan shape. Paint the fans with lemon juice so they do not discolour.

Lay a large slice of smoked salmon or smoked meat on to each of four small plates. Insert a small piece of smoked salmon or smoked meat between the slices of the fans. Set the fans on top of the large slice of salmon or meat.

Serves 4.

Feijoa relish

Serve this with cold meats, quiches and savoury pies.

3 feijoa
juice ½ lemon
2 teaspoons mustard seeds, crushed

Chop the feijoa, and mix with the lemon juice and mustard seeds.

FIG

FICUS CARICA

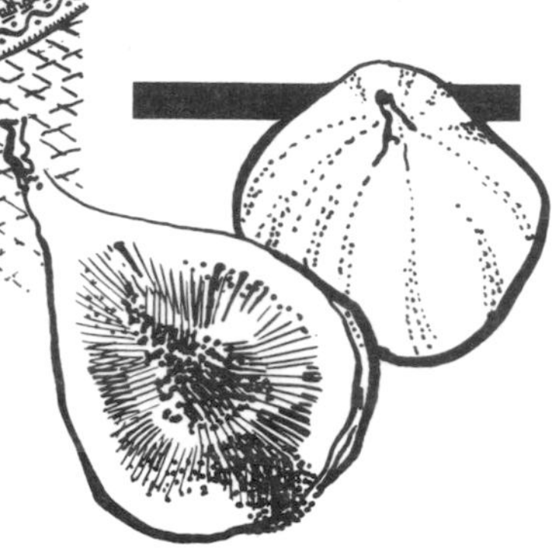

WHAT COULD BE more tempting than a fresh fig, soft and plump, a pleasing shape, and full of crimson, delicately sweet flesh? Apart from their sensual qualities, figs, like dates, have long been appreciated for their high nutritional value and ability to be easily dried and stored.

Figs were one of the first fruits to be cultivated. It is thought that they were originally found in western Asia, and gradually spread through Smyrna in Turkey westwards to Greece, Syria, Biblical Palestine and Egypt. They have been growing round the shores of the Mediterranean for thousands of years. Baskets full of dried figs have been found in Egyptian tombs and, in about 400 BC the Greek writer Aristophanes wrote: 'Nothing is sweeter than figs.'

The Romans also loved figs, and took both the dried fruits and fig trees wherever they conquered. They were eaten by rich and poor alike, in sweet and savoury dishes. After the Romans, fig trees were planted in monastery gardens. In the middle ages, dried figs were imported to Britain from southern Europe along with dates. They were very much prized for their sweetness and were particularly enjoyed during Lent when they were put into both sweet and savoury pottages and into sauces for fish. They were also an important ingredient in the mid-Lent fish pie.

Figs were taken to New Orleans by the French in the eighteenth century and, in 1882, Spanish missionaries took them to California which became one of the most important growing areas for dried figs. Most of the dried figs imported into Britain are the sweet, plump, yellow-brown Smyrna figs, grown around Izmir in Turkey and packed under the name of Izmir figs. Those of the same variety grown in California are called Calimyrna figs. Some also come from Calamata in Greece.

Fresh figs are imported from Brazil from March to April; Greece in June; and Brazil, France and Turkey in October and November. There are many different varieties, some elongated, and some wider and squatter. European figs mainly have purple skins, but those from Brazil are greener. They can also be almost white, pink or light brown, but the flesh is always a deep crimson.

To produce Smyrna figs, thick mats are left under the trees and the fruit drops onto them as it ripens and is left in the sun for a few days to dry. When sufficiently dried, the figs are taken into the towns on camels to be sterilized in boiling water and graded, sorted and packed. As figs dry, a sugar forms on the surface, preserving them naturally in their own syrup with no need for any further preserving agents.

Nutrition

Unlike most fruits, figs have a significant protein content, 1 g per ounce (3.6 g per 100 g), are rich in iron, and by weight contain more calcium than milk. They are also rich in sugars, the dried more so than the fresh. Dried figs contain 60 kcal to the ounce (213 per 100 g). They have no significant Vitamin content.

Buying and storing figs

The skin of a fresh fig should be firm and smooth, with a delicate bloom, and the fruits should just give to the touch. As they age, the skin shrivels, becomes wrinkly and feels slightly sticky, and the flesh turns brown and loses its flavour. The skin of figs is very fragile, so always put them on top of the rest of your shopping. They are best eaten on the day that you buy them, but they will keep for up to two days in the refrigerator, in a paper rather than a polythene bag.

Dried figs should be fat and look succulent, not thin and squashed with more skin than flesh. The more yellow they are the better, as sometimes the darker ones will be a little dry and even bitter. They keep in an airtight container for at least six months in a cool larder.

Figs in the kitchen

Fresh figs are such a delicacy that, if you are only able to get hold of one or two, serve them absolutely plain and enjoy them as they are. Every part is edible, so no preparation is needed. As a first course, accompany them with thin slices of Parma ham or with a portion of savoury cream cheese. As a dessert, sweeten the cheese with honey and beat in a little rose water. Cut into thin lengthways slices, figs make a perfect garnish for ice-creams and other desserts. Chopped raw figs make an exotic addition to salads based on grains and pulses.

To cook fresh figs, simmer them gently in a sugar or honey syrup; or a mixture of syrup and red or white wine, or a natural fruit juice. Add flavourings such as a twist of lemon peel or a cinnamon stick and simmer the figs for no more than 15 minutes. They can be served alone or as part of a fruit salad with fresh fruits such as pineapple or orange, added to the syrup after it has cooled.

Dried figs can also be cooked whole, and are best done in fruit juice or wine with only a little extra sweetener added to the wine and none to the fruit juice. Soak them in the liquid for at least eight hours and then simmer gently for fifteen minutes or until they look soft and plump. Add the sweetener and cook for a further five minutes. This will keep the skins soft. Again, serve them alone or with fresh fruits.

Whole and uncooked, dried figs can be filled with blanched almonds or other chopped nuts and served after dinner.

Chopped dried figs can be added to bread, cakes, tea breads or steamed puddings. They can also be added to pies of tart fruits such as apples or gooseberries, to give both sweetness and flavour, and can also be an ingredient in chutney and mincemeat.

In Greece, figs are made into a heavy wine and in the Middle East into a cough syrup with dates, raisins and jubejubes, known as the 'four fruits'. Fig leaves are used in some Middle Eastern countries like vine leaves, and stuffed with various savoury fillings.

Fresh fig and parsley salad

This is a lovely looking salad with pieces of crimson fig among the green of the parsley. Serve it as a main course, with a green salad.

8 oz (225 g) green lentils
8 oz (225 g) burghul wheat
1 oz (25 g) parsley
6 spring onions
8 fresh figs
juice ½ lemon
4 tablespoons olive oil
1 garlic clove, crushed
½ teaspoon ground cinnamon
freshly ground black pepper

Soak the lentils in cold water for 1 hour and then boil for 45 minutes or until tender. Drain. Soak the wheat in warm water for 20 minutes. Drain, and squeeze dry. Finely chop the parsley and spring onions. Chop 4 of the figs.

In a bowl, mix together the lentils, wheat, parsley, onions and figs. Beat together the lemon juice, oil, garlic, cinnamon and pepper, and fold the dressing into the salad.

Arrange the salad on a serving dish. Cut each of the remaining figs into 8 segments, keeping them joined at the base. Open them up so they look like stars, and place on the top of the salad.

Serves 4.

Roman ham

1 whole gammon, boned and tied

FOR BOILING

4 dried figs
2 celery sticks, roughly chopped
2 carrots, roughly chopped
1 large onion, halved
2 teaspoons black peppercorns
2 teaspoons juniper berries, coarsely crushed
2 teaspoons cloves, coarsely crushed
bouquet garni
2 bayleaves

GLAZE

8 oz (225 g) honey
grated rind of 2 oranges and juice of 1
1 teaspoon black peppercorns, coarsely crushed

Whether you are boiling a small joint of bacon or a whole gammon for Christmas, a few dried figs added to the water give an additional richness to the flavour. For a smaller joint, halve all the boiling ingredients.

Soak the gammon overnight. Drain, and place in a large saucepan with fresh water to cover and all the boiling ingredients. Bring to the boil, cover, and simmer for 4 hours or until the meat is tender.

Lift out the gammon. Remove the string and cut off all the rind. Heat the oven to 400F/200C/gas 6. Put the gammon on a rack in a roasting tin and score the surface fat into squares. Put the ingredients for the glaze into a saucepan and set them on a low heat for the honey to melt. Coat the gammon with half the glaze and put into the oven for 15 minutes. Baste with the remaining glaze, and bake for another 15 minutes so it is a good dark brown.

Cool the gammon on a rack for 12 hours, then transfer to a serving plate.

Figgy pudding

8 oz (225 g) dried figs
2 oz (50 g) candied peel, finely chopped
4 fl oz (125 ml) brandy
1 small cooking apple
1 medium carrot
2 oz (50 g) fresh wholemeal breadcrumbs
2 oz (50 g) wholemeal flour
1 teaspoon ground cinnamon
¼ nutmeg, grated
grated rind and juice 1 lemon
2 eggs, beaten
butter for greasing a 1½-pint (850 ml) pudding basin

A traditional English pudding, once served on Mothering Sunday, this is lighter than a Christmas pudding but sweet, and well-flavoured with the brandy.

Finely chop the figs. Put them into a bowl with the candied peel. Pour in the brandy, and leave to soak overnight.

Peel and finely grate the apple. Finely grate the carrot. Mix into the soaked figs.

Put the breadcrumbs and flour into a mixing bowl. Add the cinnamon, nutmeg and lemon rind. Add the brandy mixture, lemon juice, eggs and mix well.

Put the mixture into the greased basin. Cover with greaseproof paper and foil, and tie down with fine cotton string, making a handle for easy lifting. Bring a large pan of water to the boil. Lower in the pudding, cover, and steam for 3 hours, topping up the water as and when necessary and never letting it come off the boil. When cooked, turn out on to a plate and serve hot with custard sauce, cream or brandy butter.

Serves 6.

Rose custards with fresh fig saucc

2 eggs
2 egg yolks
¾ pint (425 ml) milk
3 tablespoons honey
4 tablespoons rosewater
6 teaspoons red currant jelly
6 fresh figs

Light-textured custards topped wth glossy red, in a sea of sweet, fragrant sauce.

Heat the oven to 375F/190C/gas 5. Beat the eggs with the egg yolks. Put the milk into a saucepan with 1 tablespoon of the honey and 2 tablespoons of the rosewater. Warm gently for the honey to dissolve. Stir it into the eggs.

Put 1 teaspoon red currant jelly into the bottom of each of 6 dariole moulds. Pour in the custard mixture. Put the moulds into a baking tin filled with enough water to come half-way up their sides. Cover the moulds all over with one large piece of foil. Cook for 40 minutes, or until set. Lift them out of the water, and cool until lukewarm.

Skin the thin outer layer from 4 of the figs. Liquidize the flesh and seeds with the remaining honey and rosewater to a smooth purée.

Turn the custards on to individual plates, tipping the plates slightly to make sure that the juice stays on one side. Spoon the fig purée on to the opposite side: the two liquids are of such different densities that they will not mix. Thinly slice the remaining figs, and use as a garnish.

Serves 6.

GOOSEBERRY AND WORCESTERBERRY

GOOSEBERRY

RIBES GROSSULARIA

GOOSEBERRIES ARE THE first of the soft fruits to ripen. They have never been grown on a large scale commercially, but have always been a welcome garden fruit. The cooking varieties are ready first. These are green and hard with a sourness that makes your tongue screw up when you eat them raw. When cooked with sugar or honey, however, they develop a rich, winey flavour. The dessert varieties are large, soft and sweet with a full flavour even when raw. They vary in colour from yellow to pale maroon. The main season is at the beginning of July.

Gooseberries are related to black, red and white currants. They came originally from the mountainous regions of northern Europe and were cultivated by the Anglo-Saxons. An easy fruit to grow, they have been a garden favourite since the thirteenth century. In some areas, after a warm spring, the first gooseberries were traditionally picked at Whitsun, although in Hertfordshire the first Sunday in July was Gooseberry Pie or Gooseberry Pudding Sunday.

Gooseberries have always been used in both sweet and savoury dishes. In Elizabethan times they were made into sweet pies and chicken and fish pies. They were also baked with chicken and, in the seventeenth century, put into meat and fish stews. There were sugary gooseberry sweetmeats, gooseberry wine and vinegar and numerous fools, creams and tansies.

In northern districts in the nineteenth century, gooseberry clubs were formed in which the members vied with each other to produce the biggest and best fruit, and it was partly due to their work in cultivating and propagating that so many varieties exist today.

Gooseberries are grown commercially in England and none are imported. They are also grown in other parts of Europe, in western Asia and north Africa and also in New South Wales.

Nutrition

Gooseberries are high in Vitamin C and potassium.

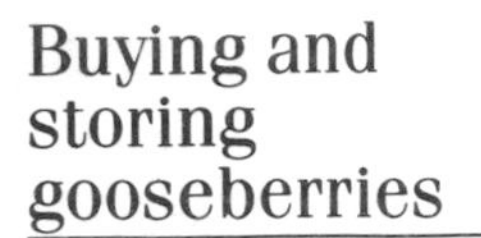

Buying and storing gooseberries

Cooking gooseberries should be hard, green and shiny. Dessert types should look shiny and almost transparent, and should yield slightly when pressed. Wrinkled skins and a dry appearance are signs of age.

Cooking gooseberries will keep for a day in a cool place and, if in punnets covered with cling film, for up to two weeks in the refrigerator. Dessert gooseberries will keep in the refrigerator for up to four days.

Freeze on trays, and pack into polythene bags. Gooseberries will keep in the freezer for six to eight months.

Gooseberries in the kitchen

Wash gooseberries before use and 'top and tail' them, either with your fingernails or with a small pair of scissors.

To cook gooseberries, put them into a saucepan with 3 fl oz (90 ml) liquid (water, fruit juice or wine), and 3–4 oz (75–125 g) sugar or honey. Cover, and set them on a low heat for 15 minutes, or until soft. A sprig of elderflowers gives them the flavour of muscat grapes. Meadowsweet and sweet cicely give gooseberries a fragrant, honeyed flavour.

Cooked gooseberries can be made into pies, tarts and crumbles, or rubbed through a sieve, as a base for fruit fools, creams, mousses and ice-creams.

Cooked with an onion and less sugar, they make a delicious sauce for oily fish such as herrings and mackerel. Chopped gooseberries can be added to stuffings for lamb, pork and chicken.

Gooseberries make a fragrant, country wine which, if bottled when the bushes are in flower the following year, will turn out light and sparkling. They also make an excellent jam.

Dessert gooseberries are usually sliced and eaten raw with sugar and cream or in fruit salads.

WORCESTER-BERRY

The Worcesterberry is a cross between a blackcurrant and a gooseberry and looks like a deep purple gooseberry. The flesh is purple, soft and sweet and usually seedless. Worcesterberries are eaten raw with sugar and cream and can be added to fruit salads and compotes.

Mackerel with cucumber, gooseberry and parsley sauce

4 small mackerel
2 pints water
juice 1 lemon
¼ pint (150 ml) dry white wine
1 oz (25 g) parsley
1 celery stick, broken
1 carrot, halved lengthways
1 small onion, peeled, left whole
4 oz (125 g) gooseberries
1 medium cucumber
2 tablespoons natural yoghurt

A light, hot dish for a cheap but rather special main course.

Fillet the mackerel, reserving one backbone. Cut the fillets into diagonal strips, ½ inch (1.3 cm) wide.

Put the reserved backbone into a saucepan with the water, lemon juice, wine, one parsley sprig and the celery, carrot and onion. Bring to the boil and simmer, covered, for 20 minutes. Strain the stock, return it to the cleaned pan, cover and simmer for a further 30 minutes.

Top and tail the gooseberries. Put half into a saucepan with 4 tablespoons of the stock and simmer for 10 minutes, or until soft. Peel and chop the cucumber and liquidize it with the cooked gooseberries, their juice, ¼ pint (150 ml) more of the stock and the yoghurt. Reserve four small parsley sprigs. Chop the rest of the parsley and add it to the sauce. Thinly slice the remaining gooseberries.

Bring the remaining stock to just below simmering point. Put in the mackerel strips and poach very gently for 5 minutes, or until cooked through but still firm.

Gently heat the sauce, without boiling it. Divide it between four dinner plates. Put a portion of the mackerel strips on top and garnish with a parsley sprig. Scatter the sliced gooseberries around the mackerel.

Serves 4.

Iced gooseberry mould

1 lb (450 g) gooseberries
3 fl oz (90 ml) white grape juice
1 sprig elderflowers
5 oz (150 g) honey
2 egg yolks
1 egg white
1 pint (575 ml) Greek-style natural yoghurt
candied angelica and crystallized violets for garnish

A luxury summer iced dessert, with a light gooseberry sorbet enclosed in a mould of rich ice-cream.

Top and tail the gooseberries. Put them into a saucepan with the grape juice, elderflowers and 3 oz (75 g) of the honey. Bring to the boil, cover, and set on a low heat for 15 minutes or until soft. Rub through a sieve.

Beat the egg yolks together. Melt the remaining honey and whip it into the egg yolks until the mixture is very thick. Whip in the yoghurt and half the gooseberry purée.

Whip the egg white, and fold it into the remaining gooseberry purée. Put each mixture separately into a freezing tray and place in the coldest part of the freezer or the ice compartment of the refrigerator, set at its lowest temperature, for 3 hours, stirring and whipping every 30 minutes to break up the ice particles. Chill a 3 pint (1.7 litre) pudding basin in the freezer for 30 minutes.

Put the egg yolk and yoghurt mixture into the

pudding basin, building it up round the sides and leaving a hollow in the centre. Put the gooseberry purée and egg white mixture in the centre and cover over with the yoghurt mixture. Freeze the mould for a further 2 hours.

To turn out the mould, dip the basin briefly into a bowl of hot water and loosen the sides of the ice-cream with a knife. Turn the mould on to a serving plate. Decorate it with angelica and crystallized violets.

Serves 6–8.

GRAPE, RAISIN, SULTANA AND CURRANT

VITIS VINIFERA

GRAPE

GRAPES, LIKE DATES and figs, have for centuries been symbols of plenty and good living. They have always been enjoyed in three ways: fresh and luscious; dried for easy storing and for their energy-giving sweetness; and made into wines, both red and white.

Grapes are such an ancient fruit that it is impossible to say for how long they have been in cultivation. They first grew wild in western Asia, southern Europe and parts of North Africa, and their cultivation probably began around the Caspian Sea. Some varieties are also native to America. Grapes were grown by the ancient Egyptians, who exploited all their uses, as did the Romans who took them to France and Britain.

The cold British climate made it virtually impossible to grow dessert grapes, but those for wine flourished after the Romans left, and were grown in Anglo-Saxon monasteries.

When the Domesday Book was written, there were thirty-eight vineyards in England and viticulture was encouraged by the Normans. When Henry II married Eleanor of Aquitaine in 1152 she brought with her the land of Bordeaux, and French wine was imported freely for the next 300 years. The Wars of the Roses, and later Henry VIII's dissolution of the monasteries, saw the end of English vineyards for centuries, until in 1945, the Viticultural Research Station was set up at Oxted in Surrey.

Their work has since enabled many vineyards to become established in England so that English wine is now of excellent quality, and able to hold its own against many foreign vintages.

Meanwhile, vines were flourishing all over Europe. Early settlers took them to America but the climate and the local pests were against them and they soon gave way to the native types.

Dessert grapes are generally larger and more succulent than the wine varieties, and there are many different varieties, generally divided into black and white, although in fact the colours vary a great deal. Some are pink, some red, some shiny black and others have a soft bloom. White grapes come in a variety of yellows and greens. Besides being of different colours, their skins vary in toughness and thickness, and flavours also vary from honey-sweet to quite sharp. Seedless grapes, once only available in October, can now be bought nearly all the year round, and these are smaller than the seeded varieties. One of the most popular varieties is the white Thompson seedless, first raised in California, but maroon ones such as Flame from Chile, are becoming better known.

Dessert grapes are imported from Israel, Australia, South Africa, Spain, Brazil, Chile, the United States, Cyprus, France and Italy and are always available.

Nutrition

Grapes are rich in potassium and have significant amounts of calcium and phosphorus. Unlike most other fruits they contain small amounts of B Vitamins, but only small amounts of other vitamins.

Buying and storing grapes

Some people prefer black grapes and some white, but underneath their skins they are very similar, and even with the skins on it can be hard to tell the difference with your eyes shut.

Grapes should be firm and their skins fresh and smooth. Do not buy them if they are becoming wrinkled, or turning brown near the stem.

Grapes for export are picked before they are fully ripe and ripened in transit. As a result, their flavour is not fully developed. To draw it out more, leave grapes on a sunny windowsill or hang them in the sun for a day.

After ripening, grapes should be refrigerated, and will keep for up to a week. Bring them up to room temperature again before using.

To remove grapes from a bunch, cut them with scissors or kitchen snippers. Pulling them off can cause other grapes to fall from the stem or become damaged.

Grapes in the kitchen

For salads, fruit salads and desserts, grapes are usually left with their skins on. Some cooked dishes, however, require them to be skinned. The skin of some varieties can be peeled off easily. Others should be immersed in boiling water first for about a minute, checking at 30 seconds. To seed grapes, cut them in half and remove the seeds with your finger tips or the point of a sharp knife.

Grapes are delicious in savoury salads. Small, seedless ones can be added whole, larger ones should be halved and seeded. Black grapes add colour to rice or white cabbage; white grapes blend into leafy salad vegetables, providing a contrast in shape and texture. Their freshness goes well with both chicken and cheese in salads.

Halved grapes make attractive garnishes for many kinds of desserts. They can also be put into mixed fruit tarts under an apricot jam or redcurrant jelly glaze, and look attractive when set in sweet or savoury aspic jellies.

The classic Veronique sauce for chicken and white fish is made by adding halved and peeled white grapes to a simple thickened sauce of stock, cream and lemon juice.

Red and white grape juice, sold in bottles and cartons, can be used as a sweet cooking liquid for fruits, as well as being made into a variety of drinks.

Vine leaves can be stuffed with savoury rice mixtures or used to cover small game birds, such as quails, before cooking. If you cannot obtain fresh ones, use those that are vacuum-packed in brine.

An oil is produced from grape seeds which can be used for salads or cooking.

RAISIN, SULTANA AND CURRANT

Raisins, sultanas and currants are referred to in the trade as vine fruits, and are all grapes that have been sun-dried. One pound (450 g) of dried fruit is produced from 4 lb (1.8 kg) of fresh grapes.

Raisins are produced from both seeded and seedless grapes. Most seedless raisins are produced in the San Joaquin Valley in California from Thompson seedless grapes, first raised from European vines and Californian root stock by William Thompson, an English gardener who emigrated to California, in 1878.

When the grapes are ripe, they are cut in bunches and placed on paper trays in the hot sun for two weeks. At packing plants, the stems are removed and the fruit is cleaned and packed. Throughout the process, no preservatives are added and the raisins are known as 'naturals'. Seedless raisins are dark brown and wrinkled, with a sweet, mellow flavour.

Raisins produced from seeded grapes are larger and often stickier, and can be sold under various names, **Lexias** from Australia, **Valencias** from Spain, **Muscats** from the USA and **Capes** from South Africa. They are sun-dried and then seeded by machine, a process which squashes them into a flat, disc shape. Once again, no chemicals are added up to this stage. Lexias are then coated with vegetable oil and Valencias are treated with sulphur dioxide to improve their colour and soften their skins. Californian Muscats receive no other treatment, and are dark coloured with a strong, treacly flavour.

Dessert raisins, known as **Muscatels**, are produced in the same way as seeded raisins, although the stones are not removed. They are left on the stems and not treated with sulphur dioxide. The best come from Spain, and are sometimes packed with Spanish almonds for the Christmas trade.

Sultanas are produced in Australia, Turkey, Greece and Crete from seedless white grapes. Before drying they are dipped briefly in an alkali solution which makes their skin wrinkle and crack and so cuts down on the drying time. After dipping, they are spray-washed and then sun-dried for about a week. Then they are packed into sweat-boxes to make the moisture content of each small fruit the same. All sultanas, except those produced in Australia, are then treated with sulphur dioxide. Mediterranean fruits are coated with mineral oil, and the Australian with vegetable oil, to prevent sticking.

Currants come from Greece (the largest producers), Australia and the USA, and Britain uses 50 per cent of the entire world crop. Currants are produced from small, black grapes which, due to a technique in the growing process, do not produce pips. Techniques for drying vary, but the best currants are produced by putting the grapes in the shade for the first part of the drying period. This produces thin skins and a natural bloom. When the currants can be shaken from the stems, they are spread out in the full sun to cure them and seal the skin. No chemical treatments are involved in any country.

Nutrition

Dried vine fruits are rich in easily absorbable fruit sugars, and give a rapid energy rise as soon as they are eaten. They have large amounts of Vitamin B1, potassium, phosphorus, calcium and magnesium.

Buying and storing vine fruits

Vine fruits should look clear coloured and soft. As they age, a sugary coating may develop. They will still be usable but they should not be bought in this condition. They will keep for up to six months in an airtight container in a cool, dry cupboard.

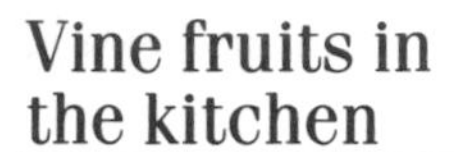

Vine fruits in the kitchen

If the vine fruits are oil-coated it is best to wash this off before using them. Put them into a sieve and run warm water over them. Drain well, and dry with kitchen paper. Uncoated fruits may be stuck together and, if so, should be pulled apart by hand.

The main use for vine fruits in Britain is in baking, where they give a combination of sweetness and moistness.

The large stoned raisins are mostly used in rich fruit cakes and puddings, such as Christmas pudding. They can be plumped before use by soaking overnight in fruit juice or alcohol such as brandy, rum or sherry.

Seedless raisins are used in cakes, breads, tea breads, scones and biscuits, and can be mixed with fresh fruits such as apples or gooseberries in pies, crumbles and other desserts. Like stoned raisins, they can be soaked in alcohol for rich cakes.

Soaked raisins together with their liquid can be mixed with chopped fresh fruits in a fruit salad. The liquid can be heated and thickened and used as a sweet sauce, with the raisins replaced.

Raisins are also good used sparingly in savoury dishes. They can be added to spiced rice as it cooks; spiced Middle Eastern lamb dishes; stuffings for turkey, chicken and lamb and salads. Simmered first in a little wine or water to plump them, they can be added to salad dressings, and are best in those flavoured with tomato puree. Raisins are also a frequent ingredient in chutney.

Currants are used more often in buns and sweet rich breads, than in cakes and puddings. They, too, can be plumped in juice or alcohol before use. Currants are the best vine fruits of all in salads, as their smallness makes them less obtrusive. They are excellent when used to give a contrast in flavour with the more bitter salad vegetables such as endive or chicory. Like raisins, they can be added to spiced rice and meat dishes and also to stuffings, sauce and chutneys.

White grape soup

2 medium onions
½ oz (15 g) butter
1 tablespoon wholemeal flour
1¼ pints (725 ml) stock
4 oz (125 g) curd cheese
¼ pint (150 ml) dry white wine
2 tablespoons chopped mint
6 oz (175 g) white grapes, halved and seeded

A savoury soup, given a fresh tang with grapes.

Finely chop the onions. Melt the butter in a saucepan over a low heat. Soften the onions. Stir in the flour and then the stock. Bring the stock to the boil, stirring, and simmer uncovered for 10 minutes.

Cream the cheese in a bowl with a wooden spoon, and gradually work in about ½ pint (275 ml) of the soup. Stir this mixture back into the saucepan. Add the wine, mint and prepared grapes and reheat gently, without boiling.

Serves 4.

Boiled beef and carrots with currants

1½–2 lb (675–900 g) skirt of beef
1½ lb (675 g) carrots
2 oz (50 g) currants
2 large onions, halved and thinly sliced
6 tablespoons chopped parsley
1 teaspoon ground cinnamon
sea salt and freshly ground black pepper
1½ pints (850 ml) stock
large bouquet garni

A delicious dish of boiled beef and carrots with a difference. The currants and cinnamon give a slight musty flavour, as well as a touch of sweetness.

Cut the beef into pieces about 1 by 2 inches (2.5 by 5 cm). Cut the carrots into ¼-inch (3 cm) thick rings. Layer the beef, carrots, onions and currants in a flameproof casserole, scattering with parsley, cinnamon, a little salt and a liberal amount of black pepper. Pour in the stock, and add the bouquet garni.

Set the casserole on top of the stove on a medium heat and bring to the boil. Cover, and simmer for 1½ hours until the beef is completely tender.

Remove the bouquet garni and either serve straight from the casserole, or tip into a warmed serving dish.

Serves 4.

Red beans, almonds and raisins with spiced wheat

BEANS

3 tablespoons olive oil
4 oz (125 g) almonds, blanched
1 medium onion, thinly sliced
1 garlic clove, finely chopped
1 teaspoon ground cumin
¼ pint (150 ml) tomato juice
juice ½ lemon
8 oz (225 g) red kidney beans, soaked and cooked until tender
2 oz (50 g) raisins
2 tablespoons chopped fresh coriander

WHEAT

1 red pepper
2 tablespoons olive oil
1 medium onion, finely chopped
1 teaspoon ground cumin
8 oz (225 g) burghul wheat
1 pint (575 ml) stock or water

An excellent blending of sweet, savoury and spiced flavours.

Heat the oil in a frying pan on a medium heat. Cook the almonds, stirring, until brown on both sides. Remove from pan. Soften the onion and garlic, stir in the cumin, and then the tomato juice and lemon juice. Bring to the boil. Add the beans, raisins and almonds. Cover, and simmer for 20 minutes.

For the wheat, core, seed and finely chop the pepper. Heat the oil in a saucepan on a low heat. Soften the onion, add the pepper and cook for 1 minute more. Stir in the cumin and the wheat. Pour in the stock or water, and bring to the boil. Cover, and simmer for 20 minutes or until the wheat is soft and all the liquid has been absorbed.

Put the wheat on to a serving plate. Spoon the beans over the top, and garnish with the chopped fresh coriander.

Serves 4.

Brandied pheasant with black grapes

1 brace pheasants
¼ pint (150 ml) stock, from the pheasant giblets if possible
1 medium onion, finely chopped
4 tablespoons brandy
7 fl oz (200 ml) dry red wine
bouquet garni
4 oz (125 g) black grapes, halved and seeded

Moist, and gently flavoured with wine and herbs, these pheasants are served in their own cooking juices. Browning them without butter works perfectly, as the reduced stock and onion provide moisture and prevent burning.

Heat the oven to 350F/180C/gas 4. Truss the pheasants. Put the stock into a large casserole and bring to the boil. Add the onion, and boil until the stock is almost reduced. Lower the heat and brown the pheasants. Warm the brandy in a small frying pan. Ignite it, and pour over the pheasants. When it has stopped flaming, pour in the wine and bring to the boil. Add the bouquet garni. Cover the casserole, and cook for 1 hour 15 minutes, or until the pheasants are tender.

Joint the pheasants. Place the joints on a warmed serving dish and keep warm. Strain the juices from the casserole into a saucepan and bring to the boil. Add the grapes, and simmer for 1 minute. Spoon the grapes and the juices over the jointed pheasants.

Serves 6–8.

Avocado, mixed lettuce and black grape salad

1 ripe avocado
1 small lolla rossa (red-edged) lettuce
½ iceberg lettuce
4 oz (125 g) seedless black grapes
4 tablespoons olive oil
2 tablespoons lemon juice
1 garlic clove, crushed (optional)
freshly ground black pepper
2 tablespoons chopped chervil (if available) or parsley

A side-salad of interesting mixed textures.

Peel, stone and dice the avocado. Tear the lolla rossa lettuce leaves into 1-inch (2.5 cm) pieces. Shred the iceberg lettuce. Mix in a salad bowl, and add the grapes. Beat together the oil, lemon juice, garlic and pepper and fold into the salad. Scatter the chervil over the top.

Serves 4.

Red cabbage, grape and Lancashire cheese salad

½ medium red cabbage
4 tablespoons olive oil
2 tablespoons red wine vinegar
2 tablespoons soy sauce
1 teaspoon Tabasco sauce
2 oz (50 g) raisins
8 oz (225 g) white grapes, halved and seeded
4 oz (125 g) Lancashire cheese, grated

Fresh grapes and sweet raisins make a delicious combination of colours and flavours in a salad. Serve this as a lunch or supper dish, accompanied by wholemeal bread.

Shred the cabbage very finely and place in a bowl. Beat together the oil, vinegar, and soy and Tabasco sauces. Fold into the salad. Mix in the raisins. Let the salad stand for 30 minutes.

Mix half the grapes into the salad, and the rest into the cheese. Put the salad on a serving plate, and arrange the cheese and grapes on top.

Serves 4.

Dried fruit and orange pashka

2 oz (50 g) dried whole apricots
4 dried figs
2 oz (50 g) sultanas
2 oz (50 g) raisins
½ pint (275 ml) natural orange juice
12 oz (350 g) curd cheese
3 tablespoons natural yoghurt
2 small oranges
4 oz (125 g) almonds, all but 4 blanched and ground

Pashka, a traditional Russian dessert served at Easter, is a delectable mixture of soaked dried fruits and soft cheese moulded together in a basin.

Finely chop the apricots and figs. Put them into a bowl with the sultanas and raisins. Pour in the orange juice, cover, and leave the fruits to soak for 8 hours. Drain. (Dilute the juice with sparkling mineral water to make a drink.)

Beat the curd cheese to a cream. Beat in the yoghurt and the grated rind of one of the oranges. Mix in the ground almonds and the soaked fruits. Put the mixture into an oiled, 1-pint (575 ml) pudding basin and chill for 2 hours.

For serving, turn the pashka on to a plate. Press the whole almonds into the top. Cut the rind and pith from the oranges, slice them thinly and arrange the slices around the pashka.

Serves 6–8.

Figgy mincemeat

350 g (12 oz) cooking apples
8 oz (225 g) dried figs
2 oz (50 g) almonds, blanched
3 fl oz (90 ml) brandy
12 oz (350 g) raisins
12 oz (350 g) sultanas
2 oz (50 g) candied peel, chopped
2 teaspoons ground mixed spice
1 oz (25 g) butter, melted

Use this as an alternative to ordinary mincemeat. It is easy to make, rich and sweet, even though it contains no sugar or suet.

Peel, core and finely chop the apples. Finely chop the figs. Put the apples, figs and almonds into a food processor with the brandy and work them to a rough, minced mixture before turning them into a bowl. Alternatively, mince the apples, figs and almonds together, put them into a bowl, and mix in the brandy.

Add the raisins and sultanas, the chopped peel, spice and butter, and mix well. Put the mincemeat into jars and seal.

This will keep for 1 month in a cool place, and for up to two months in the refrigerator.

GUAVA

PSIDIUM SPECIES

THE GUAVA HAS the most tantalizing aroma of any fruit. It is musky, heady, sweet and syrupy, with a hint of cloves and other sweet spices. Its flavour is rich and fruity, again with a hint of spice. The flesh is granular in texture, but creamy when ripe.

There are various types of guava, differing in colour and, to a certain extent, flavour. All are small and oval, usually from 1½–3 inches (4–7.5 cm) long. They have a thin, edible skin; hard granular flesh about ½ inch (1.3 cm) thick; and a number of small seeds in the centre.

The lemon guava (*P. guajava*) is the best known type. It is native to both Peru and the West Indies and is lemon-coloured with a hint of lemon about its scent and flavour. The strawberry guava (*P. catleianum*) is said to be the best. It comes from Peru, is small, round and maroon-red and has moist flesh with a similar texture and flavour to a strawberry. The yellow guava (*P. catleianum licidum*), related to the strawberry guava, is yellow and highly aromatic. In South America and Australia it is grown as a garden shrub.

Guavas are now grown in most tropical and sub-tropical areas of the world including India, Hawaii, Florida, California, Australia, south east Asia and Cuba. They have never been particularly popular in Europe, probably since they do not travel well. If they are picked ripe, they are past their best when they arrive. When they are picked just before they are ready and ripened in transit, their flavour does not develop properly. A ripe guava direct from the tree would be a treat indeed.

The Spaniards first introduced guavas to Europe, and strawberry guavas were grown in England in 1820, but did not catch on. It is only comparatively recently, since the West Indian population began to hanker for the foods they had left behind, that fresh guavas have been imported to Britain on any large scale. They now come mainly from Brazil and Israel.

Nutrition

Guavas are exceptionally high in Vitamins A and C, and also in potassium, calcium and phosphorus.

Buying and storing guavas

Guavas should be firm, with a smooth skin and a strongly aromatic scent. Wrinkling, or brown patches around the stalk, are signs of age. Guavas will keep for up to two days in the refrigerator, but should be wrapped in cling film to prevent their pervading scent from affecting the rest of the contents.

Guavas in the kitchen

When peeled, and with the seeds removed, ripe guavas can be served raw. Serve them in fruit salads, with ice-creams and cream desserts and also with sliced poultry, ham or pork or mixed into a green salad. The halves of the fruit can be stuffed with cream cheese mixtures, to be served either as a first course or as a dessert.

The best way to serve guavas, however, is to poach them very gently in a light syrup. Use four guavas, unpeeled and sliced, ½ pint (275 ml) water, 3 oz (75 g) sugar or honey, and two thinly pared strips of lemon rind. Stir the water, sugar or honey and lemon rind on a low heat until the sweetener has dissolved, bring to the boil and boil for 2 minutes. Simmer the guavas for 2 minutes. Check to see if they are soft. If not, simmer for a very little longer and check again, as they can very easily become over-soft. This compote can be used as a base for a fruit salad or other dessert, and can also be puréed to be used as a sauce. In their countries of origin, guavas are used like apples in crumbles and pies.

Despite tales of the last war, when masses of guava jam was imported, it can be delicious. You can also make guava cheese and a guava jelly which is clear pink or gold, depending on the type of guava used, with a honeyed flavour. Always add lemon juice to jams and jellies to help them set.

To make a guava drink, wash and slice 1 lb (450 g) guavas and put them into a saucepan with 1 pint (575 ml) water. Bring to the boil, simmer covered, for 45 minutes and strain through a cloth. Served chilled, this is remarkably refreshing.

Stuffed guavas

4 ripe guavas
4 oz (125 g) sweet cream cheese or a mild-flavoured, low fat soft cheese
1 garlic clove, crushed
2 pieces preserved stem ginger, finely chopped
8 small parsley sprigs or coriander leaves

The slight sharpness of guavas goes beautifully with mild soft cheeses. The garlic in this mixture makes it ideal for a first course. Without it, the same dish could easily be a dessert. The colours can be brightened by placing the guavas on a bed of herb sprigs, or leaves such as parsley, coriander or lemon balm.

Halve and peel the guavas and remove the seeds. Cream the cheese in a bowl and mix in the garlic and ginger. Pile the mixture into the guava shells. Garnish each one with a parsley sprig or coriander leaf.

Serves 4.

Guava yoghurt dessert

4 guavas
3 oz (75 g) honey
½ pint (275 ml) water
2 thinly pared strips lemon rind
juice up to ½ lemon
2 tablespoons arrowroot
½ pint (275 ml) Greek-style natural yoghurt
1 tablespoon chopped toasted hazelnuts or mixed nuts

A creamy dessert based on a guava compote.

Make a compote as described on page 114 with the guavas, honey, water and lemon rind. Strain and reserve the syrup, discard the lemon rind, and divide the guavas between 4 small bowls or dishes.

Add lemon juice to taste to the syrup. Put the arrowroot into a small bowl and stir in 8 tablespoons of the syrup. Return the remaining syrup to the saucepan, and warm it on a medium heat. Stir in the arrowroot mixture, and stir until it comes to the boil and thickens to make a translucent sauce. Take the pan from the heat.

Stir 2 tablespoons of the syrup into the yoghurt and pour the rest over the guavas. Spoon the yoghurt over the syrup and scatter the chopped nuts over the top.

Serves 4.

Tropical fruit salad

compote made with 4 guavas and honey as on page 114
2 carambola, thinly sliced into star-shaped pieces
24 lychees, peeled and stoned
1 mango, peeled and diced
flesh of 1/2 pineapple, diced

This is another way to use a guava compote. The syrup makes an aromatic juice for a fruit salad. Almost any tropical fruits can be added in varying proportions.

When the guavas are cooked, drain and reserve them. Put the sliced carambola into a bowl. Boil up the syrup from the compote again. Pour it over the carambola, and cool completely. Mix in the reserved guavas and the other raw fruits.

Serves 6.

KIWANO

CUCUMIS METULIFERUS

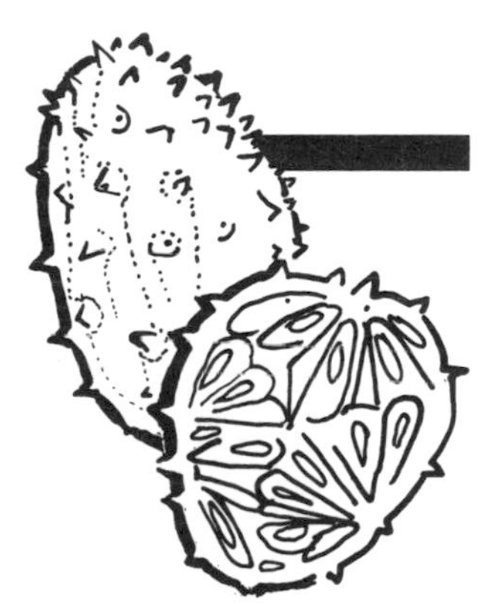

THE KIWANO IS one of the latest fruits to come on to the commercial market, and is certainly one of the most spectacular that you will ever buy. When it first appeared in 1984, each fruit cost £4–5, but now the price has been reduced considerably, making this versatile and unusual fruit far more accessible.

Kiwanos available in Britain are usually about 3–4 inches (7.5–10 cm) long and 1½ inches (4 cm) in diameter and oval, but they can grow to the size of a small melon. Their skin is golden yellow, similar in texture to that of a melon, but covered with blunt spines or horns, some of which may have a thorn-like prickle on the end. There may be the remains of a thin, prickly stalk on one end, and the small, round base of a calyx on the other. If you can get your nose between the prickles you will discover a pleasant, sweet, fresh scent, but it is when you cut a kiwano in half that you get the most amazing surprise of all. Inside, are soft, creamy-coloured edible seeds, like tiny melon seeds, covered in bright green, transparent, juicy flesh. What a temptation. If ever you needed a fruit to brighten up your table, then this is it. The flavour of this bright green delight has been described as being like a cross between a banana and a lime. It is also very much akin to a sweet gooseberry. Whichever fruit you care to compare it with, the flavour is fresh, sweet and 'green', with no hint of bitterness or sharpness.

The kiwano came originally from Africa, and its other names are African Horned Cucumber, Horned Melon or Jelly Melon. Small quantities of the fruit were imported into Britain from Africa in the early 1980s, but at the same time commercial growing was begun in New Zealand and it was New Zealand growers who gave it its new name of kiwano. Their first crop was sold to Japan in 1984, and at the time of writing most kiwanos that now reach British markets come from New Zealand from February to June. Small amounts still come from Africa at other times of the year, and also from California during September to December.

Nutrition

Kiwanos are exceptionally high in potassium, and contain significant amounts of calcium, magnesium and Vitamin C.

Buying and storing kiwanos

The skin of a kiwano should look smooth and unblemished, not wrinkled and dull. Kiwanos are best kept in a cool larder, and will stay fresh for up to two weeks.

Kiwanos in the kitchen

As a dessert fruit or a thirst-quenching snack, the flesh and seeds of the Kiwano can be eaten just as they are, straight from the shell. Either cut the shell in half and scoop out the seeds, or cut the fruit into lengthways quarters and pick up the shell with your fingers.

Kiwano pulp makes an instant, spectacular garnish. Spoon it out of the shell and use it on cheesecakes, ice-creams and water ices, meringue nests, or over other fruits such as bananas (with which it goes extremely well) or peaches.

Make use of the attractive shells. Scoop out the pulp, fill the shells with ice-cream or a whipped syllabub, and spoon the pulp back over the top; or mix the pulp with other fruits such as melon balls and pile it all back in. Kiwano can also make refreshing drinks. Try blending it with yoghurt, honey and crushed ice.

Kiwano pulp can be used as a base for salad dressings, for relishes to go with curries, and for sauces for fish and seafood.

Kiwano salad dressing

2 kiwanos
2 tablespoons olive oil
juice ½ lemon or lime
1 garlic clove, crushed
2 red or green chilli peppers, seeded and finely chopped

Spoon this dressing over other ingredients rather than mixing it in, for a stunning effect. You can vary the number of chillies, according to taste, and if fresh are unavailable, replace them with about ¼ teaspoon chilli powder.

Use the dressing with blander ingredients such as chickpeas, haricot beans and flageolets, or waxy new potatoes cooked until just tender. It is also good with cold, skinned breast of chicken or turkey, diced cooked pork, prawns or any other seafood, or poached salmon or trout and can also be used as a relish with hot foods such as grilled white fish or poultry.

Halve the kiwanos. Scoop out all the flesh, juice and seeds and put them into a bowl. Stir in the remaining ingredients.

Kiwano-topped banana whip on a biscuit base

4 oz (125 g) digestive biscuits
4 oz (125 g) unsweetened oatcakes (Walkers are the best)
3 oz (75 g) butter, melted
½ oz (15 g) gelatin
one 12 oz (350 g) pack silken tofu
1 large banana
juice ½ lime
4 kiwanos

This looks and tastes spectacular, with a very light, fresh flavour and a natural sweetness from the fruits. You can use extra banana as a garnish.

Tofu is smooth and creamy yet deliciously light in desserts. Make sure that you use silken tofu, that comes in sealed 12 oz (350 g) packs, not the heavy, more granular type used in savoury dishes. Silken tofu is pure white and very smooth. The little water packed around it must be drained off before use.

Heat the oven to 400F/200C/gas 6. Make the biscuits into crumbs and mix with the melted butter. Press the mixture into the bottom of an 8-inch (20 cm) diameter tart tin. Bake for 10 minutes and cool completely in the tin.

In a small pan, soak the gelatin in 4 tablespoons cold water. Drain the tofu and chop the banana. Liquidize them together to make a smooth purée. Add the lime juice and blend again.

Cut the kiwanos in half lengthways, and scoop the seeds into a bowl. Gently melt the gelatin and quickly mix half into the tofu mixture and half into the kiwano. Spoon the tofu mixture evenly over the biscuit base. Leave it for 10 minutes, but no longer, as the kiwano flesh will set quickly. Carefully spoon the kiwano all over the surface of the tofu. Leave the cream to set completely, about 2 hours. This is best eaten on the day of making as, even with the lime juice, the banana will start to discolour after about 4 hours.

Serves 6.

KIWI FRUIT

ACTINIDIA CHINENSIS

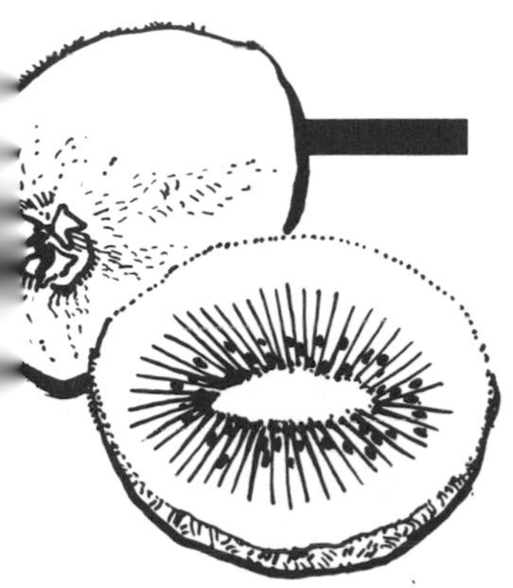

THE KIWI FRUIT shot to fame in the 1970s. Sliced to reveal its black sunray pattern among shining green flesh, it was the perfect decoration for dishes prepared in the 'nouvelle cuisine' style and adorned dishes from the first course through to the dessert.

Eventually, nouvelle cuisine fell from favour and with it went the poor kiwi fruit. Now that the razzmatazz has died down, let us appreciate it for what it is: attractive, colourful, with a delicious soft texture with an underlying crunch, a flavour so sweet that you need only a minimum of sugar, and yet tart enough to go with savoury ingredients. It is packed full of Vitamin C and children love it. It is the most successful of all the exotic imports and is now being grown under glass in Sussex. We should welcome it as being here to stay.

The kiwi fruit came originally from China, where it grew wild in the Yangtse Valley and was later cultivated. It was brought to Europe in 1900, where it was grown in conservatories and greenhouses and given the name of Chinese gooseberry, because it was hairy and green, and had a flavour similar to that of a sweet gooseberry. Soon after this, the first seeds reached New Zealand, and were grown successfully at Wanganui. All kiwi fruit now grown in New Zealand are descended from these vines.

With its name changed and a new image, the first kiwi fruits arrived in London in 1953. It would be interesting to know who bought them, as few people in Britain ever knew of their existence before the 1970s.

Kiwi fruits are now grown in Israel, France, Italy, Spain and the USSR, and it probably will not be long before more British fruits reach the shops. They are now a familiar favourite, reasonably priced, easy to prepare, versatile and with a not-too-exotic flavour that appeals to British palates.

Nutrition

Kiwi fruit are rich in Vitamin C, iron, calcium and phosphorus, and also contain proleolytic acid which, according to the growers, removes cholesterol from the circulation.

Buying and storing kiwi fruit

The thin, brown, hairy skin of a kiwi fruit prevents you from telling its age, so gently press the fruit with your thumb. If it yields slightly, it is ready to eat, if it is hard, it needs a few days in a warm room to ripen. Kiwi fruit keep for so long that over-ripe ones are extremely rare, but should you happen to find one, it will be very soft.

An under-ripe kiwi fruit can be kept in a cool place for up to a month, and sometimes even longer. In the refrigerator it can keep up to six months. Ripe fruit will keep in the refrigerator for up to two weeks.

Kiwi fruit in the kitchen

Always remove the skin of the kiwi fruit. First, cut off each end and then thinly pare away the skin in lengthways sections, using a small, sharp knife. Kiwi fruits are usually sliced crossways to show off the dark, rayed pattern of their tiny black seeds.

Arranged attractively on small plates, using one kiwi fruit per person, the slices can make numerous small, first course dishes: slices can be topped with mild fish pâtés and tiny pieces of lemon; or with soft cheese, scattered with sunflower seeds or hazelnuts. Slices can also be used to garnish pâtés and terrines, but take care than the flavours blend well besides looking good. Kiwi fruit tends to be best with milder ingredients.

Cold chicken and turkey, some types of cheese and nuts all go well with kiwi fruit in salads, but hot meat dishes garnished with the cold fruit are not so good. Diced and mixed with raw onions, ginger, cayenne pepper and vinegar, they make an unusual relish.

Slices of kiwi fruit are superb for decorating desserts. Not only do they look attractive, but do not discolour or look tired if left for some time in the air. Decorate ice-creams and cheesecakes, mousses and cold soufflés with kiwi slices alone, or a mixture of kiwi fruit and other fruits, such as halved strawberries.

A purée of kiwi fruits can simply be made by liquidizing kiwi fruits, stirring in honey or sugar, letting the purée stand for 30 minutes for the sweetener to dissolve and then sieving. This makes an excellent base for ice-creams, sorbets and water ices, but uncooked kiwi fruit contains an enzyme which breaks down gelatin so, for desserts that need to be set, either cook the kiwi fruit first or use agar-agar, which is made from seaweed, and will withstand the enzyme.

To cook and purée kiwi fruit, peel and chop four and put them into a saucepan with 1–2 tablespoons honey or sugar. Cover, and set on a low heat for 10 minutes or until they become very soft, then rub them through a sieve. This makes a very liquid purée that can be used as a base for cream desserts or thickened with a little arrowroot to be used as a topping for cheesecakes or a sauce for ice-creams and puddings.

If you have enough kiwi fruits, you can make them into jam or add them to chutney.

You do not even have to waste the skins. The same enzyme that breaks down the gelatin will tenderize meat. Lay the skins over steaks and chops, and leave for several hours before grilling.

Kiwi fruit and feta cheese salad

6 kiwi fruit
6 oz (175 g) feta cheese
½ cucumber
¼ pint Greek-style natural yoghurt
1 tablespoon lemon juice

Serve this refreshing salad as a first course on its own, or with a side salad as a light lunch or supper.

Peel and dice 4 of the kiwi fruit. Dice the cheese and the cucumber. Mix with the kiwi fruit in a bowl. Beat together the yoghurt and lemon juice, and fold into the salad. Peel and slice the remaining kiwi fruit, and lay the slices over the salad.

Serves 6 as a first course, 4 as a main course.

Kiwi fruit cream

6 kiwi fruit
2 oz (50 g) clear honey
agar-agar or gelozone to set 1 pint (575 ml) liquid
½ pint soured cream
1 ripe mango, or 4 oz (125 g) strawberries, or other fruits to garnish

Puréeing kiwi fruits raw preserves the fresh flavour of the fruits. Do not sieve them, as the dark seeds look attractive in the pale green cream. The mixture could also be served in a baked, 8 inch (20 cm) flan case.

Peel 4 of the kiwi fruit and liquidize. Put the purée into a saucepan and stir in the honey. Sprinkle in the agar-agar or gelozone, and stir it on a low heat until melted. The agar-agar may have to be brought to boiling point, but the gelozone will melt as soon as it gets warm and is best not boiled.

Take the pan from the heat, and immediately beat in the soured cream. If the mixture looks lumpy, it can be worked again in the blender or food processor. Pour the mixture into a shallow, 8 inch (20 cm) diameter dish, and leave it in a cool place until it is set.

Peel and slice the remaining 2 kiwi fruit. Peel and chop the mango, or halve the strawberries. Use the freshly prepared fruits to decorate the top of the cream.

Serves 4–6.

LOQUAT

ERIOBOTRIA JAPONICA SYN. PHOTINIA JAPONICA

WE WILL PROBABLY see more of the loquat in the future, as its cultivation is increasing around the Mediterranean, particularly in Spain. It is also grown in India, Africa, Australia, South America and California but, as the season is so short and the fruits do not travel well, it is the European varieties that are most likely to be in British shops.

The loquat takes its name from the Chinese *lu-kwyit*, meaning rush orange. When it first came to Britain in 1787, it was thought to be a medlar and called the Japanese medlar as well as the Japanese loquat. The loquat was, in fact, a native of China, which was taken to Japan and cultivated centuries ago. The first plants in Britain were planted in Kew Gardens and were grown more as ornamental trees with lush evergreen foliage, strongly scented, yellow-tinged white flowers and bright orange fruits.

The fruits must ripen on the tree in order to be pleasant to eat, and so initially were never thought of as being a valuable commercial crop. The trees, however, thrive best under plantation conditions and in recent years more have been planted.

Loquats are about the size of an apricot only more oval, with a slight point at one end. The skin is orange and slightly downy, the flesh a similar colour and, in texture, slightly firmer than a peach. They are sweet with no hint of sharpness or bitterness and can be quite bland, although their juiciness makes up for this. In the centre of the flesh are two or three large, shiny, brown seeds with the outside texture of a horse chestnut.

Spanish loquats, or nisperos, are grown without chemicals and are picked daily by hand, so that each fruit reaches the market in perfect condition. Fresh loquats are available only in May, although some are tinned or bottled.

Nutrition

Loquats are high in potassium and Vitamin A, and have significant amounts of calcium and phosphorus. They have a very little Vitamin C.

Buying and storing loquats

Loquats should also have a slight shine, and their skin should be smooth and firm. As they age they can become wrinkled, and brown patches may occur.

Loquats are best eaten on the day that you buy them, but they will keep for up to three days in the refrigerator.

Loquats in the kitchen

Loquats can be eaten raw, without peeling, but cut them in half and remove the seeds first. As a dessert, on their own or in a fruit salad, loquats need no sugar, but a squeeze of lemon juice will bring out their flavour. In China they are one of the fresh fruits included in a watermelon basket, and they are also served with almond jelly, like lychees. To serve loquats as a cooked fruit, simmer the slices in a natural fruit juice, or a light sugar syrup to which you have added lemon juice.

Loquats are excellent in savoury dishes, particularly in salads where the vinegar or lemon juice in the dressing creates a sweet and sour flavour. Raw slices can also be used as a garnish with spiced, stir-fried or sautéed meat. Chopped and mixed with raw onion, vinegar and spices, they can be made into a fruity relish.

In their countries of origin, loquats are made into jelly and are also candied. A loquat liqueur is made in Bermuda, and loquat juice is sold as a drink in Spain.

Pork tenderloin with sweet and sour loquats

1½ lb (675 g) pork tenderloin, in two even pieces
8 loquats
3 tablespoons cider vinegar
1 tablespoon clear honey
4 sage leaves, chopped
4 allspice berries, crushed
freshly ground black pepper

A little vinegar sharpens the flavour of loquats, and makes them suitable for serving with rich meats.

Heat the oven to 350F/180C/gas 4. Slit each piece of tenderloin almost in half lengthways, leaving it joined down one side. Peel, stone and slice the loquats. Mix together the remaining ingredients, and fold in the loquats. Fill the pork with the loquats, reshape it, and tie with fine cotton string at regular intervals along its length. Wrap each piece of pork separately in foil, sealing the ends tightly and rolling them upwards. Put the packets of foil into a roasting tin and cook for 1 hour.

Unwrap the pork, reserving any juices in the foil. Remove the ties and cut each piece of pork into two pieces. Serve on separate plates, with any juices spooned over the top.

Serves 4.

Chickpea, rice and loquat salad

8 oz (225 g) chickpeas, soaked, cooked and drained
8 oz (225 g) long grain brown rice, cooked and drained
8 loquats
12 oz (350 g) tomatoes
4 tablespoons olive oil
juice ½ lemon
1 teaspoon paprika
pinch cayenne pepper
1 garlic clove, crushed
2 teaspoons chopped fresh coriander
2 teaspoons chopped parsley

The lemon in this dressing once again draws out the flavour of the loquats. For a more substantial salad, add one flaked smoked mackerel fillet with the chickpeas. Serve the salad as a complete main course.

Mix together the chickpeas and rice. Stone and slice the loquats. Cut the tomatoes into small wedges. Add the loquats and tomatoes to the rice and chickpeas. Beat together the oil, lemon juice, paprika, cayenne pepper and garlic and fold into the salad. Mix in the herbs.

Serves 4.

LYCHEE, LONGAN, RAMBUTAN AND MANGOSTEEN

LYCHEE

LITCHI CHINENSIS

LYCHEES HAVE BEEN cultivated in China for 2,000 years or more. The main growing area has always been around the dykes and canals in Kwangtung.

Lychees have always been a highly valued fruit in China, so much so that they were once the downfall of an Emperor. In the eighth century, the Emperor Hsuan Tsung had a concubine called Yang Kue-fei whose passion, apart from himself, was fresh lychees. The Emperor's palace was in Peking, 300 miles from Kwangtung and yet he arranged for a daily supply of fruits to be brought to her on horseback, punishing the riders if they did not make the return journey in five days. His cruelty, and the extravagantly high price that he paid for the lychees, so infuriated the people of Peking, who had to make do with the occasional dried fruit, that they ultimately rebelled and overthrew him.

From China, cultivation of the lychee gradually spread and new cultivars were developed. They are now successfully grown in Israel, Australia, New Zealand, South Africa, Japan, India, Africa, Thailand and the Philippines.

For many people in Britain, their first introduction to a lychee has been a canned one in a Chinese restaurant, and this is no bad thing for lychees suffer very little in the canning process. The raw fruits are available in Britain mostly from September to December, although a few do come into the country at other times. A large part of the total imports come from Israel, South Africa and Madagascar.

From the outside skin through to the seed, the lychee is a surprising fruit. It is about ¾ inch (2 cm) in diameter and grows in clusters rather like cherries. The hard, thin skin is dull brown with a red blush and covered in pimples. It can be cracked open by squeezing the fruit very gently. Immediately, clear, sweet juice flows out and the white, translucent flesh can be seen. It is rather like a firm grape in texture and the flavour, too, is grape-like. Fitted snugly inside is one, oval, shiny

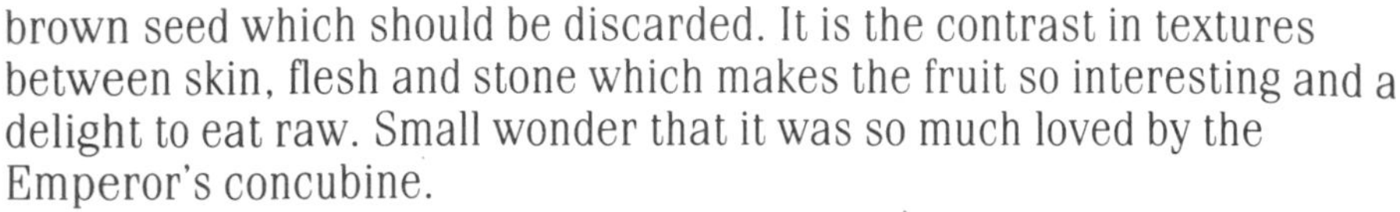

brown seed which should be discarded. It is the contrast in textures between skin, flesh and stone which makes the fruit so interesting and a delight to eat raw. Small wonder that it was so much loved by the Emperor's concubine.

Dried lychees can be bought in shops specializing in Chinese ingredients. They are usually stoned, look and taste like small prunes, and are sometimes called lychee nuts. They are used in Chinese sweet dishes and as fillings for Chinese steamed buns.

Nutrition

Lychees are high in Vitamin C, potassium and phosphorus.

Buying and storing lychees

The skin of lychees should always be unbroken, full-looking and fresh coloured. Do not buy them if a slight white bloom or mould covers the skin.

Lychees will keep for up to two days at room temperature and up to one week in the refrigerator.

Lychees in the kitchen

Before using raw or cooking, lychees must be skinned and stoned. The thin skin cracks and peels off easily. The flesh is wrapped around the stone in a dome shape at one end, and tucks in at the other, rather like a button mushroom. The stone can be extracted from the underside of the dome if it is loosened with a hairpin, a short skewer or the point of a small, sharp knife.

Whole raw lychees look wonderful in a fruit salad among other fruits of contrasting colours, such as black grapes or strawberries. They are frequently served in China with squares of almond jelly and slices of mandarin orange.

Lychees give a freshness to sweet and sour dishes and can also be pickled or put into chutneys.

LONGAN

NEPHELIUM LONGANA

The longan in China is called 'lychee's little brother'. It is smaller, and not as fully flavoured as the lychee, but in China is often grown alongside it, coming into season when the lychee has finished.

The longan is small and round, with a brown or yellow-red skin, similar in texture to that of the lychee, but with rougher pimples. The flesh is similar to that of the lychee, with an aromatic, grape-like flavour. The main drawback of the fruit is that the stone is large in comparison to the amount of flesh.

The longan is grown in China and India, and in both countries is often sold on the stem. Like the lychee, it can be canned and dried.

In the kitchen, it is used in exactly the same ways as the lychee.

RAMBUTAN

NEPHELIUM LAPPACEUM

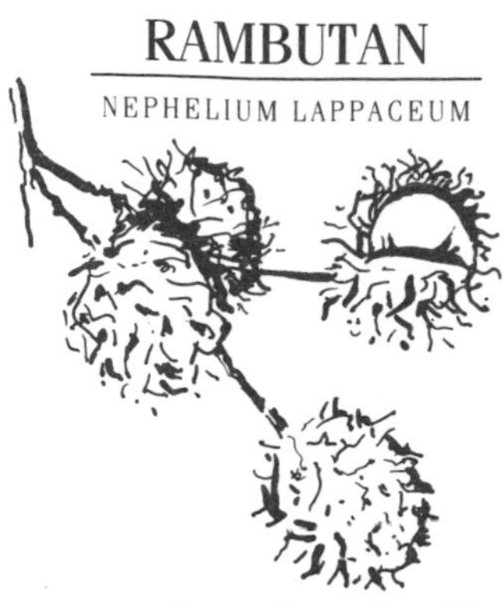

The rambutan is often called the hairy lychee and, in all but its coarsely hairy skin, closely resembles that fruit.

The rambutan came originally from Malaysia and is now also grown in Thailand and the Philippines, central America and Australia. Those arriving in Britain come from Thailand in March. The fruits are slightly larger and more oval than a lychee, and their skin is red and covered with thick, coarse, shiny hair, making it look rather like a large burr. The skin is quite soft to the touch, and peels off easily.

In flavour, the rambutan closely resembles the lychee and has the same shiny stone. Its Vitamin C content, however, is much lower.

Rambutans are sometimes tinned with pineapple.

Use rambutans in exactly the same ways as the lychee.

MANGOSTEEN

GARCINIA MANGOSTANA

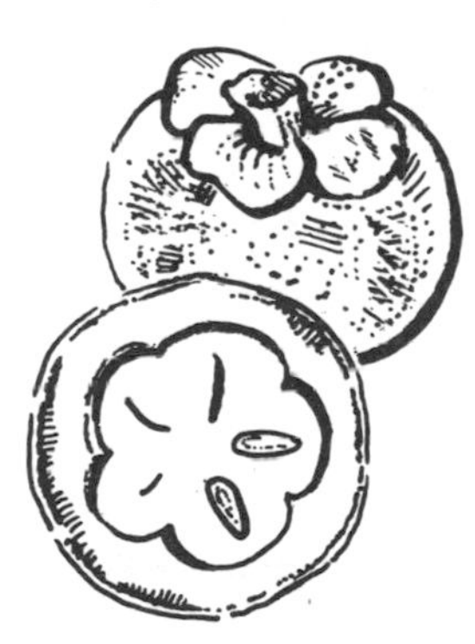

The mangosteen (or mangistan) is in some ways quite unlike a lychee or rambutan, but its flesh is so similar in both flavour and texture that they are often placed together. It is still a rare fruit, because it is difficult to grow even in tropical countries, and usually only reaches Britain in May, from Thailand. Mangosteens are also grown throughout Malaysia, in the Philippines and the East Indies and also in Java and the West Indies.

A mangosteen is about the size of a medium eating apple. It has a hard, fibrous shell, ranging in colour from crimson to dull purple, mottled to a greater or lesser extent with dull brown. On top is a short stem and four stiff, leaf-like parts of a calyx. Underneath is a beautifully formed flower pattern about ½ inch (1.3 cm) in diameter. The shell is about ¼ inch (6 mm) thick and, when the fruit is fresh, the inner lining is bright pink. As the fruit passes its peak, the shell becomes harder and browner.

The fruit inside the shell is small, about the size of a peeled satsuma, and consists of seven segments. Embedded in them are two irregularly shaped, flat stones. The flesh is pure white, translucent and in texture like a cross between a grape and a ripe greengage. The flavour is delicious, very fresh and sweet, similar to that of a lychee.

Nutrition

Although refreshing and thirst quenching, the nutrient count in the mangosteen is low.

Mangosteens in the kitchen

Mangosteens are so rare that you can seldom pick and choose, but ideally the thick skin should have as few brown patches as possible.

Removing the skin is tricky. If it is cut too deeply its tannin may affect the flavour of the flesh. Score it all round, but not right through, with a sharp knife and twist the two halves apart.

The present scarcity of mangosteens in the west at the time of writing makes it difficult to do anything but eat them raw and enjoy their flavour and texture. You can also add them to an exotic fruit salad, where they go well with mangoes. If you have several, you can purée their flesh to be used as an exotic, sweet sauce.

Sweet and sour chicken with lychees

A mild sweet and sour dish, with a delicious combination of textures and flavours.

one 3½ lb (1.6 kg) roasting chicken
16 fresh lychees
2 tablespoons arrowroot or cornflour
2 tablespoons soy sauce
1 tablespoon white wine vinegar
½ pint (275 ml) chicken stock
6 oz (175 g) carrots
2 celery sticks
4 tablespoons sunflower or groundnut oil
1 garlic clove, finely chopped
2 medium onions, finely chopped

Joint the chicken. Remove all the meat from the bones, and cut it into ¾-inch (2 cm) dice, removing the thicker skin. Peel, halve and stone the lychees, catching as much juice as possible. Put the arrowroot or cornflour into a bowl and gradually mix in the soy sauce, vinegar, stock and lychee juice. Cut the carrots and celery sticks into matchstick pieces.

Heat the oil and garlic in a large frying pan on a high heat. Stir-fry the chicken pieces until they are beginning to brown and any moisture is driven off. Remove from pan. Stir-fry the carrots, celery and onions for 2 minutes. Replace the chicken and stir-fry for 2 minutes more. Add the lychees. Give the arrowroot mixture a final stir and pour it into the pan. Simmer gently, stirring, until the sauce thickens.

Serves 4.

Fruit and almond jelly

1 lb (450 g) lychees
as many small seedless black grapes as lychees
3 satsumas, or other small soft citrus fruits
4 oz (125 g) almonds, blanched and ground
1 pint water
2 drops almond essence
2 tablespoons honey
½ oz (15 g) gelatin

In a traditional Chinese recipe, cubes of plain almond jelly are mixed with lychees and other fruits. Here, the fruits are set in the jelly.

Almond jelly has a rich, almost oily, texture like an old-fashioned milk jelly. The refreshing lychees make a superb contrast.

If you need to be quick, substitute ½ pint (275 ml) evaporated milk and ½ pint (275 ml) water for the almond mixture.

Skin and stone the lychees, catching as much juice as possible. Reshape the fruits and put a grape inside each one. Arrange in a shallow, 8-inch (20 cm) diameter dish, such as a small flan dish, with segments of satsuma in between.

Put the ground almonds, any reserved lychee juice and the water into a saucepan. Bring to the boil and let the liquid bubble up. Take from the heat, cool slightly, then return to the heat and bubble up again. Strain the liquid through muslin or an old, washed out tea towel, squeezing hard to extract as much as possible.

Return the liquid to the rinsed out pan. Add the almond essence (be careful not to add too much) and honey. Reheat without boiling and sprinkle in the gelatin. Stir for the gelatin to dissolve, again without boiling. Cool the liquid. Pour over the fruits and chill until set.

Serves 4–6.

MANGO

MANGIFERA INDICA

THE MANGO LIVES up to its reputation of being the world's most delicious fruit, and it is certainly one of the most prolific.

Mangos grow in all tropical countries of the world, both cultivated and semi-wild. They are now so widespread that their exact origin has been obscured, but it is believed to have been somewhere around the East Indies and Malaysia many thousands of years ago. They are one of the oldest tropical fruits and have been cultivated in India for over 4,000 years. Portuguese traders took mangos to Africa and South America in the sixteenth century. In the eighteenth century the fruit reached central America and the West Indies, in the nineteenth century the Canary Islands and, in the twentieth century, southern Italy, Florida, California, Hawaii, Australia, Egypt, Israel, Iran, Iraq, Madeira and the Philippines, in fact anywhere in the world where the climate is suitable.

The first British to appreciate mangos were members of the East India Company in the 1670s. To them, the fruit was mainly a chutney and pickle ingredient, and they began exporting jars of pickled mangos to Britain. Attempts were made at this time to grow mangos under glass at home, but they met with little success, although one tree in Kew Gardens bore fruit in 1818.

In many countries where mangos now grow, they are picked freely by the local populations, to whom they are as common as apples are to us. In parts of south America, mango trees line the streets, and the ripe fruits belong to those who can catch them as they fall.

There are numerous varieties, all slightly different in shape and colour and in the flavour and texture of the flesh. Most fruits are about 6 inches (15 cm) long and either kidney-shaped or rounded at one end and 'beaked' at the other. Some are rounder than others and some, called banana mangos, long and narrow. All unripe mangos are green, but they differ as they ripen. Some simply become flushed with red, some become yellow or orange with a red blush, and some turn red almost all over. In India small green mangos are grown, used mainly for chutneys and relishes.

The flavour of a mango does not compare with any other fruit. It is sweet and aromatic, with a fresh, sherbet fizz. The texture is always soft and luscious when the fruit is ripe but it is also naturally fibrous, how much so depending on the variety. In the centre of the fruit is a large, flat stone surrounded by stringy flesh.

Nutrition

Mangos are exceptionally high in potassium and Vitamin A, and have significant amounts of Vitamin C and some B Vitamins.

Buying and storing mangos

If you are buying for chutney and pickles, the mango should be firm. If you want a dessert fruit, it should yield very slightly when pressed with your thumb.

Mangos are best used as soon as possible, but keep in a cool place for two days and in the refrigerator for up to a week.

An unripe mango can be ripened at room temperature.

Mangos in the kitchen

According to Rupert Croft-Cooke in his book of *Exotic Food*, the best way to eat a mango is in the bath, as it is so juicy. Even then, you have to know the best way to cut it, as the skin is not edible, unless of course you are slicing the fruit for a chutney.

To prepare a mango, hold it upright on a board with one narrow side pointing towards you. With a sharp knife, cut off two thick slices from either side of the stone. The flesh can be spooned out of these, or they can be cut into slices and the skin removed from each slice. Then cut away the skin from the centre part and cut the flesh from the stone. Even with the non-fibrous types, there is bound to be some stringy flesh clinging to the stone. Don't waste it, but pick the stone up and suck it. It is messy, but definitely worth it.

Sliced or chopped mango makes a perfect dessert with no additions, although you can scatter it with nuts or chopped dates. Mango can also be mixed with other fruits in a tropical fruit salad. A simple combination of mango and kiwi fruit is wonderful. The same raw fruits can fill a tart on a base of whipped cream or thick Greek yoghurt.

Mango flesh is easily puréed and the naturally sweet purée can form the base of many different desserts. Whip it with an equal quantity of whipped cream or thick yoghurt for a fool, or add eggs for a mousse or a cold soufflé. Make it into ice-creams and water ices, or use it as a sauce.

Liquidized with yoghurt or milk and crushed ice, mangos make a refreshing drink. Mango juice is sold alone or mixed with the juice of other tropical fruits.

Mangos are too expensive and rare to be used in cooked desserts in the West, but in their countries of origin, particularly the West Indies, they are put into pies like apples. They are also made into jams and fruit jellies. In South America they are made into thick fruit pastes that are cut into pieces and sold as sweetmeats.

Slightly under-ripe mango can be added to spiced and curried meat dishes, particularly chicken or lamb. It can also be added to spiced rice to go with curries. More simply, lay slices of firm mango over lamb or pork chops, or over chicken breasts as they are grilled.

Raw chopped under-ripe or green mango can be mixed with coconut, chilli, spices and yoghurt to be served as an accompaniment to curries.

Curried rice and vegetables with mango

1 large aubergine
2 teaspoons sea salt
12 oz (350 g) potatoes
1 green pepper
1 firm mango
3 tablespoons olive oil
1 large onion, thinly sliced
1 garlic clove, finely chopped
1 teaspoon hot Madras curry powder
1 teaspoon ground cumin
1 teaspoon ground turmeric
8 oz (225 g) long grain brown rice
1 pint (575 ml) stock
2 tablespoons tomato purée

Mangos in a curry make a fresh contrast to the other ingredients. This dish can be served with meat curries, or you can add some blanched and fried almonds to make it a meal in itself.

Dice the aubergine. Put it into a colander and sprinkle with the sea salt. Leave to drain for 20 minutes. Rinse in cold water and dry on kitchen paper. Scrub and dice the potatoes. Core and seed the pepper, and cut into thin, 1 inch (2.5 cm) strips. Cut the mango into strips and remove the skin.

Heat the oil in a large saucepan on a low heat. Soften the onion and garlic. Stir in the curry powder, spices and rice. Pour in the stock and bring to the boil. Add the tomato purée. Cover, and simmer for 30 minutes. Slice the mango flesh and lay it on top of the rice. Cook for a further 10 minutes. Gently fold in the mango before serving.

Serves 4.

Mango chutney

4 mangos, just beginning to ripen
4 oz (125 g) dark Muscovado sugar
2 teaspoons sea salt
2 teaspoons ground ginger
2 teaspoons ground cumin
2 teaspoons ground coriander
½ pint (275 ml) white malt vinegar
1 garlic clove, crushed

If you like mango chutney, it is well worth making your own. This is mellower and less syrupy than any bought variety.

Thinly slice the mangos, without peeling. Put into a saucepan with the remaining ingredients. Bring to the boil and simmer for 45 minutes to 1 hour until the mixture is thick. Cool the chutney slightly. Put it into warm jars and seal tightly.

Makes about 1½ lb (675 g).

Mango ice

3 ripe mangos
juice 1 lime or lemon
1 egg white

Mangos are so sweet and full of flavour that only the minimum of ingredients are needed in order to make a tropical water ice.

Remove the flesh from two of the mangos and purée it together with the lime or lemon juice. Put the purée into an ice-cream maker, and follow the manufacturer's instructions. Alternatively, pour into a freezing tray and freeze for 2 hours, either in the coldest part of the freezer or in the freezing compartment of the refrigerator, set at the coldest temperature.

Stiffly whip the egg white. Whip the slushy purée to break up the ice particles. Fold it into the egg white. Return the mixture to the ice tray and freeze for 2 hours, breaking up the ice crystals every 15 minutes. Scoop out portions with an ice-cream scoop and freeze on a tray.

Serve straight from the freezer, garnished with slices from the remaining mango.

Serves 6.

MEDLAR

MESPILUS GERMANICA

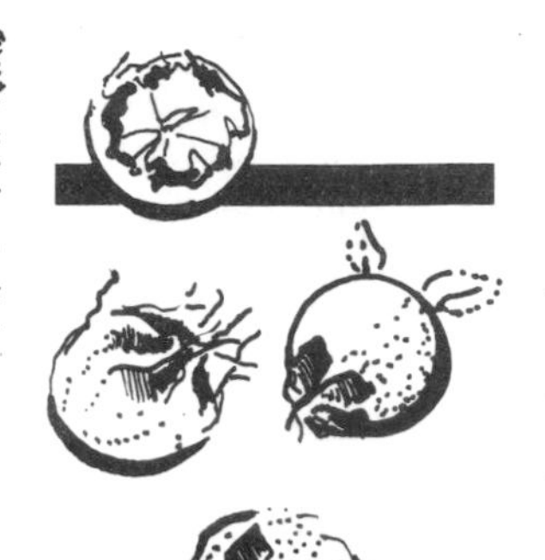

THE MEDLAR IS an old-fashioned fruit, much more appreciated in times gone by than it is today. Today, we like everything clean and hygienic and certainly do not want our fruit to be rotten which a medlar has to be, in order to be edible. Medlars are small like a plum, brown like a russet apple, and in shape like half a rounded fruit, with a point at one end and the other open to reveal the seeds crowned with a pointed calyx. Medlar trees have a tangle of twisted branches and leaves that turn deep red in the autumn. The original medlar trees had thorns, but later varieties were thornless. They grow wild and make a good garden tree, but none are now grown in orchards.

A native of south-east Europe, the medlar quickly spread westwards and became naturalized as far as Britain. Medlars were grown in Anglo-Saxon gardens and medieval orchards, and in Tudor and Stuart times the fruits were made into marmalades and sweet fillings for tarts. They remained popular right through to the beginning of the twentieth century, and in Victorian times were kept in a silver dish of moist sawdust on the sideboard. Since then, medlar trees have survived in obscurity in the corners of gardens, the fruits enjoyed by their owners but seldom reaching the markets.

It is because the medlar involves keeping carefully after it has been picked that it has never been a popular commercial fruit. When ripe, the flesh is hard and acid. In order for it to soften and sweeten, the fruits must be kept in a cool place, such as an outbuilding, laid on straw or hay until they are 'bletted', which means that they have to ferment inside. They look awful: squashy, brown and rotten, but their flavour is sweet and aromatic. They will not all be ready together, so after a week or so they must be looked at every day and those that are ready taken away and eaten as soon as possible.

Nutrition

Medlars are high in potassium. Their vitamin content is unknown.

Buying and storing medlars

See above.

Medlars in the kitchen

The best thing to do with a medlar is to scoop out the flesh with a teaspoon and eat it as it is. It is apparently good with port. Dorothy Hartley in her fascinating book, *English Food*, recommends mixing the scooped out flesh with cream and brown sugar. Her recipe for baked medlars is to arrange them on a shallow dish with butter and cloves, and put them into the oven for a few minutes.

If you have your own tree, you can make medlar cheese, jelly and jam.

Medlar jelly

4 lb (1.8 kg) medlars
4 inch (10 cm) cinnamon stick
thinly pared rind and juice 1 lemon
12 oz (350 g) sugar to each pint (575 ml) strained liquid

Put the medlars into a preserving pan with the cinnamon stick, lemon rind and juice, and just cover with water. Bring to the boil and simmer until very soft, about 45 minutes. Strain the liquid through a jelly bag, without pressing down, and measure it.

Return the liquid to the cleaned pan. Add the sugar, and stir on a low heat for it to dissolve. Bring to boiling point, and boil until setting point is reached.

Pour the jelly into warmed jars, cover and leave until cool.

Makes about 2 jars.

MELON AND WATERMELON

MELON

CUCUMIS MELO

MELONS ARE AN ancient fruit that have refreshed the palate and quenched thirsts since the days of the ancient Egyptians. Related to the gourd, squash, pumpkin and cucumber, their origin is uncertain, but is thought to be either from Asia or tropical Africa.

Melons did not reach Europe until the beginning of the fourteenth century. They were grown first in Italy, where Pope Paul II is said to have eaten so many he died of them, and also in Spain. Columbus took them to the Americas where his men first planted them on 29 March 1494. A year later they reached France, probably taken by Charles VIII of France after his Italian campaign.

According to Mrs Beeton, the first melons came to England in the fifteenth century, were forgotten during the Wars of the Roses, and then arrived permanently from France in the sixteenth century. The favourite plants were called musk melons, as their aroma was like that of the musk used in perfumes and pot-pourris. Since then, melons have been grown widely in English country houses. They were particularly popular in the seventeenth century and again in Victorian times, when they were grown in hot houses. Melons can be grown quite easily under glass in the garden, but they have never been a commercial crop in Britain until recently, when Guernsey growers started to grow the Galia melon on a small scale.

Melons are grown in most of the warmer countries of the world, including southern Europe. Those arriving in Britain are sent from South America, Israel, South Africa, Spain, the Canary Islands, Holland and France.

There are many different varieties of melon and sometimes it is hard to tell the difference. The most popular in Britain seems to be the **Honeydew**, sometimes called the winter melon because of its excellent keeping qualities. Honeydew melons are a pointed oval shape and their skins are usually bright yellow or dull, dark green. Yellow ones have a smoother skin with shallow, lengthways ridges; green ones are rougher, with deeper ridges. White honeydew melons are grown in South America and these can occasionally be bought in the spring. The flesh of all honeydew melons is pale green and fairly solid. It is hard when under-ripe, but when ripe it is soft, although solid, and very juicy. Honeydew melons are not as sweet and rich as other types, but are extremely refreshing.

The sweetest and best of all the melons is reputed to be the **Charentais**, which originally came from Holland but which received its name from Charentes in France where it was developed. Charentais melons are round, with a smooth, green skin and soft, orange flesh. Only a few are sent to England, and these are available from June to October.

Round melons that have a rough, pale biscuit-coloured network pattern over their skins, are known in Britain as **Musk**, **Netted** or **Nutmeg** melons and in the United States as **Cantaloupe** melons. Under the netting, the skin of this type of melon can be yellow or green. The flesh is always soft, sweet and aromatic and can be green, orange or pink.

The **Galia** and the **Rock** melon are the two varieties of musk melon most widely available in Britain. The Galia, named after the daughter of the man who first raised it and coming from Italy, Spain, Holland and Guernsey, has a thin yellow skin under its network. Its flesh is bright green, smooth, sweet and juicy. The Rock melon is smaller and firmer, and almost totally covered with its net-like pattern. Its flesh is salmon pink, more solid and less watery than most melons, and almost syrupy sweet. It comes mainly from South Africa.

Ogen melons are closely related to the musk melons, but have no network pattern. Their skins are thin, yellow and marked into sections with green stripes. Like the Galia melons their flesh is bright green, but it is slightly fibrous and has a hint of sharpness.

The **Tiger** melon or **Pepino** is the latest addition to the melon family and, at present, comes only from Colombia in very small quantities. It is small and round, and its skin is dull yellow with black or purple stripes. Unlike most melons, it contains only about five small seeds. The flesh is firm and sugary in texture and, when under-ripe can be quite crisp with an apple-like flavour. As it ripens it remains solid but becomes very juicy, sweet and aromatic. At the time of writing, Tiger melons are scarce and expensive but they could easily become more popular over the next few years.

Nutrition

All melons are about 95 per cent water, but they are rich in potassium and have significant amounts of Vitamin C, calcium and phosphorus.

Buying and storing melons

Most melons are ripe if they yield under your thumb when pressed on the end. Look out for darker patches on the skin of the Galia and Ogen types which signify that they might be over-ripe. All melons should smell sweet and fresh when they are ready to eat.

Honeydew melons can be kept for up to two weeks in a cool, dark larder. When cut, they should be wrapped in cling film and placed in the refrigerator, where they will keep for up to four days.

Other types of melons will keep for up to three days in a cool place and, when cut, for a day in the refrigerator wrapped in cling film.

Melons in the kitchen

Although there are so many different varieties of melon, there are not many melon recipes. Mostly, they are served raw, often at the beginning of the meal to refresh the palate and wake up the taste buds. Larger types are served in wedges, the smaller types in halves.

If you are serving wedges of honeydew melon, scoop out the seeds, and fill the middles with a portion of cream cheese topped with a nasturtium flower; yoghurt scattered with chopped nuts and preserved ginger; yoghurt mixed with tahini (sesame paste) and sprinkled with sesame seeds. All these richer ingredients provide a good contrast in flavour to the light, watery melon, besides making it look more attractive.

Halved round melons can be filled with a mixture of other fruits such as grapes and kiwi fruit, either plain or first marinated in port or sherry.

When you have small, single-portion melons, slice off the top and fill them with fruits in the same way.

For large round melons, which can serve four people, slice off the top, scoop out the flesh with a melon baller and mix it with other fruits and alcohol, before piling them all back in. In the summer, a mixture of melon and stoned red cherries with a sprinkling of mint looks very pretty and fresh.

Melon flesh can be puréed and used as the base for water-ices and ice-creams.

Honeydew melons go well with savoury ingredients such as fish and seafood, ham, or chicken and can be mixed with them in salads. A little diced melon added to a carrot salad gives it a freshing lift. The sweeter types can be served with a wedge of prosciutto ham, smoked duck or venison, or with good quality salami.

Melons can be used to make jams, especially melon and ginger jam and can also be pickled.

WATERMELON

CITRULLUS VULGARIS

The watermelon is the most refreshing of all fruits and can serve as a drink as well as a snack. It arrives in Britain in the summer and its high water content makes it a great reviver on hot days.

Watermelons consist of a large round or oval shell enclosing sweet refreshing flesh, yet they are a different species from other melons. Their seeds are arranged within the flesh rather than in a cavity in the middle, and the flesh has a texture that is a cross between sugar candy and crushed ice.

Whether the watermelon originated in tropical Africa or India is uncertain, but it features in ancient Sanskrit literature and Egyptian art, and seeds have been found in Egyptian tombs so it must have been cultivated for many thousands of years. It was not heard of in Europe until the thirteenth century and none reached Britain until Elizabethan times. African slaves took the watermelon to America, and it was first cultivated there at the beginning of the seventeenth century. Watermelons are now cultivated all over the world. Those reaching Britain come mainly from Israel, Italy, Greece, Spain and Cyprus.

Some watermelons are round and others oval. Their skin is dark green and waxy and the oval varieties may have darker stripes. The flesh of most watermelons is crimson red, although there are some in which it is creamy yellow. The seeds are dark brown or black. In Britain, the smaller watermelons, such as the Israeli Sugar Baby are the most popular. They weigh 6–10 lb (2.7–4.5 kg) and are sold whole or in halves or wedges. Other varieties can be much larger.

The **Golden** or **Pineapple** watermelon has recently made a brief appearance from Israel. This has a golden skin with a netted pattern and yellow flesh. At the time of writing, bad weather in the growing areas had put a stop to the crop, but it could well be a variety to look out for in the future.

Nutrition

Although watermelons are 92 per cent water, they are exceptionally high in Vitamin A and potassium, and have significant amounts of Vitamin C, calcium and phosphorus.

Buying and storing watermelons

Watermelons should be hard when bought, and should give a muffled sound when tapped. Their skin should look waxy, perhaps with a yellow patch, but certainly with no brown blemishes. When buying them cut, the flesh should look firm and sugary. After a slice has been cut for some time, the colour darkens and the flesh begins to soften and take on a cotton-wool texture. This can also happen to a whole melon, but only after it has been stored for about three weeks.

Keep an uncut watermelon in a cool dark place for up to two weeks. Once cut, wrap it in cling film and store in the refrigerator for up to two days.

Watermelons in the kitchen

To bring out the full flavour and freshness of a watermelon, serve it slightly chilled, but not icy. In the Caribbean, wedges are served on a bed of ice. Many people like to eat wedges of watermelon from the shell, however messy this may be. The seeds can be picked out first with the handle of a teaspoon, or can be eaten or spat out.

The flesh can be cut from the wedges and diced, mixed with other fruits and laced with rum to be served as a first course or dessert. It can also be mixed with natural yoghurt or soured cream and served scattered with toasted nuts, or with lemon juice, honey and ground cinnamon. In China, the whole fruit is cut into a basket shape and the flesh scooped out, diced and mixed with other fresh fruits before piling back into the basket.

Once the seeds are removed, watermelon flesh can liquidize to a thin purée. Unsweetened, this makes a refreshing base for a water-ice.

The diced flesh can be used in salads with seafood and chicken, or as a garnish for slices of cold meat.

Melon brose

Serve this for a special breakfast.

6 oz (175 g) jumbo oats
3 oz (75 g) dried whole apricots
3 oz (75 g) raisins
½ pint (275 ml) natural apple juice
1 small Galia or Ogen melon
3 fl oz (90 ml) creamed smetana or soured cream

Put the oats into a bowl. Quarter the apricots, and add them to the oats with the raisins. Pour in the apple juice and leave to soak for 6 hours or overnight.

Just before serving, dice the melon flesh and mix it into the oats with the smetana or soured cream.

Serves 4.

Chicken, tarragon and melon salad

one 3½ lb (1.6 kg) roasting chicken
5 large tarragon sprigs, plus extra for garnish if wished
½ oz (15 g) butter, softened
¼ pint (150 ml) dry white wine
1 egg yolk
½ teaspoon mustard powder
freshly ground white pepper
4 fl oz (125 ml) oil
4 teaspoons tarragon vinegar
1 tablespoon chopped tarragon
1 honeydew melon

Diced melon adds a light touch to salads with mild flavours and creamy dressings.

Heat the oven to 350F/180C/gas 4. Truss the chicken, putting one tarragon sprig inside. Spread skin with the butter. Lay the remaining tarragon sprigs over the legs and breast, spreading out the leaves as much as possible. Put the chicken into a roasting tin and cover completely with foil. Roast for 1 hour. Increase temperature to 400F/200C/gas 6. Remove foil and pour the wine into the tin. Continue cooking for 30 minutes, until the chicken is golden brown. Remove from tin and cool completely.

Pour all the juices from the pan into a cup or small bowl and refrigerate until they cool and the fat rises to the top.

Put the egg yolk into a bowl with the mustard powder and pepper. Work them together and gradually beat in 1 tablespoon of the oil. Beat in 1 teaspoon of the tarragon vinegar and then the rest of the oil. Mix in the remaining vinegar and the chopped tarragon. Skim all the fat from the surface of the chicken juices. If the juices have set to a jelly put the bowl into a saucepan of water and set it on a low heat until they melt to a liquid again. Beat them into the mayonnaise.

Dice the melon flesh or scoop it into small balls and coat with the mayonnaise. Put the melon into the bottom of a flat serving dish. Cut the chicken into small joints and set them on the top. Garnish with extra tarragon sprigs if wished.

Serves 4.

Watermelon with cherries and curd cheese

½ medium watermelon
6 oz (175 g) sweet red cherries
2 tablespoons chopped mint
6 oz (175 g) curd cheese
8 juniper berries
8 allspice berries

A light, refreshing summer first course.

Chop the watermelon flesh, removing as many seeds as possible. Stone the cherries. Divide fruit between 4 small bowls and scatter with the mint. Put a portion of the curd cheese on top. Crush the juniper and allspice berries together and scatter over the cheese.

Serves 4.

Watermelon basket

1 medium watermelon
1 small cantaloupe melon
8 oz (225 g) lychees or rambutans (page 125)
6 oz (175 g) loquats, if available (page 122)
3 peaches
20 maraschino cherries
¼ pint (150 ml) sweet sherry
2 tablespoons clear honey
4 oz (125 g) black grapes, in one bunch

This is a traditional Chinese dish. The mixture of fruits can be varied according to your taste and what is available. For example, two medium oranges can be used instead of the loquats.

Stand the watermelon on its side. Make a cut from the top end, to within ½ inch (1.5 cm) from the centre. Make a similar cut from the base. Then make 2 cuts down, round half the circumference of the melon, to meet the first cuts. Remove the wedges of melon that are now cut away. Cut away the flesh from the remaining strip of melon, so that you are left with a 1-inch (2.5 cm) handle, made from the rind.

Scoop the flesh of the water melon from the wedges and also from the base of the basket into balls, discarding the seeds. Cut the cantaloupe melon in half. Remove the seeds and scoop the flesh into balls. Peel and stone the lychees, catching as much juice as possible. Stone and slice the loquats. Halve, stone and dice the peaches. Put the prepared fruits into a large bowl. Add the maraschino cherries, lychee juice, sherry and honey.

Put the melon basket on to a serving dish. Fill with the fruits and hang the grapes on the handle.

Serves 6.

MULBERRY

MORUS NIGRA

'HERE WE GO round the mulberry bush' – we have all sung it, but how many of us have ever tasted a mulberry? Probably only those lucky enough to have a mulberry tree growing in the garden.

There are two types of mulberry, the black, which produces large purple fruits, and the white, the leaves of which are used to feed silkworms. The black mulberry originated in either Iran or Nepal, was taken to Europe by the Greeks, and spread further by the Romans. It was grown in British orchards in medieval times and was a familiar garden tree in the sixteenth century.

Mulberries are attractive trees with spreading branches, but are often the last to leaf in spring and the first to lose leaves in the autumn. In the thirteenth and fourteenth centuries, mulberries were known as murreys and gave their name to meat pottages that were coloured with their dark, wine-red juice. Later they were mixed with spices, sugar and wine in tarts, and boiled with sugar to make stiff jelly drops.

Mulberries have always been essentially a garden fruit in Britain and have only been grown in ones and twos in orchards among other fruit and kept for private use.

Mulberries are about 1 inch (2.5 cm) long, oval and dark purple-red and very succulent and juicy. They are sweet yet acid, and deliciously aromatic.

Nutrition

Mulberries are exceptionally high in potassium and have significant amounts of calcium, phosphorus and Vitamin C.

Picking and storing mulberries

If you are lucky enough to own a tree, you will need to learn the right way to harvest the fruits. Picking them from the tree is difficult and besides, the fruit drops off by itself when it is ripe. It is best to spread mats, tarpaulin or paper under the trees so that fruits drop on to them and can be easily picked up. Check the mats at least once a day to ensure that the fruit is used in its peak condition. The fruits will go on falling over a period of several weeks.

The berries should all be a deep, purple-red colour. Under-ripe ones may still be red and over-ripe ones are squashy. Mulberries are delicate, and should be handled as little as possible. They will stain anything they touch dark red.

They will keep for up to two days in the refrigerator. Freeze them on trays, and pack into polythene bags. They will keep for up to six months.

Mulberries in the kitchen

Mulberries are a delight eaten raw, sprinkled with sugar or with clear honey spooned over them, and topped with cream or a creamy, mild yoghurt. To make a mulberry purée as a base for fruit fools, mousses, soufflés, water-ices or ice-creams, rub them raw through a sieve, stir in honey or sugar to taste and leave for 30 minutes for the sweetener to dissolve.

Simmered very gently with sugar or honey, until the juice begins to run, mulberries can be tipped into a bread-lined pudding basin to make a late summer pudding. They can also be put into pies, or pickled and made into sharp sauces for pork, lamb, poultry or game.

Mulberry juice has often been used to colour wines and cordials and in France it is mixed with mead. It can also be mulled with wine.

PASSION FRUIT

PASSIFLORA SPECIES

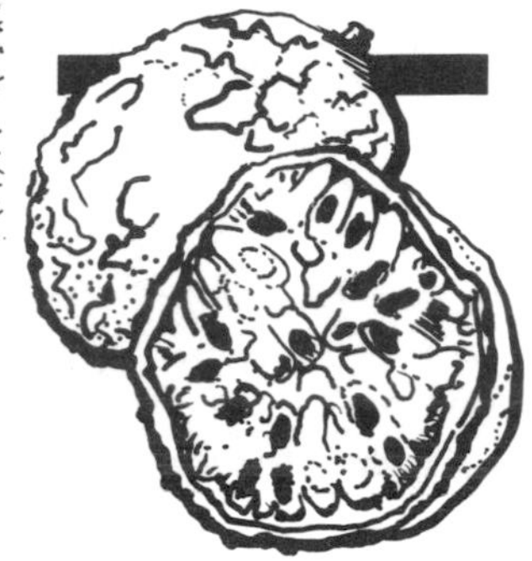

CONTRARY TO WHAT might be thought on first hearing its name, the passion fruit is not a famed aphrodisiac, but is so called because Spanish priests who first found it growing in South America could use its spectacular flower to preach to the local Indians about the crucifixion. There are many different varieties, but in all of them, the three styles represent the nails; the five stamens Christ's wounds; the filaments are the crown of thorns; the ovary the sponge soaked in vinegar; and the ten petals the apostles, excluding Judas and Peter.

Since then, the passion fruit has been carried to all the warmer parts of the world, where it is a favourite garden plant besides being cultivated commercially. It has been particularly popular in Australia, where the meringue-based dessert known as pavlova was devised especially for it. The passion fruit did not arrive in Britain until the nineteenth century and it is only recently that it has become more readily available.

There are eleven species with edible fruits and, although all different in size and colour they all contain edible seeds enclosed in a soft, transparent pulp which has an acid, aromatic, sherbet flavour.

The first to arrive in Britain, and still the most common was the *Passiflora edulis*, a small fruit, round or egg-shaped and about 1½ inches (4 cm) in diameter. The smooth green skin turns to purple and gains dimples as the fruit ripens, and the inside is lined with deep pink. The seeds are dark and the flesh bright orange with a sharp, aromatic flavour.

The original Spanish name for the passion fruit was granadill, or little pomegranate, and **granadilla** is the name for the other species that you are now quite likely to find in Britain. The yellow granadilla is closely related to *P. edulis* and is similar in size, shape and flavour. The main difference is that it is yellow or orange instead of purple.

The **sweet granadilla** (*P. lingularis*) is very different. It comes from Peru and looks like an orange maraca. It is about the size of a medium orange, with a hard, smooth thick skin, dull orange in colour, thickly speckled with paler patches. Inside is a mass of dark grey seeds encased in pale orange flesh that has a sweet, plum-like flavour, more mellow but less acidic than that of the purple passion fruit. The seeds can be swallowed whole, but if crunched they make the flavour sharper.

Nutrition

All passion fruit are high in potassium and Vitamin A, and have significant amounts of Vitamin C, phosphorus, sodium and calcium.

Buying and storing passion fruit

The skin of the small, purple passion fruit, although dimpled, should not look dry and wrinkled, but moist and slightly shiny. Granadillas should be shiny and light orange, with no brown or darker patches.

Both keep well for up to a week in a cool place.

Passion fruit in the kitchen

To remove the seeds from a small passion fruit, cut it in half with a sharp knife and scoop them out with a spoon. Do not throw away the shells, for they can make a delicious conserve (see below). To cut a thick-skinned granadilla, insert the point of a sharp knife into one side and gradually work it down.

Small passion fruit and granadillas can be interchanged in recipes. Because of their size, use two passion fruit to one granadilla. You may need less sweetening when using a granadilla because of its milder flavour.

Passion pulp can simply be spooned out of the shell and eaten as it is. The seeds will slip down easily. Passion fruit seeds, in small amounts, can be spooned over fruit salads, meringue-based dishes, cheesecakes, ice-creams and cream desserts as a decoration.

By rubbing the seeds in a sieve, the juice can be extracted and this can be used as a base for soufflés, mousses, ice-creams, water-ices and other desserts where purée or juice is required.

The juice can also be used as a drink, either alone or mixed with other fruit juices.

Passion fruit shell jam

shells from 6 purple passion fruit
juice ½ lemon
1½ pints (850 ml) water
10 oz (300 g) granulated sugar to every ½ pint (275 ml) liquid

This is a deep pink, fragrant jam. It is delicious with scones and in tartlet cases, and can also be used as a topping for cakes or sponge flans.

Put the halved shells into a saucepan with the lemon juice and water. Bring to the boil and simmer for about 30 minutes, or until every part, including the white pith, has turned a deep, pinky maroon colour and the pith is soft, translucent and almost gelatinous in texture.

Strain and measure the liquid and put it into a saucepan. Using a teaspoon, scrape the pulp from the passion fruit shells. Cut it into thin strips and add to the liquid. Discard the shells.

Add the sugar to the liquid and stir on a low heat for it to dissolve. Bring the syrup to the boil, and continue boiling until setting point is reached.

Pour the jam into warmed jars, cover with waxed greaseproof paper and seal.

Makes about 1 lb (450 g).

Granadilla and cream nests

3 oz (75 g) butter
8 fl oz (225 ml) water
4 oz (125 g) wholemeal flour
3 eggs, beaten
2 granadilla
7 fl oz (200 ml) double cream
¼ pint (150 ml) Greek-style natural yoghurt

Nests of choux pastry filled with a light-as-air mixture of cream, yoghurt and the sweet, mellow juice of the granadillas.

Heat the oven to 400F/200C/gas 6. Put the butter and water into a saucepan, set on a medium heat and bring to the boil. Sprinkle in the flour all at once, and beat to make a smooth paste. Take from the heat and cool for a few minutes. Beat in the eggs a little at a time, and beat to make the mixture smooth and glossy. Put the mixture into a forcing bag and pipe 8 choux nests on to a floured baking sheet. Bake for 25 minutes, raising the heat to 425F/220C/gas 7 after the first 10 minutes. Lift the cooked nests on to a wire rack and pierce them to release the steam. Cool completely.

Put the seeds of one of the granadillas into a sieve over a bowl, and rub to extract all the juice and flesh. Stiffly whip the cream. Whip in the yoghurt and the granadilla juice.

Just before serving, pile the cream mixture into the choux pastry nests and spoon the seeds from the remaining granadilla over the top.

Serves 8.

Passion fruit cheesecake

BASE

6 oz (175 g) plain oatcakes (Walkers are best)
½ teaspoon ground mace
1 oz (25 g) dark Muscovado sugar
3 oz (75 g) butter, melted

FILLING

3 passion fruit
½ oz gelatin
4 tablespoons pineapple juice
2 oz (50 g) honey
1 egg, separated
6 oz (175 g) fromage frais
½ pint (275 ml) Greek-style natural yoghurt

TOPPING

2 passion fruit
1 tablespoon honey
¼ pint (150 ml) pineapple juice
1 tablespoon arrowroot

With the juice for flavour and the seeds for decoration, a passion fruit cheesecake makes a splendid dessert.

Heat the oven to 400F/200C/gas 6. Crumble the oatcakes and mix with the mace, sugar and butter. Press into an 8 inch (20 cm) diameter flan ring, and bake for 10 minutes so they make a firm base. Cool completely in the tin. With the base still in the tin, line the sides only with oiled greaseproof paper.

For the filling, sieve the passion fruit. In a small pan, soak the gelatin in the pineapple juice. Put the passion fruit juice and honey into a saucepan and warm them together until the honey has melted. Melt the gelatin on a low heat, and stir it into the passion fruit juice. Beat in the egg yolk and stir on a low heat, without boiling, until the mixture thickens. Remove the pan from the heat and leave the mixture until it is almost set. Stiffly whip the egg white. Fold first the fromage frais and the yoghurt into the setting mixture, and then the egg white. Pour the mixture over the biscuit base.

Scoop the seeds from the remaining two passion fruit and put them into a saucepan with the honey and all but 4 tablespoons of the pineapple juice. Mix these 4 tablespoons with the arrowroot. Warm the passion fruit mixture, stir in the arrowroot and keep stirring until you have a thick, translucent sauce. Cool slightly, stirring to prevent setting, and spoon over the cheesecake.

Leave the cheesecake in a cool place for 2 hours to set.

Serves 6.

PAWPAW (PAPAYA)

CARICA PAPAYA

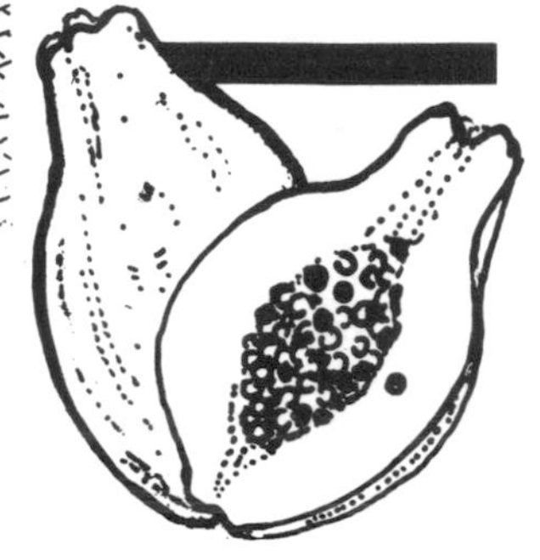

THE PAWPAW IS a tropical fruit, mostly now associated with the Caribbean. In their countries of origin every part of the fruit, even the leaves, is used, and in every stage of ripeness the fruit has different culinary uses.

Pawpaws grow on a small, unbranched tree that has a tuft of star-shaped leaves at the top. Fifty or more pear-shaped fruits hang down under the leaves, at various stages of ripeness. Those reaching Britain are the smaller ones, about 6–7 inches (15–18 cm) long, but some can grow up to 20 inches (50 cm). They are all green at first, some stay green, and others ripen to yellow or orange. Insidc, thc flesh turns from pale yellow to a deep salmon pink. When ripe it has a sweet, creamy, aromatic flavour and a texture like soft butter. Inside a pear-shaped hollow in the centre of the fruit is a cluster of tiny, round, shiny, black seeds encased in a gelatinous membrane.

Pawpaws have never grown wild. The Portuguese found them being cultivated by the South American Indians, and took them to the Caribbean Islands where the Carib Indians called them *ababai*, from which pawpaw and papaya both come. Cultivation quickly spread to all the tropical parts of the world, including India, Malaysia, Africa, the United States and Australia. The smaller types that now reach British markets were developed in Hawaii in 1919.

Nutrition

Pawpaws, like many orange-coloured fruits, are exceptionally high in Vitamin A and also in potassium. They have significant amounts of Vitamin C, calcium and phosphorus.

The leaves, stalks and unripe fruits contain an enzyme known as papain which tenderises meat. This is extracted, processed, and used as an ingredient in commercial meat tenderizers.

Buying and storing pawpaw

The skin of a pawpaw should look very slightly shiny, and the colour should be fresh. There should be no soft, bruised spots and no browning round the stalk end.

Unripe pawpaws should feel hard, like an unripe avocado. As they ripen, they will become softer and should give under the thumb when pressed.

To ripen a pawpaw, leave it at room temperature for a few days. When ripe, it will keep in the refrigerator for up to a week.

Pawpaws in the kitchen

To appreciate a ripe pawpaw for the first time, cut it lengthways in half, scoop out the seeds, and sprinkle the flesh with a little freshly squeezed lime juice. Eat it as it is, or fill the seed cavity with creamy yoghurt. Served in this way, pawpaws can be a first course or a dessert. The flesh can also be peeled and diced, tossed with lime juice and topped with yoghurt and some chopped stem ginger. Cut into long, thin, melon-like slices it can be served with prosciutto ham or smoked salmon. Diced or sliced, it can be added to fruit salads or used as a garnish for dessert dishes. Pawpaw will not deteriorate or change colour when it is cut, and so can be prepared in advance if necessary.

The flesh can also be puréed. Add a dash of lime juice to lift the flavour, and mix it with whipped cream or thick yoghurt to make a fruit fool. Use it for jellies, soufflés, mousses, ice-creams and water-ices.

The skin of an under-ripe pawpaw can be used as a meat tenderizer. Peel it away, cover the meat with it, and leave for several hours before cooking. The meat can also be placed in a liquid marinade at the same time.

Under-ripe pawpaws can be treated as a vegetable. Peel, and remove the seeds. Cut the fruit into slices, grate over a little nutmeg, add a pinch of salt and steam for 15 minutes or until tender. Serve with melted butter. They taste rather like squash. Unripe pawpaws can be pickled and made into chutney.

Pawpaw seeds have a peppery flavour, and can be used whole or crushed in salad dressings.

The leaves, in their countries or origin, are boiled and served as a vegetable. They have a bitter flavour like dandelion leaves or spinach.

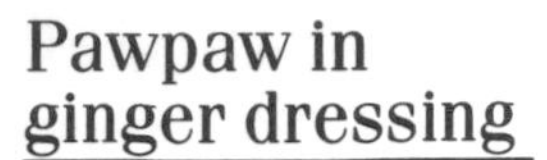

Pawpaw in ginger dressing

2 ripe pawpaws
4 tablespoons white wine vinegar
1 oz (25 g) fresh ginger, grated
4 tablespoons sunflower oil
coriander leaves for garnish

Serve this as a first course.

Halve the pawpaws. Scoop out and reserve the seeds, and put each pawpaw half on a small plate.

Put the seeds into a small blender with the vinegar, ginger and oil and work until you have a smooth dressing. Serve the dressing separately in a small dish, garnished with coriander leaves.

Serves 4.

Pork stir-fried with pawpaw

1 lb (450 g) lean, boneless pork
juice 1 lime
½ teaspoon cayenne pepper
8 oz (225 g) long grain brown rice
1 firm pawpaw
3 tablespoons sunflower oil
1 large onion, roughly chopped
1 garlic clove, finely chopped
½ oz (15 g) fresh ginger, peeled and grated
3 tablespoons soy sauce

An economical, all-in-one dish where the pawpaw acts as a built-in relish.

Cut the pork into ¾ inch (2 cm) dice. Put the lime juice and cayenne pepper into a bowl. Add the pork and coat in the juice. Cover, and leave at room temperature for 4–8 hours. Boil the rice in lightly salted water for 40 minutes, or until tender. Drain, run cold water through it, and drain it again. Peel the pawpaw and cut into thin, lengthways slices.

Heat the oil in a large frying pan on a high heat. Stir-fry the pawpaw for about 3 minutes, or until it looks bright and translucent and is beginning to soften. Remove, and keep warm. Drain the pork, add to the pan, and stir-fry for 5 minutes, or until cooked through and beginning to brown. Add the onion, garlic and ginger and stir-fry for a further 3 minutes. Mix in the rice and the soy sauce and stir quickly until heated through.

Put the rice mixture on to a serving dish, and garnish with the strips of pawpaw.

Serves 4.

Pawpaw and lime fool

2 ripe pawpaws
juice 2 limes
¼ pint (150 ml) Greek-style natural yoghurt or double cream, whipped
small amounts of other fruits, such as passion fruit seeds or kiwi fruit
slices for garnish (optional)

Like mangos, pawpaws need very few ingredients in order to make delicious desserts.

Halve the pawpaws and remove the seeds. Scoop out the flesh with a spoon and purée, or mash with a fork. Fold the yoghurt or cream into the fruit purée.

Pile the fool into dishes and garnish it with fruit.

Serves 4.

PEACH AND NECTARINE

PEACH

PRUNUS PERSICA

ALL OVER THE world, people love fruits with generous amounts of sweet, juicy, melting flesh. In tropical countries there is the mango; in temperate regions, there is the peach.

Peaches came originally from China, where they have been cultivated for thousands of years. They were taken along the old silk routes to Persia and from there to ancient Greece and Rome. The Romans planted peaches in a few sheltered spots in the south of England. These were found by the Anglo-Saxons, but no more trees were planted here until Crusaders brought them back from the Holy Land. Peaches were set in the royal gardens at Westminster in the thirteenth century, but for many years they were exceptionally rare throughout the rest of the country. It was not until the sixteenth century that they became more common and were planted in sheltered corners of gardens by south-facing walls to be enjoyed mainly by the rich owners of country houses.

In the seventeenth century peaches moved into the new and fashionable greenhouses, and in the nineteenth century several varieties were raised in Britain. Peaches were taken to South America by the Spanish in the sixteenth century, established in California in the seventeenth, reached Australia in the nineteenth and South Africa at the beginning of the twentieth. They spread so far and so fast that, after the apple and the orange, they have become one of the most widely cultivated of all fruits.

Peaches have never been a successful commercial crop in our cool climate, and fewer are grown here now than 100 years ago. Our supplies come mainly from Italy, Spain, France, Greece and Israel in the summer and, increasingly, South Africa in the winter.

There are thousands of different varieties of peach, differing in size, shape, colour, texture and whether they are freestone (with stones that easily drop out when the fruit is cut), or clingstone (with flesh that clings to the stone).

Nutrition

Peaches are high in potassium and Vitamin A, and have significant amounts of Vitamin C.

Buying and storing peaches

When peaches are ripe, their skins should be yellow, flushed with red. Any showing green through the down are likely to be hard and inedible. Peaches should just give when pressed with the thumb, but should not be too soft. There should be no bruises or blemishes, and the skin should be undamaged.

The skin of a ripe peach is soft and easily damaged, so take care to put the fruit at the top of your shopping bag. Peaches will keep in the refrigerator for up to four days.

To freeze peaches, skin them, cut them in half and remove the stones. They can be sliced if you wish. Freeze them on a tray, and pack into polythene bags. They will keep for up to two months. They can also be frozen in a sugar syrup for up to four months.

Peaches in the kitchen

Peaches can be eaten straight out of your hand, but it is probably less messy to halve and stone them first. Run a knife all the way round the groove of the peach, cutting down as far as the stone, then pull the two halves apart. If they are obstinate, twist them slightly.

If peaches need to be skinned for a recipe, do it before halving and stoning. Place in a bowl, cover with boiling water, leave for 2 minutes (very ripe peaches may need less), then drain. The skins should slip off easily.

A peach half cries out for a filling. You can simply swirl on a portion of whipped cream, plain or flavoured with honey and vanilla; or put a few raspberries, chopped strawberries or chopped preserved ginger in first. As a first course, fill the peach with a herb and garlic flavoured soft cheese, or soft cheese mixed with finely diced ham.

For a hot dessert, fill the peach halves with mixtures of nuts and dried fruits, and bake in a medium oven for 10 minutes.

Sliced peaches can be added to fruit salads; poached in syrup, made into fritters; baked under rich, sweet batters; and topped with cream and sugar and placed under the grill to make a brulée. Diced peaches can be threaded on to skewers and grilled on a barbecue.

Diced or sliced, peaches can be added to side salads and salads of meat or beans. They go particularly well with chicken, turkey, pork and ham and also with chickpeas, or in refreshing, green summer salads of lettuce, cucumber, spring onions and herbs. Slices of peach can be laid on lamb or pork chops for grilling or baking.

To purée peaches, skin and dice them and work them in a blender. The purée can be mixed with an equal quantity of whipped cream and eaten as a fool, or used as a topping for strawberries or other soft fruits. A little honey can be added if you wish. Mixed with yoghurt, the purée can be made into a jelly.

Peaches make an excellent chutney and slices or halves can be pickled, or preserved in sweetened brandy.

Dried peaches

Dried peaches can be bought in health food and other specialist shops. They are plump and golden, but their slightly sharp flavour makes them better for cooking than for eating as a snack.

Dried peaches are produced, mainly from freestone varieties, in the Sacramento and San Joaquin Valleys of California, in Australia, South Africa and, increasingly, China. They are hand-picked to avoid damage and only firm, unbruised and fully ripe fruits are used. The peaches are halved, stoned, placed cut-side-up on trays, and put through sulphur dioxide fumes to preserve their colour and prevent fermentation. They are then placed in the sun for four to eight days or until they are golden yellow, and then the drying is finished in the shade to prevent them from shrivelling.

NECTARINE

PRUNUS PERSICARIA VAR. NECTARINA

Nectarines are similar to peaches in many ways. The main differences are that the skin is shiny and smooth instead of downy, and the flavour is slightly sharper. The texture is very much the same.

It is often thought that a nectarine is a cross between a peach and a plum, but this is not true. Most peach trees at some time bear a few fruits that are more like a nectarine than a peach, and the nectarines we know today are descended from one of these. Nectarines, like peaches, travelled the old silk routes to Persia and reached Europe from there. They arrived in Britain later than the peach, in the sixteenth century, and were grown in sheltered gardens and later in glass houses. After the nectarine reached America, its cultivation was established along the Pacific coast and also in the more southerly eastern states.

The nectarine was familiar to Mrs Beeton, who writes that it 'received its name from nectar, the particular drink of the gods.' Peaches and nectarines are now sold side by side and both are available for most of the year.

Hot peach and walnut salad

4 ripe but firm peaches
1 small lettuce
4 tablespoons olive oil
3 oz (75 g) walnut pieces
1 garlic clove, finely chopped
1/8 nutmeg, grated
2 tablespoons white wine vinegar

This is a delightful first course. The colours are lovely, deep orange and golden brown on a bright green bed; and the textures are part crunchy, part soft and juicy. All the flavours are rounded together with nutmeg.

Stone and slice the peaches. Arrange a bed of lettuce on each of four small plates.

Heat the oil in a frying pan on a medium heat. Cook the walnuts and garlic, stirring, until the garlic is brown. Mix in the peaches and immediately grate in the nutmeg. Pour in the vinegar and let it bubble. Spoon over the lettuce and serve immediately.

Serves 4.

Broad bean and nectarine salad

3 lb (1.35 kg) broad beans, weighed in their shells
1 mint sprig
3 tablespoons dry white wine (optional)
3 tablespoons olive oil
2 tablespoons lemon juice
2 large nectarines
1 tablespoon chopped mint
1 tablespoon chopped chives
1 tablespoon chopped parsley

Use this as a side salad with cold meats or quiches. To turn it into a more substantial salad for a buffet table, add diced ham or a mixture of red and white kidney beans.

Shell the beans. Steam them with two of the best pods and the mint sprig for 20 minutes, or until just tender.

While the beans are cooking, beat together the wine, oil and lemon juice. Fold the dressing into the beans while they are still warm and leave to cool completely.

Stone and dice the nectarines, reserving a few whole slices for garnish. Mix the nectarines and herbs into the beans, and garnish.

Serves 4.

Peach and raspberry jellies

4 peaches
½ oz (15 g) gelatin
8 oz (225 g) raspberries
¼ pint (150 ml) pineapple juice
2 oz (50 g) honey
2 oz (50 g) low fat soft cheese
4 tablespoons double cream

In the classic combination of peaches and raspberries the flavours go exceptionally well together.

Put the peaches into a bowl. Pour boiling water over them and leave for 2 minutes. Drain and peel. Halve, stone and dice, and divide between four small dishes.

In a small pan, soak the gelatin in 4 tablespoons warm water. Put all but four of the raspberries into a saucepan with the pineapple juice. Cover, and set on a low heat for 10 minutes or until soft and very juicy. Rub through a sieve. Return to the cleaned pan and add the honey. Stir on a low heat for it to dissolve. Gently melt the gelatin, and stir into the raspberry purée. Leave the purée to cool, but not set, and pour over the peaches.

Leave the jellies in a cool place to set. Beat together the cheese and cream. Top each jelly with a portion of the mixture, and decorate with the remaining raspberries.

Serves 4.

Dried peach and yoghurt brulée

6 oz (175 g) dried peaches
½ pint (275 ml) natural orange or apple juice
3 oz (75 g) dark Muscovado sugar
½ pint (275 ml) Greek-style natural yoghurt

A simple but delicious combination of textures and flavours, slightly chewy peaches in a dark brown syrup, topped with creamy yoghurt and with a crisp caramel over all.

Soak the peaches in the orange or apple juice for 8 hours. Drain and quarter them. (Use the juice for soaking other dried fruits, or drink it diluted with sparkling mineral water.)

Put the peaches into a shallow, ovenproof dish. Sprinkle with 1 oz (25 g) of the sugar, and leave for 2 hours for the sugar to become syrupy.

Spoon the yoghurt evenly over the top of the peaches and sprinkle on the remaining sugar. Put the dish under a pre-heated high grill for 3–4 minutes, or until the sugar caramelises. Serve hot.

Serves 4.

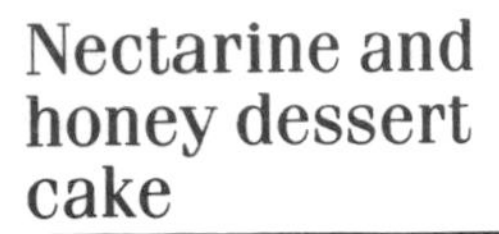

Nectarine and honey dessert cake

3 ripe nectarines
4 oz (125 g) butter, plus extra for greasing
4 oz (125 g) honey
4 oz (125 g) wholemeal flour
1 teaspoon bicarbonate of soda
2 eggs, beaten
few drops almond essence
¼ pint (150 ml) double cream

A moist cake, containing refreshing pieces of nectarine.

Heat the oven to 350F/180C/gas 4. Line an 8-inch (20 cm) tart tin with buttered greaseproof paper. Scald, skin and chop two of the nectarines.

Cream the butter with 3 oz (75 g) of the honey. Toss the flour with the bicarbonate of soda and beat it into the butter and honey, alternately with the eggs. Beat in the almond essence. Fold in the chopped nectarines.

Put the mixture into the flan tin. Bake for 15 minutes, or until firm. Turn the cooked cake on to a wire rack to cool, leaving it upside down.

Put the cake on to a flat plate. Put the remaining honey into a saucepan with 4 tablespoons water. Bring it gently to the boil, stirring, and simmer for 1 minute. Cool for 2 minutes, then spoon it over the cake. Leave to cool completely.

Whip the cream and either pipe or spread it over the cake. Slice the remaining nectarine and use it as a decoration.

Serves 4–6.

PEAR AND ORIENTAL PEAR

PYRUS COMMUNIS (AND OTHER SPECIES)

WHO KNOWS WHAT I have got? In a hot pot? Baked wardens, all hot.' 'Wardens' were pears, raised first in a Cistercian abbey in Bedfordshire in the Middle Ages and one of the many varieties to have come in and out of favour during this fruit's long history.

Pears are indigenous to Britain and Europe, Western Asia and the Himalayas. They were enjoyed in ancient Greece, and wild varieties were improved by the Romans, who regarded them as both medicine and food. New Roman varieties were taken to Britain and harvested, after the Romans left, by the Anglo-Saxons. The Normans were great fruit growers, and planted small orchards of pears around their manors. Pears and ale are said to have hastened the death of King John, and pears in syrup were served at the wedding feast of Henry IV. Research into grafting methods was carried out in the fifteenth century, and by 1629 there were at least sixty-two known types.

Pears were eaten fresh and dried. Some were grown especially for making perry, the pear equivalent of cider, called locally merrylegs or devil-drink because of its intoxicating effects.

Of the many different varieties that have been grown in Britain, the Conference and the Comice have proved to be the modern favourites. (Wardens are sadly no more, although by all accounts they were an excellent and versatile fruit, used for perry as well as being baked and made into preserves.) The **Comice**, called originally the Doyenne du Comice, was first raised at Angers in 1849 and was brought to Britain by Sir Thomas Dyke Acland in 1858. Comice pears are large and oval and their skin is pale yellow with russet speckles and occasional pink tinges. Their pale yellow flesh has a melting, juicy texture and a delicate spicy flavour.

The **Conference** pear was raised in England in 1874 by the firm of Rivers from the pip of a French cooking pear. It was exhibited at the International Pear Conference at Chiswick in 1895. The committee of judges, who awarded it first prize out of 10,000 entries, requested that it be called Conference. The Conference pear is medium-sized and long-shaped, with a dark green, russet-speckled skin, and pale yellow flesh that may have a pink tinge when ripe. It is both a cooking and a dessert pear. Some like to eat it raw when it is soft, but it is best when still crisp. Conference pears store better than most other varieties, and are available for much of the year.

Other home-grown varieties that you might well find in the shops are the Beurre Hardy, Dr Jules Guyot, Laxton's Superb and William's Bon Chrétien. These are rarely stored and only available soon after they are picked in the autumn.

The **Beurre Hardy** is another French pear, introduced in 1840. It is large, conical and slightly irregularly shaped, with a rough, yellow-green skin, covered with russet dots and with thick russet patches at top and bottom. The flesh is pinky coloured and very soft and sweet.

Dr Jules Guyot, French again, is large with a rough, pale yellow skin, red-flushed and with russet patches. Its flesh is delectable, very soft and with a musky flavour, but the fruit does not keep well and must be eaten as soon as possible.

The **William's Bon Chrétien**, despite its name, was raised by a Mr Stair at Aldermaston in 1770, and was nicknamed Stair's Pear. Mr Enoch Bartlett took it to the United States where it became the Bartlett pear, popular in the American canning market. It is a large, oval, even-shaped fruit, with yellow-gold, russet-dotted skin, that may also have russet stripes and red flushes. It has a smooth, buttery flesh and a sweet musky flavour.

The **Laxton's Superb** is a hybrid of the William's Bon Chrétien raised by the Laxton Brothers. It is slightly smaller than the William's but very similar in flavour and a more consistent cropper.

Besides these British grown pears, others come in from Europe, South Africa, Australia, New Zealand, South America and the United States.

Nutrition

Pears are high in potassium, with significant amounts of calcium and phosphorus. Their vitamin count is fairly low.

Buying and storing pears

Pears are picked and put into commercial cold storage when slightly under-ripe, so that they reach the shops in peak condition. They do not keep well once in a warm atmosphere, and should be eaten as soon as possible. When bought they should ideally be on the hard side rather than soft, and there should be no brown blemishes on the skin or around the stalk.

Pears keep for up to three days in a cool place. Always handle them very carefully, as their skins are very thin and easily damaged.

To freeze uncooked pears, slice and dip in lemon juice, pack into containers and top up with sugar syrup. They will keep for up to two months. If you need to keep them for longer, poach in a syrup before freezing and they will keep for up to eight months.

Pears in the kitchen

Raw pears can be eaten as they are, or sliced before serving. They are excellent with cheese, particularly the soft, mild types such as Brie or Lymeswold. Served as a first course, pear halves can be coated in a tarragon cream dressing, and slices of fruit are good with a French dressing and chopped nuts. Chopped firm pears can be added to side salads, and go particularly well with watercress.

Pears for cooked dishes are usually poached or baked in a sugar syrup. The medieval dish of pears baked in a spiced red wine is still popular. With a chocolate sauce, poached pears become *Poire Belle Helene* and they can also be topped with fruit sauces, such as raspberry. With creamy sweetened rice, they make Pear Condé. You can also make pear charlotte or tart; bake whole pears in pastry cases, or make pear fritters.

All types of pear can be bottled in syrup. Dessert pears can be added to sweet chutneys, and cooking varieties can be pickled in a sweet, spiced vinegar. Besides perry, pears can be made into a light, sparkling country wine. Pear brandy, known as Williamine, Poire William or Poire is made in Switzerland, Germany, the Alsace district of

France, and Eastern Europe. Some varieties have a mature pear in the bottle, achieved by putting the bottle over the pear as soon as the blossom has dropped.

DRIED PEARS

Dried pears can be bought in health food and other specialist shops. They are sweet and chewy, with a pleasant granular texture. Diced, they can be used as sweetmeats. Soaked for eight hours in fruit juice and chopped, they can be added to cakes.

Dried pears are produced mainly in California and also in South Africa, Australia and China. The main type for drying is the Bartlett pear. The fruit is picked by hand, washed, halved and cored but not peeled, and laid on trays in the sun for up to two days. They are then moved into the shade to dry further. No chemicals are added.

ORIENTAL PEAR

Oriental pears, or nashi as they are sometimes known, are a relatively new addition to the British market. In 1988 they were tipped to become the most popular of the new fruits but they have yet to share the spectacular success of, for example, kiwi fruits.

There are two types, Chinese and Japanese. The Chinese pears are round with yellow skins, dappled closely with light brown. Their skin is bitter, but the flesh is light, crisp, sweet and granular, creamy coloured and slightly translucent. When you bite into the fruit, the juice splashes on your tongue. They are best eaten raw, slightly chilled and peeled, and are also excellent in fruit salads.

Japanese pears are barrel-shaped, with a slightly smaller top than bottom. The skin is yellow, with small, even brown spots; the flesh is the same colour and texture as the Chinese type but less sweet. It is very similar in texture to a water chestnut, but granulated.

The Japanese pear is excellent in savoury salads, and its delicious crispy texture makes it a good addition to stir-fried vegetables, particularly bean sprouts, Chinese cabbage, celery, carrots and green peppers. Do not over-flavour the dish with soy sauce, or the delicate pears will be overpowered. Sherry, vegetable stock or rice wine are the best liquids.

A partridge in a pear tree

shortcrust pastry made with 6 oz (175 g) wholemeal flour

FLAKY PASTRY

6 oz (175 g) wholemeal flour
pinch salt
5 oz (150 g) butter
4 tablespoons iced water
1 tablespoon lemon juice

FILLING

1½ lb (675 g) small, firm Conference pears
¼ pint (150 ml) dry cider
1 tablespoon clear honey
2 inch (5 cm) cinnamon stick
small chip nutmeg
approximately 4 oz (125 g) mincemeat

GLAZE

1 small egg, beaten

A very special pie for Twelfth Night.

For the flaky pastry, put the flour and salt into a bowl. Chop the butter and divide it into 4 portions. Rub one portion into the flour, and mix to a dough with the iced water and lemon juice. Knead the dough lightly until smooth, then roll it out into an oblong. Dot one portion of chopped butter over two-thirds of the dough. Fold the dough into 3, give it a half turn to bring the edge towards you, and roll it out again. Dot with the butter as before, and fold. Refrigerate, wrapped in a polythene bag, for 15 minutes. With the edge of the dough towards you, roll out again, dot with butter, and fold. Chill again, then roll and fold twice before returning to the refrigerator.

Peel and halve the pears, and cut away the tougher parts of the cores. Have the cider ready in a saucepan and, as each pear is ready, drop it in. When all the pears are done, add the honey, cinnamon and nutmeg. Set the pan on a moderate heat, bring to the boil and simmer for 10 minutes. Take the pan from the heat and cool, keeping the pears cut-side-up if possible.

Heat the oven to 375C/190F/gas 5. Line a 10-inch (25 cm) diameter tart tin with the shortcrust pastry and put in the pears, rounded side up. Spoon the juice over the top, discarding the spices, and fill the gaps between the pears with mincemeat.

Roll out the flaky pastry and cut out a 10-inch (25 cm) round. From this, cut the shape of a branching tree that will cover the pears. From the flaky pastry trimmings, cut 8 thin circles about 1½ inches (4 cm) in diameter, and one oval shape 3 inches (7.5 cm) long, and 1½ inches (4 cm) across. Put a tiny portion of mincemeat into the centre of each round. Bring the edges up and pinch them together at the top to make a pear shape. Lay them on the flan with the top of each one touching a branch, so they look as though they are hanging from the tree, leaving room in the middle for the partridge. Put about 2 teaspoons of mincemeat in the centre of the oval and draw the sides to the middle a bit like a Cornish pasty. Pinch them together. Pinch the ends together and raise them up to make a tail at one end and a head and beak at the other. Put the partridge in the middle of the pear tree.

Brush the pastry with the beaten egg and bake the pie for 40 minutes or until it is golden brown. Serve it warm, with double cream.

Serves 6–8.

Glazed tarragon chicken with pears

one 3½ lb (1.6 kg) roasting chicken
1 oz (25 g) butter
¼ pint (150 ml) chicken stock
2 tablespoons tarragon vinegar
2 teaspoons chopped tarragon, or 1 teaspoon dried
4 small, firm Conference pears

A well-reduced glaze adds flavour to this simple dish.

Joint the chicken. Heat the butter in a large frying pan on a medium heat. Cook the chicken pieces, skin side down first, until golden brown on both sides. Set them aside. Pour off all but a thin film of fat from the pan, and set it back on the heat. Pour in the stock and vinegar and bring to the boil. Replace the chicken joints, add the tarragon, cover, and cook on a very low heat for 15 minutes.

Peel, quarter and core the pears. Add to the chicken and cook for another 20 minutes, turning once or twice. The liquid should reduce to 4–6 tablespoons of glaze.

Transfer to a serving dish and spoon any glaze over.

Serves 4.

Chinese cabbage, beansprout and Japanese pear salad

½ Chinese cabbage
1 Japanese pear
6 oz (175 g) beansprouts
4 tablespoons sesame oil (or olive oil)
juice ½ lemon
1 tablespoon soy sauce
1 teaspoon clear honey
1 garlic clove, crushed
½ teaspoon ground ginger
2 tablespoon sesame seeds

A light, refreshing salad with a crisp texture. The main salad can be prepared up to an hour in advance, but don't peel and add the pear until just before serving, otherwise it could discolour or lose its texture.

Finely shred the cabbage. Peel and core the pear, and cut it into thin, lengthways slices. Put the cabbage and beansprouts into a salad bowl.

To make the dressing, beat together the oil, lemon juice, soy sauce, honey, garlic and ginger. Fold into the salad. Put the sesame seeds into a heavy frying pan and stir on a medium heat until they begin to jump. Tip on to a plate and cool.

Arrange the slices of Japanese pear over the salad and scatter with the sesame seeds.

Serves 4.

Dried pear and ginger pudding

6 oz (175 g) dried pears
7 fl oz (200 ml) natural apple juice
7 fl oz (200 ml) water
6 oz (175 g) wholemeal flour
1 teaspoon ground ginger
1 teaspoon ground mixed spice
3 fl oz (90 ml) corn oil, plus extra for greasing
6 oz (175 g) pear and apple spread
6 fl oz (175 ml) natural yoghurt

A moist, dark, winter pudding full of deliciously sticky dried pears. Serve it warm, with yoghurt or soured cream.

Put the pears into a saucepan with the apple juice and water. Bring to the boil, remove from heat, and leave to soak for 4 hours. Drain, reserve liquid and four of the best halves, and chop the rest.

Heat the oven to 350F/180C/gas 4. Put the flour into a bowl with the ginger, mixed spice and bicarbonate of soda, and make a well in the centre. Put in the oil, 3 fl oz (90 ml) of the soaking liquid, the pear and apple spread and the yoghurt. Gradually beat all these ingredients together, taking in flour from the sides of the well, to make a thick batter.

Line an 8-inch (20 cm) diameter cake tin with oiled greaseproof paper. Place the pear halves, cut-side-up, in the bottom and pour the batter over them. Bake for 45 minutes or until a skewer inserted in the centre comes out clean. Turn on to a plate and leave upside down so the pear halves show.

Serves 6.

Steamed chinese pears

4 Chinese pears
2 oz (50 g) stoned dates
2 oz (50 g) walnuts
1 teaspoon ground ginger
2 tablespoons honey

This is a traditional Chinese recipe. If you cannot find any Chinese pears, use Conference pears instead. In most Chinese recipes, the pears are left unpeeled. The skins, however, can be bitter and mask the delicate flavour, so here they are removed

Peel the pears. Cut a 1-inch (2.5 cm) 'lid' off the tops, leaving the stalks intact. Core the pears using an apple corer.

Finely chop or mince the dates and walnuts. Mix in the ginger and honey. Fill the pears with this mixture and replace the tops, anchoring with cocktail sticks.

Put the pears into a heatproof dish that will fit into a steamer. Bring the water in a large saucepan to the boil. Put in the steamer with the dish of pears inside. Cover, and steam the pears for 25 minutes or until tender. Serve warm.

Serves 4.

PERSIMMON AND SHARON FRUIT

DIOSPYROS SPECIES

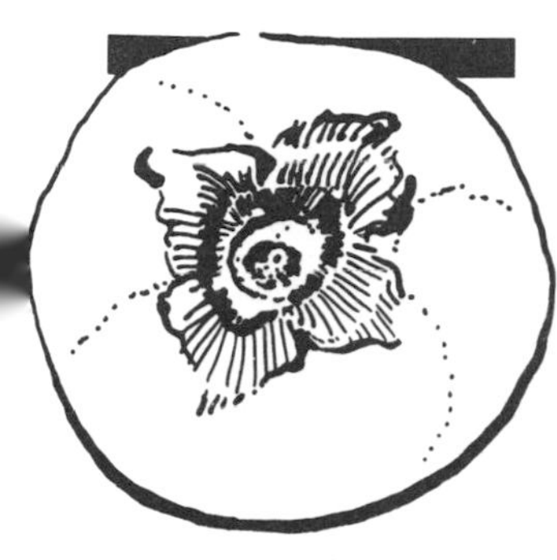

IMAGINE A SMALL, drooping tree like one in a Japanese painting; covered with pale blossoms in the spring and in the autumn, after the leaves have fallen, bearing hundreds of round, orange-red, tomato-like fruit. That is the persimmon, or kaki fruit tree.

The persimmon is native to Japan and China, where it has been cultivated for centuries as an important autumn source of Vitamin C. It also grows wild in western Asia and the Himalayas, and varieties were found in north America by the early settlers. It has never been grown in Britain, which is surprising, as the tree is a hardy one, growing as far north in America as the Great Lakes and able to withstand the Japanese snows. It is also suited to very warm climates, and has been grown all round the Mediterranean for almost as long as it has been in Japan. Over all these years, the fruit has never been grown widely for commercial purposes.

There are many different types of persimmon, over a thousand in Japan alone, but always the fruit looks like an orange-red or orange-yellow tomato, with a shiny skin and a stalk in the slight depression at the top. The base of the fruit can be either rounded or flattened, and there may be slight ridges or indentations running from top to bottom. The different types vary in size, but those reaching Britain are about 2½ inches (6 cm) in diameter. The flesh is a similar colour to the skin, and the texture is also like that of a tomato. Embedded in it are eight almond-shaped seeds.

The one drawback of the original persimmon is that before it is ripe the flesh has a pithy texture and is extremely astringent. When ripe, however, it is totally different, very soft and incredibly sweet, with no hint at all of sharpness or bitterness. This was the quality that encouraged the Israelis to develop the sharon fruit (named after the valley where it was first cultivated), a golden-orange variety of the persimmon, sweet even when firm, and virtually seedless. It is much easier to use as you do not have to guess when the fruit is sweet enough for eating; and more versatile, as it can be used firm or soft.

Nutrition

All varieties of persimmon and sharon fruit are high in Vitamins A and C and potassium. They also have significant amounts of phosphorus and calcium.

Buying and storing persimmon and sharon fruit

A fruit labelled 'persimmon' should be eaten when soft. It can, however, be bought under-ripe and ripened off at room temperature. A sharon fruit can be used when either firm or soft. However, some sharon fruit are sold under the name of persimmon. If in doubt, check the country of origin. All fruit from Israel (sometimes labelled 'Carmel') are sharon fruit.

Persimmon and sharon fruit in the kitchen

To eat either fruit in its soft, ripe state, for the first time, simply cut off the top and eat the flesh with a small spoon. The ripe flesh can be puréed and used as a sweet sauce for other fruits or ice-creams. Use it as a base for fools, water-ices and sorbets, or thicken it with arrowroot as a filling for pre-cooked tartlet cases. Puréed persimmon or sharon fruit can also be used as a base for a salad dressing. It is excellent mixed with the juice of citrus fruits to bring out its flavour. With vinegar, it can be made into a sweet and sour sauce for raw seafood or stir-fried meats.

The firm flesh of sharon fruit should be peeled before use. Cut it into wedges to use in fruit salads, or serve with diced melon as a first course. Thin slices can be used to decorate cakes and cream desserts. They are good in savoury salads with seafood; and chopped and mixed with raw onion and lemon juice they make a relish for cold meats.

Prawn salad with sharon fruit

2 boxes mustard and cress
8 oz (225 g) shelled prawns
3 ripe sharon fruit
2 tablespoons white wine vinegar
1/4 teaspoon cayenne pepper

Persimmon or sharon fruit, puréed and mixed with vinegar, make a simple sweet and sour sauce that is ideal for delicately flavoured seafood. Use sharon fruit for this recipe, as they can be sliced whereas the persimmon cannot.

Arrange a bed of cress on each of four small plates, with the leaves pointing outwards. Place the prawns in the centre. Peel one of the sharon fruit and mash it with a fork. Mix in the vinegar and cayenne pepper. Spoon over the prawns.

Peel the remaining sharon fruit and slice thinly lengthways. Arrange round the prawns.

Serves 4.

Sharon fruit and grapefruit salad

1 small lettuce
4 sharon fruit
2 medium grapefruit
1 garlic clove, crushed with a pinch sea salt
freshly ground black pepper
3 tablespoons chopped mint

Mixed with grapefruit, the flavour of the sharon fruit becomes almost melon-like. No dressing is needed, as the fruits provide all the juice and flavours themselves.

Shred the lettuce, and arrange it on four small plates. Peel the sharon fruit and cut into thin, lengthways slices. Cut the rind and pith from the grapefruit. Cut the flesh from the skin in segments and halve each segment. Mix with the sharon fruit. Mix in the garlic, pepper and mint. Pile the salad on top of the lettuce.

Serves 4.

PINEAPPLE

ANANAS COMOSUS

EXOTIC IN APPEARANCE and with sweet-sharp juicy flesh, the pineapple has become one of the most popular and commonly known of all tropical fruits. It is also very widely travelled.

The first Europeans to discover the pineapple were the Spaniards, who found it in South America and the West Indies, and who brought it back to Europe. It was first grown commercially in Hawaii by an English captain, at the end of the nineteenth century. This is where the main canning industry was later situated, so taking pineapples, in this form at least, into kitchens all over the world.

Pineapples first reached England at the time of Cromwell. One was grown in the royal gardens in 1661, and very gradually the idea of hot-house growing became fashionable. Hot houses were expensive to maintain and highly labour intensive, and the fruits that came out of them were greatly valued, so much so that even the core was eaten, and the peels were boiled to make jellies and preserves. But the 1870s, steam ships were bringing pineapples from the West Indies, which were cheaper to buy than the hot-house ones were to produce, so pineapple growing fell from favour.

Pineapples are now grown all over the world and come to Europe from Ghana, the West Indies, the Azores and the Canary Islands. There are three main commercial types: the queen, the cayenne and the Spanish type. Queen pineapples are very small and golden yellow, and have recently been coming into Britain in larger quantities from South

Africa. Cayenne pineapples are the large types, and Spanish pineapples have deep yellow flesh and are mainly grown in Cuba and Puerto Rico for the United States market.

Each pineapple forms in the centre of a clump of spiky leaves. They were christened pineapple by the Spaniards, who thought they looked like large pine cones.

Nutrition

Pineapples are high in potassium and have significant amounts of magnesium, chlorine and Vitamin C. They also contain an enzyme known as bromeline, which aids in the digestion of meat, making them an ideal dessert after a rich, meat meal. However, the enzyme also breaks down gelatin if the puréed fruit is used raw in jellies and mousses, so either cook it first, or use vegetarian equivalents such as agar-agar or gelozone.

Buying and storing pineapples

Pineapples should always be ripe when you buy them as, even if kept in a warm place, they will not ripen successfully. Usually the darker the colour, the riper and sweeter the pineapple. A ripe fruit will be orange all over, with no parts turning brown. The leaves should look a fresh pale green and, if the fruit is ripe, you should be able to pull them out singly.

Pineapples can be stored for up to four days in a cool place. Once cut, they should be wrapped in cling film and put into the refrigerator, where they will keep for up to two days.

Pineapples in the kitchen

To remove the husk from a pineapple, first cut off the top crown of leaves and then the base just above the indentation for the stalk. Hold the pineapple down on a board and, using a long, serrated knife, slice off the husk in strips, taking thick enough pieces to include the 'eyes'. Slice the pineapple and stamp out the cores with an apple corer to give uniform round holes.

The whole husk of a pineapple can be used as a container for a mixed fruit salad, for pineapple ice-cream or even a flambéed mixture of pineapple and other fruits. To preserve the husk, slice off the top crown but leave the stalk end intact. If the pineapple does not stand up on its base, trim the small piece of stalk. Once the top has been sliced off, cut between the flesh and the husk with a sharp knife, and then gradually cut away the flesh in as large pieces as possible, until you are left with a shell.

Raw pineapple can be added to fruit salads with other fresh fruits, but needs the sweetness of sugar syrup or honey. It is excellent in compotes of dried fruits, where it provides a contrasting freshness.

Finely chopped, sweetened and chilled it can be folded into vanilla-flavoured whipped cream or into syllabubs. Pineapple slices, fresh or canned, make an attractive topping for upside-down cakes and are also good in sweet rice dishes. Rings or half-rings are delicious grilled or fried in butter and flambéed.

Slices of raw pineapple, topped with cream cheese or a yoghurt-based dressing, can be served as a first course. Diced pineapple can be added to green salads and rice salads; or half-slices can be served as a garnish in salads of rich meats or cottage cheese.

In Chinese cookery, pineapple is stir-fried in meat dishes. In Britain it is baked with gammon and served with roast duck, and in the Caribbean it is chopped and made into a relish.

Crystallized pineapple can be bought in many specialist shops. Chop it and mix it into fruit cakes or use it as a garnish for desserts.

Pineapple juice is made commercially and can be used for soaking dried fruits and as a liquid for cooking other fruits, besides being made into drinks.

Stilton and pineapple salad

6 oz (175 g) Stilton cheese
8 tablespoons (125 ml) olive oil
4 tablespoons white wine vinegar
pinch cayenne pepper
1 garlic clove, crushed
1 small pineapple
4 oz (125 g) watercress
6 celery sticks

An attractive salad for a light main meal. The Stilton blends with the rest of the ingredients to make a thick and creamy dressing. Serve with wholemeal rolls or a potato salad.

Finely grate or crumble the Stilton cheese, depending on its texture. Cream it in a bowl and gradually work in the oil. Beat in the vinegar, cayenne pepper and garlic.

Cut the husk from the pineapple and cut the flesh into 8 slices. Remove the cores and cut the slices in half.

Chop the watercress and divide it between four plates. Chop the celery and scatter it over the top. Put a portion of the Stilton mixture in the centre of each bed of watercress. Arrange the pineapple pieces around it.

Serves 4.

Pineapple in orange caramel sauce

1 medium pineapple
2 medium oranges
1½ oz (45 g) dark Muscovado sugar
1 oz (25 g) butter

Warmed pineapple slices in a rich sauce of orange juice and dark sugar.

Cut the husk from the pineapple. Cut the flesh into 8 slices and stamp out the cores. Cut each slice in half. Lay the pieces of pineapple in a shallow, heatproof dish, overlapping as little as possible.

Thinly pare the rind from one of the oranges, and cut it into thin slivers. Put it into a saucepan with a small amount of water, bring to the boil, boil for 2 minutes and drain. Squeeze the juice from both oranges. Put juice into a saucepan with the sugar, and set on a low heat, stirring for the sugar to melt. Remove the pan from the heat. Melt the butter on a low heat. Brush it over the pineapple and pour the orange syrup over the top.

Heat the grill to medium. Put the pineapple under the grill, about 2 inches (5 cm) away from the heat. Brown the first side. Turn the slices over and brown the second side.

Put the cooked pineapple slices on to warmed, individual plates and spoon over any syrup from the dish. Scatter the orange rind over the top.

Serves 4.

Queen pineapple sherbet

4 queen pineapples
3 oz (75 g) honey
¼ pint (150 ml) creamy yoghurt
2 tablespoons chopped candied peel (optional)

A light and refreshing dessert, made special by being frozen inside the pineapple shells. Children prefer it plain but, for adults, the candied peel adds a bitter-sweet contrast in flavour.

Slice the tops from the pineapples and reserve them. Scoop out the flesh, reserving the shells. Remove the cores and liquidize the flesh. Add the honey and yoghurt and blend again.

Put the sherbet into an ice-cream machine, or else pour into a freezing tray and place in the coldest part of the freezer or the freezing compartment of the refrigerator, set at the coldest temperature, for 3 hours. Whip the mixture every 30 minutes to break up the ice particles. After the final freezing, whip it again and mix in the candied peel if you are using it. Pile the sherbet into the pineapple shells. Wrap each pineapple separately in cling film to prevent any sherbet oozing out, and return to the freezer for 2 hours. Leave at room temperature for 10 minutes before serving.

Serves 4.

PLUM, GREENGAGE, DAMSON, SLOE, BULLACE AND PRUNE

PRUNUS SPECIES

PLUM AND GREENGAGE

PLUMS NEED A whole summer of sun to ripen and soften and to develop their characteristic rich flavour. They come with the early apples in the last weeks of summer, and are just as good in warming autumn puddings as they are in summer desserts.

Although the wild plum, the bullace, is native to Britain, the many varieties that have been cultivated here over the centuries came originally from the Middle East, Eastern Europe and Armenia. They were grown by the Romans and Anglo-Saxons, and were a popular fruit in medieval orchards. In Tudor times they were put into tarts and pies and made into marmalades and sugary sweetmeats. Plums were most popular in the seventeenth and eighteenth centuries, when there was a great vogue for preserving and jam-making.

One of the earliest known plums was the **cherry** plum (*P. cerasifera*), also called the myrobalan plum. It is small and round, with sweet, yellow flesh and sharp crimson skin. In Britain and Europe, the cherry plum is not grown on any large scale and is available only in local shops and markets.

About 90 per cent of all the plums now grown in Britain, Europe and Western Asia are of the variety *Prunus domestica*, which is a cross between the cherry plum and the wild bullace. These plums are much larger now than either of their parents, and there are countless varieties, differing in sweetness and sharpness, size and colour. They can be roughly divided into dessert plums and cooking plums, but some are dual-purpose and can be eaten raw when they are ripe and soft.

One of the first to ripen in late July and early August is the dual-purpose **Early Laxton**, which has a golden, blushing skin and sweet, juicy golden flesh. Next come the **Early Rivers**, which are small and round with a purple skin and deep yellow flesh. They are a dual-purpose plum although they are best for bottling and making jam. **Czar** plums also come near the beginning of August. They are larger than the Early Rivers, with a dark blue skin and yellow-green flesh. Again, they are dual-purpose, but best of all in pies. **Yellow Egg** plums with their bright yellow skins come in mid-August. They look as though they should be a dessert plum, but in fact can be quite sharp, and are best for making jam and cooking. The **Purple Pershore** is the wine-maker's plum, oval and red-purple in colour with yellow flesh. It also makes delicious jam. The **Victoria** is everyone's favourite dessert plum, large and oval with blushing golden skin and sweet golden flesh. It can also be made into delicious compotes and other delicate desserts.

Burbank plums are oval and ripen in September. When their skin is yellowish red use them for cooking; when they have turned deep red, eat them raw. **Monarch** plums are large, round and purple, and best for cooking and preserving. **Marjorie's Seedlings** are similar in appearance to Monarchs, but their flesh is juicier and they make a good dual-purpose plum. The egg-shaped **Warwickshire Drooper** has yellow skin, speckled brownish-red, and yellow flesh. It is thought to be the best of all for preserving. One of the best jam-making plums is the **Blaisdon Red**, oval and wine-red with hard, acid flesh.

The Gage plums or **greengages** are all of the species *Prunus institia*, related to the wild bullaces. They are small, very sweet and almost all fragrantly scented. They are thought to have originated in Armenia and from there travelled across Europe, reaching France in the seventeenth century. In 1725 a Sir Thomas Gage brought a variety known in France as the *Reine Claude* to Britain, and it became known as the Green Gage. The true greengage is primarily a dessert fruit, but others, the **Bryanston Gage** and the **Cambridge Gage**, are dual-purpose. Gage plums, besides being grown in Britain, are imported from Spain, France and Italy throughout the summer.

Mirabelle plums are closely related to the Gage plums, and are grown in France and Germany particularly in the border district of Alsace. They are small, round and a blushing yellow with a sweet scent. They are mainly used for cooking and preserving and for making a liqueur.

Types of plum that are exported to Britain include the light red, sweet **Gaviota** and the red-skinned **Harry Pickstone**, both coming from South Africa in January and February. Other imported plums include the deep red **Santa Rosa**, first developed in California but coming from South Africa and Chile in the winter and Spain in the summer, and the golden yellow **Songold** which comes from South Africa in the spring. Other types come from the United States from July to October.

Nutrition

Plums are high in potassium, and have small amounts of calcium, magnesium and Vitamin A.

Buying and storing plums

Plums should be firm when fully ripe, and the skins should not be broken or blemished. Dessert varieties should yield to the touch and should not be green or pale-coloured.

Plums keep in the refrigerator for up to four days.

To freeze plums, halve and stone them, freeze on trays and pack into polythene bags. They keep for up to three months. To keep them for up to six months, pack in a sugar syrup.

Plums in the kitchen

Plums need to be stoned for most recipes. Run a knife all round the groove in the fruit and pull the two halves apart. For some jam recipes, the stones are left in and skimmed off as they float to the surface when the fruit has softened. Leave the stones in for jelly-making, as the juice will be strained off.

Raw plums are good eaten plainly as a dessert fruit, and can also be sliced and added to fruit salads or savoury salads, either with green vegetables or cold meats.

Dessert plums are also good halved, sprinkled with a little Muscovado sugar and grilled. Prepared in the same way they can be baked in a dish with sherry or cider. They also make good compotes and can be puréed once cooked to use as a base for jellies, ice-creams and cream desserts.

The cooking varieties are good for compotes and purées and make the best pies, crumbles, puddings, dumplings, cobblers and turnovers.

Plums can be bottled in syrup and made into jam and jelly. They make delicious chutneys, relishes and savoury sauces, and a superb country wine.

Plums can also be cooked with meat. They are good in pork and other savoury cold pies, and slices can be laid on lamb and pork chops for grilling or roasting. Put plums with spices and a little red wine into a casserole with a pot roasted piece of beef, then skim and sieve the juices to use as a savoury sauce.

Greengages can be used in the same ways as plums. They are particularly good puréed, and used as a base for cream desserts such as mousses and cold soufflés.

DAMSON

PRUNUS DAMASCENA

Damsons are small, oval fruits, about ⅝ inch (1.5 cm) in diameter, dark purple or black with a soft, blue bloom. Their flesh is yellow-green and, when raw, very astringent. Although they have been growing wild in British and European hedgerows for centuries, they are not indigenous to this country, but were found in Damascus by Crusaders in the twelfth century. They brought back stones which were eventually planted in their homelands.

By the fifteenth century, most country houses boasted a damson tree in the garden and the fruits were thought to be good appetizers if eaten before dinner. They were also put into pies and, in later centuries, made into jellies, jams and country wines.

Damson trees have never been cultivated on a large scale. A few trees are grown among plum orchards and the fruits from these reach local greengrocers' shops and markets rather than supermarkets.

Nutrition

The nutritional quality of damsons is similar to that of plums.

Buying and storing damsons

Damsons should look firm with a fresh bloom, and their skins should be neither split nor blemished.

Damsons in the kitchen

When damsons are ripe they can be easily stoned in the same way as plums. They are best used in warming autumn dishes such as pies, puddings and crumbles. They make excellent jams and jellies, chutneys and sauces and produce a good wine.

Finely chopped, they can be added to stuffings for pork and lamb; laid on chops before grilling and roasting; and put into raised pies.

SLOE

PRUNUS SPINOSA

The sloe is the fruit of the blackthorn, which grows wild in woods and hedgerows in Britain, Europe and Scandinavia. The fruits are very small, about ⅜ inch (1 cm) in diameter, black with a blue bloom and with hard, greenish-red flesh.

Sloes are mostly used for making sloe gin, but they also make a superb jelly when mixed with apples.

BULLACE

PRUNUS DOMESTICA

The bullace is the wild ancestor of most of the plums that we know today, and can be found in hedgerows throughout Britain and Europe. Bullaces are similar to sloes but slightly larger, and can be used in the same ways.

PRUNE

Large, dark, rich-tasting prunes are in fact dried plums. The plums used have to be of a type that will not ferment either during or after drying.

Prunes were first produced around Turkey and Iran from plums. Twelfth century Benedictine monks discovered them and carried them back to their monasteries in Bordeaux in France. Eventually their cultivation spread to other regions of France, particularly Agen, and the tree became known as the d'Agen prune.

In 1848, Louis Pellier, a French nurseryman, went to California in search of gold. He did not find any but instead bought himself a farm in the Santa Clara Valley. His brother sent him cuttings of d'Agen prune trees which he grafted onto American plums. This was the beginning of the Californian prune industry.

French prunes are still the best, although they are very expensive and available only in specialist shops. Most prunes imported into Britain come from California, and others from South Africa, South America and eastern European countries.

Plums that will eventually become prunes are fully ripened on the tree and then shaken mechanically into wooden trays. The fruit are washed and then subjected to a flow of warm air in drying tunnels, where they stay for up to 24 hours. Before packing they are dipped in potassium sorbate to prevent them from going mouldy. Potassium sorbate is a natural preservative found in rowan berries, and it can be completely metabolised in the body without harm. After dipping, the fruits are graded to size.

Tenderized prunes are large prunes which have been through a special cooking process. They are softer than the usual types and, when cooked, become juicy and plump in a very short time. They are also a delicious dessert fruit.

Nutrition

Prunes are high in potassium and calcium and have significant amounts of magnesium and phosphorus. They are exceptionally high in Vitamin A.

Buying and storing prunes

Buy large prunes which look dark and glossy and keep them in an airtight tin for up to six months. Even with the potassium sorbate dip, all prunes will develop a sugary coating if they are kept for too long. They can still be used but will not be as moist as they should be.

Prunes in the kitchen

Prunes should always be softened before use. If you have time, soak them in fruit juice or black tea for eight hours. You can also put them into a saucepan, cover with juice or tea, bring to the boil and then soak for 4 hours.

To stone prunes, slit the fruit down one side, remove the stone and reshape the fruit. If the fruit is to be halved or chopped, you can simply cut the flesh from the stone.

Prunes can be put into fresh fruit salads to give sweetness and a contrast in flavour and texture. They can also be soaked, and served with other dried fruits. Chopped, they make an excellent addition to cakes and tea-breads.

Prunes, either whole or chopped, can be added to stuffings for poultry, and are excellent when mixed into braised red cabbage. They can also be added at the last minute to savoury rice dishes.

Spiced plum sauce

This keeps in the refrigerator for up to three weeks. Serve with cold meats or nut roasts.

1 lb (450 g) dark cooking plums
1 small onion
2 tablespoons sunflower oil
1 teaspoon ground ginger
1/4 teaspoon cayenne pepper
1/4 teaspoon ground cloves

Stone and slice the plums. Thinly slice the onion. Heat the oil in a saucepan on a low heat and soften the onion. Stir in the plums and spices. Cover, and simmer for 15 minutes or until the plums are very soft. Cool completely and put into a jar.

Pork and plum pie

shortcrust pastry made with 6 oz (175 g) wholemeal flour
1 lb (450 g) belly of pork rashers
8 oz (225 g) dark cooking plums
½ oz (15 g) pork dripping or soft lard
1 medium onion, finely chopped
2 teaspoons chopped rosemary
sea salt and freshly ground black pepper
1 egg, beaten

A rich but economical pie for the cold table.

Remove rind and bones from pork and finely dice the meat. Stone and chop the plums and add to the pork.

Melt the dripping in a small frying pan on a low heat. Soften the onion. Mix the onion, rosemary and seasonings into the pork and plums.

Heat the oven to 350F/180C/gas 4. Line an 8-inch (20 cm) diameter tart tin with two-thirds of the pastry. Fill with the pork mixture. Cover with the remaining pastry, and brush the top of the pie with the beaten egg.

Bake for 30 minutes. Cover with damp greaseproof paper, and bake for a further 30 minutes. Cool completely before serving.

Serves 4–6.

Herrings in oatmeal with damsons

4 small to medium herrings
6 tablespoons coarse oatmeal
8 oz (225 g) damsons
1 oz (25 g) bacon fat, pork dripping or butter
1 medium onion, finely chopped
pinch cayenne pepper
1 tablespoon red wine vinegar

Damsons make a sharp sauce that goes well with oily fish.

Fillet the herrings and coat in the oatmeal. Halve and stone the damsons. Melt the fat in a large frying pan on a medium heat. Brown the herring fillets, cut side down first, on both sides. Remove to a serving plate and keep warm.

Lower the heat and soften the onion in the pan. Add the damsons and cook, stirring, until soft and deep red. Add the cayenne pepper and wine vinegar and mix well. Let the sauce bubble and spoon it over the herrings.

Serves 4.

Cockie leekie

one 3½ lb (1.6 kg) roasting chicken
½ lemon
8 prunes
1 small onion, halved, not peeled
1 small carrot, halved lengthways
1 celery stick in three pieces
bouquet garni
1 teaspoon black peppercorns
1 lb (450 g) leeks
12 oz (350 g) carrots
12 oz (350 g) parsnips
1 oz (25 g) butter
3 tablespoons wholemeal flour
¾ pint (425 ml) stock
6 tablespoons chopped parsley

Every cook has a version of this poached chicken dish. It is an excellent example of how sweet and savoury flavours blend, and has probably been handed down and altered since medieval times, when such recipes were very popular.

Thinly slice the lemon and place it inside the chicken together with the prunes. Truss the chicken, and put it into a large saucepan or flameproof casserole with the onion, carrot, celery stick, bouquet garni and peppercorns. Pour in water to just cover the legs. Bring to the boil, cover, and simmer for 40 minutes.

Wash the leeks and cut them into 1-inch (2.5 cm) pieces. Thinly slice the carrots and parsnips. Remove the carrot, onion and celery from the pan. Add the leeks, carrots and parsnips, cover again and simmer for a further 20 minutes. Lift out the chicken and vegetables and keep them warm. Strain and reserve the stock.

Melt the butter in a saucepan on a low heat. Stir in the flour and then ¾ pint (425 ml) stock. Bring to the boil, stirring. Add the parsley and simmer for 2 minutes.

Joint the chicken. Arrange it on a serving dish and pour over the sauce. Garnish with the prunes and serve the vegetables separately.

Serves 4.

Plums with rich vanilla custard

1 lb (450 g) cooking or dual-purpose plums
4 tablespoons sweet sherry
¼ teaspoon vanilla essence
2 oz (50 g) demerara sugar

CUSTARD
6 fl oz (175 ml) milk
¼ pint (150 ml) double cream
1 vanilla pod or ½ teaspoon vanilla essence
3 egg yolks
1 oz (25 g) demerara sugar

A dish for late summer evenings, with cold baked plums under a rich, hot custard.

Heat the oven to 400F/200C/gas 6. Halve and stone the plums and put them into an ovenproof dish with the sherry, vanilla essence and sugar. Cover with foil and bake for 20 minutes. Cool completely.

Put the milk and cream into a saucepan with the vanilla pod or vanilla essence. Bring to just below boiling point. Remove the vanilla pod. Beat the egg yolks in a bowl. Beat in about 6 tablespoons of the hot liquid, and stir the mixture back into the saucepan. Stir on a very low heat, without boiling, until the mixture thickens. Pour the custard into a bowl, cover with wet greaseproof paper and cool completely.

Cover the plums with the custard. Sprinkle the sugar over the top. Heat a grill to high. Put the dish under the grill until the sugar has melted and browned. Serve immediately.

Serves 4.

Greengage tarts

shortcrust pastry made with 4 oz (125 g) wholemeal flour
12 oz (350 g) greengages
3 oz (75 g) light Muscovado sugar

These little tarts are moister, tastier, sweeter and altogether more delicious than jam tarts. Eat them plain for tea, or dress them up with swirls of whipped cream and a garnish of toasted flaked almonds and serve them as a dessert.

Heat the oven to 400F/200C/gas 6. Roll out the pastry and line 12 tartlet tins.

Halve and stone the greengages. Put them into a saucepan with the sugar. Cover, and set on a low heat for about 15 minutes, or until very soft. Remove from the heat and rub through a sieve.

Put about 1½ teaspoons of the purée into each tartlet case. Bake the tarts for 10 minutes, and cool on a wire rack.

Makes 12.

Damsons with raisin cobbler

1 lb (450 g) damsons
5 oz (150 g) dark Muscovado sugar
4 oz (125 g) wholemeal flour
½ teaspoon bicarbonate of soda
pinch fine sea salt
1 oz (25 g) butter
2 oz (50 g) raisins
4 tablespoons cold milk

A dish of rich, dark damsons sizzling under sweet pastry rounds that soak up the sweet-sharp juice deliciously.

Heat the oven to 400F/200C/gas 6. Halve and stone the damsons. Put them into a saucepan with 3 fl oz (90 ml) water and 4 oz (125 g) of the sugar. Cover, and set on a medium heat for 15 minutes or until soft and juicy. Transfer to a 1½-inch (4 cm) deep, 8-inch (20 cm) diameter ovenproof dish.

Put the flour, bicarbonate of soda, salt and remaining sugar into a bowl, rub in the butter, add the raisins and mix to a dough with the milk. Divide the dough into 8 even pieces. Form them into flat rounds and place on top of the damsons. Put the dish into the oven for 20 minutes, or until the cobblers are beginning to brown.

Serves 4.

Sloe gin

1 bottle gin
175 g (6 oz) sloes
125 g (4 oz) granulated sugar

A warming, rich crimson liqueur to make with ripe sloes in early October, that will be ready to drink by Christmas.

Pour all the gin from the bottle. Prick the sloes all over with a fork, and put them into the gin bottle. Cover with the sugar and pour as much gin as possible back into the bottle. Cover tightly. Turn the bottle upside down and shake it, so the sugar begins to dissolve and the gin gradually begins to turn pink. Do this every day for two months, and then let the bottle stand undisturbed for three weeks, before opening.

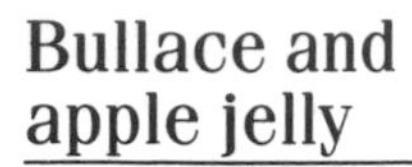

Bullace and apple jelly

2 lb (900 g) bullaces
2 lb (900 g) dessert apples, chopped complete with skins and cores
2 lb (900 g) cooking apples, chopped complete with skins and cores
2 pints (1.15 litres) water
1 lb (450 g) sugar for every 1 pint (575 ml) strained liquid

This clear, deep red jelly is excellent with scones for tea. With chopped mint stirred in as it cools, it can also make an accompaniment for roast lamb. If you can't get bullaces, use damsons or dark cooking plums.

Put the bullaces and apples into a preserving pan with the water. Bring to the boil and simmer gently until very soft, 1½–2 hours, skimming off any stones that come to the surface. Strain through a jelly bag and measure the liquid. Return it to the cleaned pan. Weigh out the required amount of sugar and warm in a low oven for 5 minutes. Bring the liquid to the boil. Stir in the sugar, and keep stirring until it has dissolved. Boil until setting point is reached. Pour the jelly into warmed jars and cover with circles of waxed paper. Cover completely when it is cold and set.

Makes about 4 lb (1.8 kg).

Dried fruit with coconut yoghurt

4 oz (125 g) prunes
1 oz (25 g) dried apple rings
3 oz (75 g) dried whole apricots
¾ pint (425 ml) natural orange juice, or mixed orange and grapefruit juice
½ pint (275 ml) natural yoghurt
2 oz (50 g) desiccated coconut
4 pieces preserved stem ginger, finely chopped (optional)
4 almonds

The creamy coconut and yoghurt topping turns simple, soaked dried fruit into a special dessert.

Put the prunes, apple rings and apricots into a bowl with the fruit juice, cover, and leave to soak for 8 hours. Mix the yoghurt and coconut, cover and refrigerate for the same amount of time.

Mix the ginger into the fruits and divide between 4 small bowls. Spoon the coconut mixture over the top, and garnish with the almonds.

Serves 4.

POMEGRANATE

PUNICA GRANATUM

WHEN YOU CUT through the hard shell of a pomegranate to reveal the hundreds of small white seeds, each encased in transparent crimson flesh, it is easy to see why to ancient peoples the fruit was the symbol of fertility. The Israelites were told by Moses that pomegranate trees would grow in the Promised Land, and the prophet Mohammed told his people to eat pomegranates to purge themselves of envy. In Greek mythology, pomegranate seeds were Persephone's only food in the underworld, and a pomegranate was given to Paris by Aphrodite.

The true home of the pomegranate was ancient Persia, although it may also have grown wild in other Mediterranean countries and even in western India. Its cultivation spread to ancient China, Greece and Egypt, and fruits eventually reached Italy and Spain.

It was from Spain that the first pomegranates reached England in the thirteenth century. They were tremendously expensive, sixpence for a single fruit, but 230 fruits arrived at Portsmouth for Queen Eleanor in 1289. They remained a rarity, and even 200 years later appeared only at the tables of the very rich. The seeds were used sparingly as a decoration, scattered over pottages and rich stews.

Since then, pomegranates have been little used in Britain. The French have been more discerning, turning the juice into jellies, desserts, and the sweet syrup known as grenadine. They have also been made much use of in Jamaica and, of course, have never ceased to be popular in the Middle East.

Pomegranates are grown all over the tropics and sub-tropics but those reaching Britain come from Israel, Egypt and Spain from August to December. Children enjoy spitting the pips at each other but, with a growing interest in exotic recipes, it is to be hoped that they are also better used.

Nutrition

Pomegranates are high in potassium and have small amounts of calcium, phosphorus and Vitamin C, but little else.

Buying and storing pomegranates

The hard, thick skin of the pomegranate should look shiny and round. As it ages, it becomes dull and dimpled and begins to shrivel very slightly.

Because of their thick skin, pomegranates keep for up to three weeks in a cool place.

Pomegranates in the kitchen

To remove the seeds from a pomegranate the Middle Eastern way, cut the fruit in half crossways. Put one half of the fruit, cut side down, in your left palm, holding your hand over a bowl. Hit the fruit with the handle of a knife and the seeds should drop out. If this does not work, cut the pomegranate into lengthways quarters, and push the seeds from each piece.

Pomegranate seeds both look and taste wonderful in salads made with rice or cracked wheat; lettuce or white cabbage, or any other leafy ingredient that shows up their colour. As a garnish, they can be scattered on to any dish, sweet or savoury. In Turkey, for example, they are scattered over a rich almond custard, and in Greece over fried eggs. They are excellent with rich meats and game, and also with fish.

Pomegranate juice is pink, sweet and fragrant, and the best way to extract it is to cut the fruit in half crossways and squeeze each half very gently on a lemon squeezer (not an electric one) taking care, if possible, not to crush the seeds.

Since ancient times, pomegranate juice has been used for both drinks and desserts. It can form the base of ice-creams, jellies and water-ices and can be mixed with other fruit juices to make refreshing, non-alcoholic drinks.

Syrop de Grenadine has long been made in France, although now may be made with pomegranate substitutes and a little alcohol. It can be mixed with iced water or wine, and can also be used as a sauce for desserts.

Hot black bean and rice salad with pomegranates

8 oz (225 g) long grain brown rice
2 pomegranates
1 large red pepper
1 large green pepper
1 large onion, thinly sliced
4 tablespoons olive oil
1 garlic clove, chopped
1 teaspoon paprika
1 teaspoon ground coriander
8 oz (225 g) black kidney beans, soaked, cooked and drained
juice ½ lemon

A tasty vegetarian dish of sparkling colours and fresh flavours, substantial enough for a main meal. Black beans look best and have a delicious mealy texture, but if they are unavailable use brown beans or pinto beans.

Cook the rice in lightly salted boiling water for 40 minutes or until just tender. Drain, run cold water through it and drain it again. Remove the seeds from the pomegranates, reserving as much juice as possible. Core and seed the peppers and cut them into thin strips.

Heat the oil in a large frying pan on a high heat. Stir-fry the red pepper for 2 minutes. Remove, and keep warm. Stir-fry the green pepper, onion and garlic for 2 minutes. Mix in the spices and then the rice, beans and pomegranate seeds with their juice. Stir to heat through. Add the lemon juice and mix well. Put the salad on to a serving plate and surround it with the strips of red pepper.

Serves 4.

Pomegranate and rose ice-cream

ICE-CREAM

2 pomegranates, plus an optional extra one for garnish
2 egg yolks
2 tablespoons clear honey
½ pint (275 ml) double cream
½ pint (275 ml) Greek-style natural yoghurt
4 tablespoons rose water

SAUCE

2 pomegranates
4 tablespoons rose water
½ tablespoon arrowroot
2 tablespoons clear honey

A refreshing, light ice-cream with the flavour of Turkish delight. The sauce is optional, but it does turn the ice-cream into an especially attractive dessert. Only a small amount is needed, as it is very rich and sweet.

For the ice-cream, squeeze the juice from the 2 pomegranates. Using an electric beater, whisk the egg yolks with the honey until the mixture is thick and fluffy. Bring the cream to just under boiling point. Pour it into the egg mixture in a thin stream, while keeping the beater turned on. Whisk in the yoghurt and then the pomegranate juice and the rose water.

If you have an ice-cream machine, fill it with the mixture and follow the manufacturer's instructions. If not, put the mixture into a freezing tray in the coldest part of the freezer or into the ice compartment of the refrigerator, set at the coldest temperature. Freeze the mixture to a slush, about 2 hours. Whisk well, put into a plastic box and cover. Return to the refrigerator or freezer for 3 hours, or until frozen completely. Before serving, put the ice-cream into the main part of the refrigerator for 45 minutes.

For the sauce, squeeze the juice from the two pomegranates and mix in a small saucepan with the rose water. Put the arrowroot into a bowl and stir in 2 tablespoons of the juice mixture. Stir the honey into the

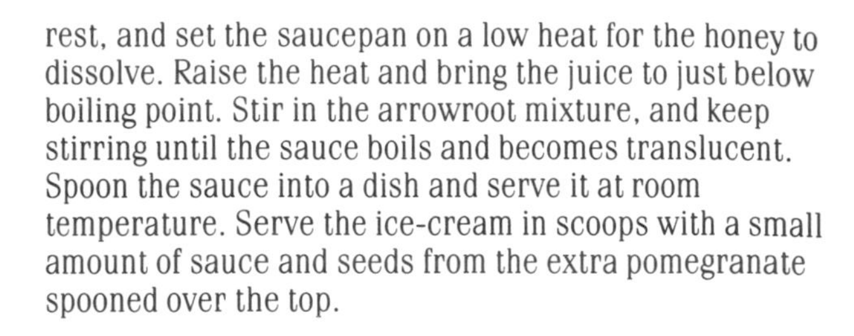

rest, and set the saucepan on a low heat for the honey to dissolve. Raise the heat and bring the juice to just below boiling point. Stir in the arrowroot mixture, and keep stirring until the sauce boils and becomes translucent. Spoon the sauce into a dish and serve it at room temperature. Serve the ice-cream in scoops with a small amount of sauce and seeds from the extra pomegranate spooned over the top.

Serves 6.

PRICKLY PEAR

OPUNTIA FICUS INDICA

THE PRICKLY PEAR grows on a prickly cactus, and the fruit itself has tiny prickles hidden deep in its greeny-orange skin, which can very quickly become embedded into yours! It is about 3 inches (7.5 cm) high and 1½ inches (3 cm) in diameter, tapering to about ¾ inch (2 cm) at the base and ⅜ inch (1 cm) at the top. When the skin is peeled away it reveals soft, deep orange flesh with a very sweet and slightly bland flavour. Buried in it are objectionable little seeds which are small, smooth and round, rather like lead shot.

The prickly pear was first cultivated by the South American Indians, who used the plant as a hedge to protect villages and to keep in animals, besides picking and eating the fruit. Columbus brought plants back to Europe, and they quickly became widespread and semi-wild around the Mediterranean. The plants also reached Africa, India and Australia, where they were used to farm the cochineal insect, to make red dye for military uniforms. The prickly pear has seldom been commercially cultivated in Europe. Those reaching Britain come mainly from South America.

Nutrition

The prickly pear is high in potassium, calcium and Vitamin A and also has significant amounts of phosphorus and Vitamin C.

Buying and storing prickly pears

The skin, between the prickles, should be smooth and firm. Prickly pears keep for up to a week in the refrigerator.

Prickly pears in the kitchen

To prepare a prickly pear, first take its skin off. Cut off a small piece from the top and bottom. Then slit all the way down one side of the skin with a sharp knife and peel it back.

Slices of prickly pear, sprinkled with lime or lemon juice to bring out the flavour, can be eaten alone or in a fruit salad. However, the best way to use it is to rub the flesh raw through a sieve to make a wonderful deep orange purée that looks stunning when used as a sauce or topping for other desserts. Add honey, sugar, lemon or lime juice to taste; leave it quite plain; or dilute with fruit juices or alcohol.

Prickly pear and soft cheese tart

The cream and cheese mixture makes a pale, mild-flavoured base which brings out both the colour and flavour of the prickly pear.

shortcrust pastry made with 4 oz (125 g) wholemeal flour
4 fl oz (125 ml) double cream
8 oz (225 g) low fat soft cheese
2 tablespoons thick honey
juice ½ lime
3 prickly pears
1 teaspoon arrowroot
1 tablespoon flaked almonds

Heat the oven to 400F/200C/gas 6. Line a 7-inch (18 cm) flan tin with the pastry. Bake the pastry blind for 10 minutes and cool it.

Whip the cream. Whip in the cream cheese, honey and lime juice. Put the mixture into the flan case and smooth the top.

Peel, chop and sieve the prickly pears. Mix 1 tablespoon of the purée with the arrowroot, and warm the rest in a small saucepan. Stir the arrowroot mixture into the saucepan. Bring the purée to the boil, stirring, and stir until it is thick and translucent. Cool slightly, and spoon evenly over the cheese mixture. Scatter with the almonds. Leave until the topping is cool and set.

Serves 4–6.

Prickly pear cocktail

4 prickly pears
juice 1 lime
4 fl oz tequila (use vodka if tequila is not available)

FOR A LONG DRINK
12 fl oz (325 ml) tonic water

Tequila is also produced from a cactus, and the flavour goes particularly well with that of prickly pear to make a before-meal appetizer or an after-meal refresher. For a longer drink, add the tonic water.

Chop, mash and sieve the prickly pears. Mix the purée with the lime juice and tequila or vodka and add the tonic water, if wished.

Serves 4.

QUINCE AND JAPONICA

QUINCE

CYDONIA OBLONGA, SYN. C. VULGARIS

THE QUINCE IS the golden apple of ancient mythology, and the golden pear of the nutmeg tree rhyme. Once dedicated to both Venus and Aphrodite, it is the symbol of happiness and love. Its very name brings to mind medieval courts and banquets, and its sharp, mysterious scent is as aromatic as a pot pourri.

The quince is a golden yellow fruit, which can be the size and shape of a small apple or a small, fat pear, depending on the variety. The flesh is hard, granular and unpleasant raw; but when cooked it becomes soft, bright pink and with an almost sherbet flavour that is sharply aromatic.

Quinces probably came originally from Iran, but were grown in ancient Greece and Rome. The first quinces to arrive in Britain were probably brought by the Romans. They were grown in gardens by the Anglo-Saxons and also by the Normans, and have been a more popular garden than orchard fruit every since.

There are references to quinces in fourteenth century cookery books and Chaucer calls them coynes. It was quinces, and not oranges, from which the first marmalade was made, and the word came from *marmelo*, the Portuguese word for quince.

Quinces have also been a popular fruit for pies, either alone or with apples and, in the sixteenth century, when oranges were served to the rich at feasts, the less well off had to make do with 'quinces baked'.

Quinces are grown commercially around the Mediterranean and also in Australia and South America. In Britain, the occasional quince tree is planted in a pear orchard to assist pollination, but they are still essentially a garden fruit. Quinces rarely reach supermarkets, and must be sought out in local country greengrocers.

Nutrition

Quinces are high in potassium and Vitamin A and have reasonable amounts of Vitamin C, calcium and phosphorus.

Buying and storing quinces

If quinces have brown speckles this means they are past their best, and must unfortunately be left alone.

Quinces in the kitchen

Quinces cannot be eaten raw. They are best peeled, cored and sliced in the same way as apples and pears. Cook the slices down to a purée with honey or sugar, and a very little water. The purée can be used in a fruit fool, or mixed with an equal quantity of whipped cream to make a syllabub. The slices can also be poached gently in a syrup and served plainly with yoghurt or cream.

Quinces make delicious jellies, fruit cheeses and butters, which turn out golden or deep pink, depending on the variety. They can be used alone or mixed with apples.

The aromatic flavour of quinces gives a lift to apples in pies, crumbles, or any sweet dish that requires the fruits to be puréed.

Add a quince to the apples when making apple sauce to serve with pork or ham, or to stuffings for lamb or poultry.

Quinces with meat are very popular in the Middle East. They are added to spiced lamb or chicken, to make a dish called a tagine. Quinces are also stuffed with a split pea and onion purée and served either as a first course or as an accompaniment to a meat dish.

If you ever have enough quinces, you can make an aromatic country wine.

JAPONICA

The japonica is an ornamental tree which bears small, round, green fruits which are sometimes called Japanese quinces. They have a quince-like scent and a sharper, more lemony, flavour than quinces and can be used in the same ways.

Quince stuffing

2 medium quinces
1 medium onion
½ oz (15 g) butter
4 oz (125 g) granary or wholemeal breadcrumbs
½ teaspoon ground cinnamon
⅛ nutmeg, grated
1 teaspoon chopped rosemary
3 fl oz (90 ml) dry white wine

This stuffing has a slightly sharp flavour. It is good with rich meats such as lamb or pork, and also with poultry.

Peel, core and finely chop the quinces. Finely chop the onion. Melt the butter in a frying pan on a low heat and soften the onion. Add the quinces and cook for 1 minute more. Take the pan from the heat and mix in the breadcrumbs, cinnamon, nutmeg and rosemary. Bind together with the wine.

Quince marmalade

4 lb (1.8 kg) quinces
2 pints (1.15 litres) water
12 oz (350 g) granulated sugar to every 1 pint (575 ml) pulp

This is an adaptation of a nineteenth century recipe. It is a thick, stiff jelly which, if put into straight-sided jars, can be eased out and sliced. Eat it with bread, tea cakes or toasted muffins.

Roughly chop the quinces without peeling or coring. Bring the water to the boil in a preserving pan. Simmer the chopped quinces until soft and pulpy. Rub quinces and liquid through a sieve. Measure the pulp and return it to the rinsed out pan. Bring to the boil and add the sugar. Stir until dissolved. Simmer, stirring frequently, for 2–3 hours until setting point is reached. Skim if necessary.

Put the marmalade into warm jars and cover with rounds of waxed greaseproof paper. Cover completely when cold.

Makes about 5 lb (2.25 kg).

RASPBERRY, LOGANBERRY, TAYBERRY, BOYSENBERRY AND OTHER BERRIES

RUBUS SPECIES

RASPBERRY

RUBUS IDAEUS

THE SMALL, SHARP, juicy raspberry is a product of the cooler northern sun and damp cold winters. Related to the blackberry, it has grown wild in Britain and northern Europe and across to Asia since prehistoric times and, according to legend, was found growing on Mount Ida by the Greek gods.

Wild raspberries must have been very prolific and widespread, since they were not brought into British gardens until Tudor times, when there was a great new interest in gardening, although they had been cultivated in France for some time before this. Raspberries have been grown commercially only since the 1920s, and one of the main producing areas is centred around Blairgowrie in Scotland.

When raspberries were first cultivated they were used mainly for making sugary sweetmeats. The seventeenth century saw the beginning of the great age of preserving and there were raspberry jams, jellies and preserves. Wine making was also very popular at this time, and raspberry juice was added to grape wines to give both flavour and colour. In the eighteenth century, raspberry vinegar became popular, both as a drink and as an ingredient in sweet and savoury sauces.

Early types of cultivated European raspberry were white, yellow and orange, besides the now more usual red. Pale yellow raspberries can be found growing wild in Scotland. They are supposed to be sweeter and better flavoured than the reds, so try them if you can. There are also black-fruited varieties, which have been developed in the United States from wild species growing there.

Raspberries are easy to gather and now that there are so many pick-your-own farms we can all enjoy harvesting raspberries in the sun.

Nutrition

Raspberries are rich in most minerals, particularly potassium, and also in Vitamin C.

Picking, buying and storing raspberries

When picking raspberries, leave the under-ripe ones, and do not put any that squash in your fingers into your punnet, or they will make the rest go mouldy. A fully ripe raspberry will slip easily off the bine. It should yield when gently squeezed, but should not squash or break. When buying raspberries, look for fruit in the same condition. They should look fresh, juicy and full, and all the berries should be quite separate.

Raspberries should be stored in their punnets. They will keep for up to two days in the refrigerator and are exceptionally easy to freeze. Put them into the freezer on trays and, when hard, pack them into polythene bags. They will keep for up to a year.

Raspberries in the kitchen

Raspberries can be eaten raw, with sugar or honey and cream, either alone or mixed with strawberries, peaches or apricots. They can also be used in fruit flans, and sandwiched between cakes or used as a decoration on top. Put them into meringue bases, large or small; pile them into tartlet cases or use them as the base for a traditional trifle. You can also add them to lettuce salads, and scatter them over cooked lamb or poultry.

Very ripe raspberries can be puréed raw, simply by rubbing them through a sieve. Raspberry purée can be used for ice-creams, water-ices and sorbets, for mousses, fools and other cream desserts and as a base for sweet sauces. Gently stewed with sugar or honey until the juice runs, raspberries, together with red and blackcurrants, make the perfect summer pudding.

Raspberries can be added to sautéed meats and rubbed through a sieve with the other juices to make a sauce. They can also be put into stuffings.

The pectin content of raspberries is high and they contain citric and malic acids, so are an excellent fruit for using alone or mixing with others to make jams and jellies. Raspberry vinegar can be diluted with iced water and used as a drink, or made into sweet or savoury sauces.

LOGANBERRY

R. LOGANOBACCUS

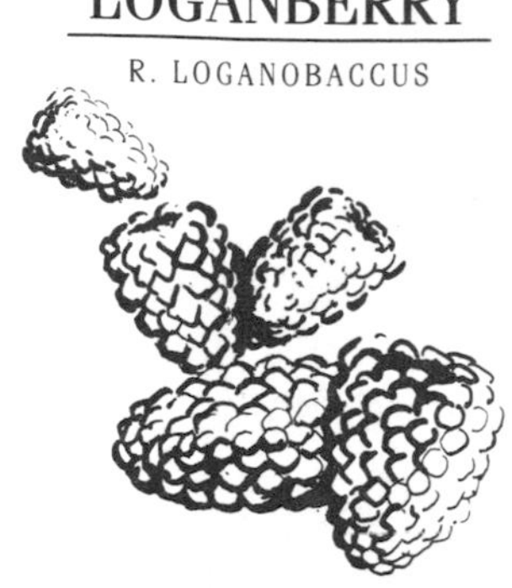

The loganberry looks like an elongated, dark raspberry. It is very juicy, and has a fuller flavour than the raspberry. It is a natural cross between a raspberry and the Pacific blackberry, and was first discovered in the garden of Judge J H Logan at Santa Cruz, California. It came to England in 1897.

The loganberry was for many years purely a garden fruit, but it has recently been cultivated commercially. Small amounts come into the shops throughout July and early August and you can also pick your own.

Loganberries are delicious raw, and are best of all served simply with honey or sugar and cream. Their size and colour makes them look particularly good in mixed fruit salads. They also make a rich, dark purée that can be used in the same ways as raspberry purée.

TAYBERRY

The tayberry is a more recent fruit, developed by the Scottish Crop Research Institute, from a cross between a high quality cultivated blackberry from Oregon in the United States, and a raspberry. Tayberries have become very popular in recent years. They are large, conical and deep purple with an aromatic flavour. They are available from early July until mid-August and can be used in the same ways as loganberries.

BOYSENBERRY

Boysenberries are long, dark red berries. They are not grown in Britain on a wide scale but a few have been reaching the shops in recent years. Like the loganberry they are a cultivar of the Pacific blackberry. Boysenberries do not have the rich flavour of loganberries or tayberries and can be quite sharp. They are best puréed, sweetened, and used as for raspberry purée.

SUNBERRY

Sunberries were first raised at the Institute of Horticultural Research at East Malling in Kent. They are another raspberry hybrid and look like large, glossy, dark red raspberries. Use them like blackberries or raspberries.

TUMMELBERRY

The tummelberry is a tayberry cross developed in Scotland. It is large, rounder than a tayberry, and red to purple in colour. The flavour is sharp and aromatic, and the fruit can be used in similar ways to loganberries.

YOUNGBERRY

This is large, wine-red and sweet, and was developed by a Mr Young in Louisiana.

OLALLIE

The olallie is popular in California. It is a cross between a youngberry and a loganberry, and is medium-sized and black.

HONEYBERRY

The honeyberry grows only in Finland, where it is known as the *mesimarja.* The fruits are like tiny raspberries, and most of the crop goes into the production of a liqueur of the same Finnish name that was once popular at the Russian court.

ARCTIC CLOUDBERRY

The Arctic cloudberry grows wild all over Scandinavia. It has large pips and a caramel flavour, and is mostly used for making a liqueur.

Green salad with raspberries

This salad has an Elizabethan flavour: it contains a good selection of herbs, a slight touch of onion and no garlic. Serve it with lamb, chicken or pork, nut roasts or cottage cheese.

1 small lettuce
1 small cucumber
8 oz (225 g) raspberries
1 tablespoon chopped tarragon
1 tablespoon chopped mint
10 sage leaves, chopped
green parts of 4 spring onions, chopped
4 tablespoons olive oil
2 tablespoons tarragon vinegar
freshly ground black pepper
pinch sea salt

Tear the lettuce into small pieces. Cut the cucumber into lengthways quarters and slice thinly. Put both in a salad bowl with the raspberries, herbs and chopped onion. Beat the oil, vinegar and seasonings together and fold into the salad.

Serves 4.

Raspberry and honey vinegar

1½ lb (675 g) raspberries, picked fresh or bought in 3 lots of 8 oz (225 g) at 4-day intervals
one 13 fl oz (369 ml) bottle white wine vinegar
honey equal to weight of the strained vinegar [see recipe method, approx 8–12 oz (225–350 g)]

Diluted with mineral water, this makes a refreshing summer drink. You can also use it as a sauce to top vanilla, strawberry or raspberry ice-creams, or as an ingredient in savoury sauces.

Put 8 oz (225 g) of the raspberries into a bowl. Pour on the vinegar (keep the empty bottle). Cover the raspberries with cling film and leave in a cool place for 4 days. Strain the vinegar through a nylon sieve. Return it to the bowl with a further 8 oz (225 g) raspberries. Leave for 4 days, strain, add the remaining raspberries and leave for a further 4 days.

This time, strain the vinegar through a jelly bag to make it clear. Weigh a saucepan. Pour in the vinegar, and weigh again. Add honey to the same weight as the vinegar. Bring to the boil on a low heat, stirring until the honey has dissolved. Boil for 5 minutes and skim well.

Pour the vinegar into an earthenware jug and cover it with a linen tea cloth folded into 4. Tie the cloth down securely and leave for 24 hours.

Pour the vinegar back into the original bottle and screw on the top. It can be used immediately, but will keep for up to a year.

Makes about 12 fl oz (350 ml).

Raspberry ripple mousse

1 lb (450 g) raspberries
3 oz (75 g) honey
½ oz (15 g) gelatin
4 tablespoons red grape juice or water
2 eggs, separated
¼ pint (150 ml) natural yoghurt

This recipe also works exceptionally well with tayberries.

Put the raspberries into a saucepan with the honey. Cover, and set on a low heat for 15 minutes or until soft and juicy. Take from the heat and rub through a sieve. Return half the raspberry purée to the cleaned pan and put the rest into a bowl.

In a small pan, soak the gelatin in the grape juice or water. Warm the raspberry purée that is in the saucepan. Beat the egg yolks into it, one at a time and stir on a low heat until the mixture becomes thick. It must not boil or it will curdle. Take the pan from the heat and stir in half the gelatin. Stir the other half of the gelatin into the reserved raspberry purée. Leave both mixtures until they are on the point of setting.

Stiffly whip the egg whites. Fold first the yoghurt and then the egg whites into the raspberry and egg yolk mixture. Pour the mixture into a glass serving bowl. Gently stir the raspberry purée into the bowl to make a streaked pattern. Leave the mousse for 2 hours to set.

Serves 4.

RHUBARB

RHEUM SPECIES

THE STEM OF a vegetable, related to the wild dock and sorrel, with poisonous leaves and a root which was grown by the ancient Chinese to be used as a purgative. Not much of a recommendation for any food, but nonetheless, a fair definition of rhubarb. Rhubarb technically is not a fruit (it does not contain seeds that will grow into another plant), but a stem. In Britain at least, however, many people have an affection for it. It arrives when there are no fresh fruits to be harvested, and those in the cold store are beginning to run out. It is so prolific that it can be picked every day during its growing season and used for countless desserts, wines and preserves. The word may be a joke, but rhubarb has many advantages.

There are many different types, all coming originally from China, Siberia, India and the area around the Himalayas. Rhubarb appears in a Chinese medical book dated around 2,700 BC, so it is very ancient. The Chinese traded it along the old silk and spice routes, and it eventually reached Europe through Constantinople. The type used medicinally was *R. officinale*, later called Turkey rhubarb, and for centuries this was the one most commonly grown and traded. The first type to arrive in Britain, however, was the Siberian rhubarb, *R. rhaponticum*. It was planted in gardens in Tudor times and, although occasionally used medicinally, was regarded more as a curiosity.

One hundred years later, probably in Italy, seeds of the Siberian rhubarb were crossed with other varieties to produce the culinary types known today. Seeds of these were sent to the garden writer John Parkinson, and he planted them in his garden. The plant was still, however, used medicinally.

In the eighteenth century, the Bath Society for the Encouragement of Agriculture encouraged growers to produce more rhubarb for medicinal use, but it was not long before the thrifty wives of these growers realized the great culinary potential of rhubarb. The first recorded rhubarb recipe dates from 1795 in a book called *The Housekeepers Instructor* by W A Henderson.

By early Victorian times, rhubarb treated as a fruit had become popular. It was grown commercially mainly around London, and it was here that one day a flower pot was accidentally left over a rhubarb plant. When it was removed, there were thin, tender sticks of pale pink rhubarb with light green leaves – the first forced rhubarb.

For some reason, the idea of forcing rhubarb caught on in the North, particularly in Yorkshire and it is still grown there. The thin, delicate stems are cut when they are about two inches (5 cm) long, by candlelight, and are very tender, with a delicate flavour.

Outdoor rhubarb can be picked from April onwards. It is crimson red, taller, thicker and altogether more robust in flavour and texture than forced.

Nutrition

Rhubarb is exceptionally high in potassium and calcium, and is rich in other minerals as well, but has only a little Vitamin C.

Buying and storing rhubarb

Rhubarb stems should be crisp and firm. Old rhubarb quickly becomes floppy. Rhubarb keeps in a cool place for one day only.

To freeze, chop the stems into short lengths and pack into polythene bags. They will keep for three months, or for six months if packed in a sugar syrup.

Rhubarb in the kitchen

The leaves of rhubarb should be discarded. They are poisonous and should never be eaten. Cut off the very ends of the stems that may have sections of leaf buds attached. Chop the stems into lengths of 1–1½ inches (2.5–4 cm).

Rhubarb is not pleasant when eaten raw. To cook it, poach the pieces gently in a syrup made with honey or sugar. Cooked rhubarb can be served plainly, hot or cold, and can be made into pies, crumbles and cobbler dishes. It is delicious served with any form of sweet rice and the cooked pieces can be baked in a rice pudding. Rhubarb can also be puréed and made into fools, ice-creams, mousses and other cream desserts.

Rhubarb can be made into jam and chutney both of which are particularly good when flavoured with ginger, and it makes a good, dry wine. Chopped rhubarb can be added to pork casseroles or sauté dishes. It makes a good sauce or relish for cooked meats or grilled mackerel.

Pork stir-braised with rhubarb

1½ lb (675 g) lean, boneless pork
7 fl oz (200 ml) dry white wine
6 allspice berries, crushed
6 sage leaves, chopped
1 large onion, thinly sliced
12 oz (350 g) rhubarb

A dish that uses rhubarb more like a vegetable than a fruit. Cooked with meat, it develops a savoury flavour.

Cut the pork into ¾-inch (2 cm) dice. Put the wine, allspice berries and sage into a bowl, and turn the pork in the mixture. Cover, and leave for 4 hours at room temperature. Drain the pork, reserving the marinade, and dry it with kitchen paper. Chop the rhubarb.

Heat a large, heavy frying pan on a high heat with no fat, stir the pork around until it browns well. Lower the heat, add the onion and rhubarb and cook gently for 2 minutes. Pour in the marinade and bring to the boil. Cover, and simmer for 30 minutes, or until the pork is tender.

Serves 4.

Rhubarb and almond creams

1 lb (450 g) rhubarb
3 oz (75 g) honey
½ oz (15 g) gelatin
2 tablespoons flaked almonds
2 tablespoons ground almonds
4 oz (125 g) fromage frais
crystallized violets or whole almonds for decoration (optional)

A light, sweet jelly with a creamy topping.

Chop the rhubarb. Put the honey into a saucepan with 6 fl oz (175 ml) water and stir on a low heat for it to dissolve. Bring the syrup to the boil and add the rhubarb. Cover, and simmer for 15 minutes or until soft. Rub the rhubarb and juices through a sieve to make a thin purée. Return the purée to the pan and set it on a low heat. Sprinkle in the gelatin and stir for it to dissolve. Take the pan from the heat.

Divide the flaked almonds between 4 6–7 fl oz (175–200 ml) glass dishes or tall dessert glasses. Half-fill the dishes with about three-quarters of the rhubarb purée. (If you are using tall glasses, this jelly can be set at an angle for extra effect.) Refrigerate for the purée to set.

Mix the ground almonds and the fromage frais into the remaining rhubarb purée. Keep the mixture in a warm place to prevent it from setting.

When the jellies in the refrigerator have set, spoon the rhubarb and ground almond mixture on top. Leave the jellies in a cool place to set completely.

Serves 4.

STRAWBERRY

FRAGARIA SPECIES

'RAWE CRAYME UNDECOCTED, eaten with strawberys . . . is a rurall mennes banket. I have knowne such bankettes hath put men in jeopardy of their lyves.' There could be no better testimony for a strawberry than that, and it was written in the sixteenth century long before the large, soft modern varieties had been developed.

Wild strawberries have grown in Britain and northern Europe since prehistoric times. They received their name long before they were taken into cultivation and covered with straw. The Anglo-Saxons called them 'streawberige', meaning a berry that put out runners and strayed. In medieval times they were taken into gardens, but no attempt was made at cultivating larger varieties. The fruits were small and hard, but still much loved, and there were enough of them to be hawked in London streets. In France at the same time, they were planted in the royal gardens at the Louvre in Paris. With pure white flowers, and leaves the shape of the sacred trefoil, the strawberry became associated with the purity and goodness of the holy family. It was taken up as a symbol of European royalty, and the leaf pattern was incorporated in the design of coronets for the nobility.

In 1714 a French naval officer named Amedée François Frazier was secretly surveying the coastline of Chile, when he discovered strawberry plants with larger berries than anyone in Europe had yet imagined. He immediately dug up some plants and sent them home. Only a few survived the journey and these, when planted, did not fruit, but by a lucky coincidence they were growing near some varieties first discovered by settlers in Virginia, and the two cross-pollinated naturally to produce the large, sweet ancestor of all our modern strawberries.

Strawberry growers now have to meet many demands. In order to extend what was once a very short season, they have produced both early and late varieties, besides those that will crop for a long time. Strawberries have to be disease-resistant, with a good shelf life, besides looking attractive and having a fine flavour. Certain types are favoured by pick-your-own farmers and special varieties are also grown for canning and jam-making.

Whichever variety of British-grown strawberries you buy, you can nearly always be sure that they will be softer and sweeter than the imported types. These can be bought quite easily all the year round, flown in from such places as Kenya and the United States. They have been specially produced to withstand long journeys, and so are much harder than those coming from local growers.

Nutrition

Strawberries are an excellent source of potassium and have a significant amount of most other minerals. They are rich in Vitamin C, but this diminishes quickly as soon as they have been picked.

Picking, buying and storing strawberries

If you are picking your own strawberries, do not pick the under-ripe ones. Make sure you know what colour the variety that you are picking is when ripe. Some are red all over, and others can be whiter. Certainly, they must not be green or hard. Do not pick them if they are soft, have brown patches or are beginning to look dry and shrivelled. Always pick strawberries without hulling them, as this helps to preserve their flavour, texture and vitamin content.

When buying strawberries, make sure they are even-shaped, fresh and shiny, and ripe but firm.

Whether buying or picking, check your strawberries when you get them home and discard any mildewed ones which may contaminate the others.

Strawberries do not have a very long shelf-life, but refrigerating them can spoil their flavour. They can be kept in a cool place for up to two days, but should always be eaten as quickly as possible.

Strawberries do not freeze very well, since they lose their shape and become very soft as they thaw. Thawed strawberries however do make an excellent puree. Freeze strawberries on trays, and pack into polythene bags. They keep for up to four months.

Strawberries in the kitchen

Raw strawberries with cream really are a banquet. They can be left unsweetened or coated with sugar or honey. Serve them alone, or mix with other summer fruits. Whole or halved, strawberries can be put into open summer tarts on top of whipped cream, a pastry cream, or silken tofu whipped with strawberry jam. They can be sandwiched between cakes and shortbreads, and laid on top as a decoration. Put them into nests of meringue, or use as a base for a summer trifle.

To make a strawberry purée, simply rub ripe strawberries through a sieve and use to make water-ices and ice-creams, fruit fools, mousses, soufflés, cheesecakes and other cream desserts. Thicken it with arrowroot to use as a sweet sauce.

Strawberry is the most popular British jam, but it can be tricky to make, as the fruits do not contain enough pectin to achieve a good set when used on their own. Always add lemon, redcurrant or gooseberry juice, or citric acid to the pan with the strawberries.

Strawberry wine is pale and delicate. You can also make a strawberry vinegar like the raspberry vinegar on page 191. Use it as a drink, or as a base for sweet sauces.

If you are ever lucky enough to find small alpine strawberries, you can use them as a decoration on cream cakes and shortcakes and on desserts made with an ordinary strawberry purée. Pile them into tartlets, or stir into sweetened whipped cream, bruising them slightly to stain the cream pink.

Strawberry, cheese and bacon salad

1 lb (450 g) strawberries
8 oz (225 g) lean unsmoked back bacon
1 lb (450 g) cottage cheese
2 tablespoons tarragon vinegar or mild white wine vinegar
1 density or cos lettuce

A light lunch dish for a summer day.

Halve the strawberries. Grill the bacon until it is cooked through and cut into ½-inch (1.3 cm) squares. Put the cheese into a bowl and beat in the vinegar. Fold in the strawberries and bacon.

Shred the lettuce and arrange it on 4 dinner plates. Arrange the salad on top.

Serves 4.

Strawberry sherbet with strawberry sauce

SHERBET

8 oz (225 g) ripe strawberries
2 oz (50 g) no-sugar-added strawberry jam
¼ pint (150 ml) water
¼ pint (150 ml) natural yoghurt

SAUCE

8 oz (225 g) ripe strawberries
2 tablespoons no-sugar-added strawberry jam

DECORATION

extra strawberries
mint leaves

A refreshing summer dessert to be made with ripe strawberries. If you cannot get the jam, use honey instead.

For the sherbet, rub the strawberries through a sieve. Melt the jam on a low heat and stir it into the strawberries. Stir in the water. Use an ice-cream machine if you have one, or else put the mixture into a freezing tray in the coldest part of the freezer, or in the ice compartment of the refrigerator, set at the coldest temperature, for 2 hours. Beat it well to break up the ice particles. Beat in the yoghurt. Pour the mixture into a bowl and freeze completely, whipping it after the first hour. Scoop the sherbet into portions, using an ice-cream scoop, and freeze them on a tray.

For the sauce, rub the strawberries through a sieve. Melt the jam on a low heat and stir it into the strawberries. Chill the sauce for at least 1 hour before serving.

To serve, either put the scoops on to individual plates, pour the sauce over and decorate with mint leaves and extra strawberries; or, for a special meal, pile the scoops into a glass bowl with fresh strawberries and a trickle of sauce in between and the rest of the sauce spooned over the top. Garnish with the mint leaves and serve immediately.

Serves 4–6.

TAMARILLO

CYPHOMANDRA BETACEA

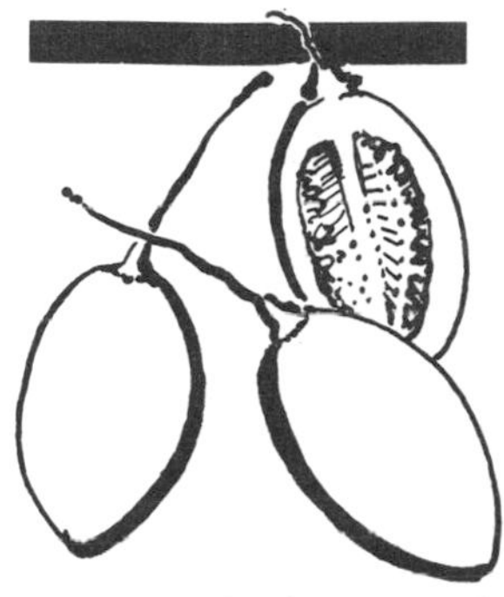

TAMARILLOS GROW ON you. At first, you may not think much of them, but after you have tried them several times you begin to find their strange flavour, like a cross between an unripe tomato and a plum, irresistible.

Tamarillos are a native of Brazil and have only recently been cultivated on a large enough scale to be exported. The trees are small and neat, with clusters of fragrant, pink and purple flowers.

In size and appearance, the tamarillo is rather like an Italian plum tomato, only less rounded and tapering to a point at the bottom. The skin has a shiny, tomato-like texture, but is a much deeper, pinker red, becoming almost maroon when the fruit is ripe. The flesh is similar to that of a tomato, but slightly pulpier. It is orange-red nearest the skin, and deepens to a rich, purply-maroon colour inside. When the fruit is very ripe, even the outer parts darken. Embedded in the flesh are soft, deep maroon pips.

Nutrition

The tamarillo is an excellent source of Vitamin A and also has significant amounts of Vitamin C. Its mineral count, however, is low, apart from a little calcium.

Buying and storing tamarillos

To be ready for dessert purposes, tamarillos should be firm but quite soft and their skin should be dark and beginning to look loose and easily peelable. If they are to be used for a savoury recipe, they need not be quite so ripe. An under-ripe tamarillo will quickly ripen off in a warm room. When ripe, the fruit keeps for up to one week in the refrigerator.

Tamarillos in the kitchen

It may not seem like it at first, but tamarillos are extremely versatile and can be used to great effect in both sweet and savoury dishes.

First of all, they should be peeled. When they are firm, use a sharp knife to take off the peel in thin strips. When they are ripe, you can easily peel it away by hand.

Tamarillos have a bitter-sweet flavour, and this makes them an excellent accompaniment to savoury dishes. For a quick relish, chop the flesh and mix with a little lemon juice. You can also cut the flesh into thin slices and lay it over lamb or pork chops, or joints of chicken or duck. If you are grilling, cook the meat completely, lay the slices of tamarillo on top, and cook for a further two minutes so they just begin to melt into the meat. If you are roasting, lay the slices on the meat for the final 10 minutes of cooking time. Tamarillos also make excellent relishes and chutneys.

To serve tamarillos as a dessert, they should be fully ripe. When sliced and eaten raw, their flavour is too strong to serve them alone, but they make interesting additions to an exotic fruit salad.

The best thing to do with a ripe tamarillo, however, is to make it into a sweetened purée. Peel the flesh first, liquidize it, and then rub it through a sieve to get rid of the pips. This will leave you with a deep maroon purée. For each fruit, stir in 2–3 tablespoons of sugar (taste after 2), and leave to stand for 1 hour.

Served plain, this sweetened purée can be used as a sweet sauce for ice-creams and cream desserts. It can even be eaten just as it is, with soured cream swirled over the top, as a sweet fruit soup. For a quick whip, beat it into Greek-style yoghurt or silken tofu, and for a drink, dilute it like squash with fizzy mineral water. You can also thicken it with arrowroot, and use it as a fruit glaze or a topping for cheesecakes. It is best of all made into an ice-cream which has a strange, musky, bitter-sweet flavour (see recipe, page 201).

Tamarillo sauce

3 tamarillos
2 tablespoons olive oil
1 small onion, finely chopped
1 garlic clove, finely chopped
2 teaspoons dark Muscovado sugar
juice 1 medium orange

This is good with tortellini or plain pasta, but use it sparingly. It is also excellent as a relish with fish, pork, poultry and cheese dishes.

Skin and chop the tamarillos. Heat the oil in a small saucepan on a low heat. Soften the onion and garlic. Add the tamarillos, sugar and orange juice. Cover, and simmer for 15 minutes or until the tamarillos are soft and pulpy. Stir well, and serve hot or cold.

Serves 4.

Tamarillo ice-cream

3 ripe tamarillos
4 oz (125 g) golden caster sugar
2 egg yolks
1 tablespoon cornflour
7 fl oz (200 ml) double cream
3 fl oz (90 ml) milk
flaked almonds to decorate (optional)

An extremely rich ice-cream, best suited to adult tastes. Savour it in small portions.

Peel and liquidize the tamarillos. Stir the sugar into the purée and leave for 1 hour, or until the sugar has dissolved naturally, stirring occasionally.

Put the egg yolks and cornflour into a small saucepan and beat them together. Stir in the cream and milk. Stir on a very low heat, without boiling, until the custard thickens. Take from the heat and dip the base of the pan into cold water. Cool slightly, and stir into the tamarillo purée.

Chill the mixture. Either freeze it in an ice-cream machine according to the manufacturer's instructions, or put it into a freezing tray and then into the coldest part of the freezer or the ice compartment of the refrigerator, set at the lowest temperature. Freeze for 3 hours, beating it every 45 minutes. Put it into a plastic box, cover, and freeze it completely.

Serve in small scoops, scattered with a few flaked almonds.

Serves 8.

TAMARIND

TAMARINDUS INDICA

THE TAMARIND IS an ancient tree, featuring in Indian mythology, that has its origins in both Asia and Africa. It is a member of the pea family, and is a tall tree with leaves similar to those of the laburnum, and yellow flowers, striped with red, that hang down in long clusters. After the flowers, come the pods which hang down from long thin stems until they are dry and crackly on the outside and the flesh on the inside is dark and sticky.

Fresh tamarinds are available quite widely in Britain. Inside those dry, biscuit-coloured pods, the flesh is compressed, sticky and a dark orange-brown. When the pod is stripped away, the flesh stays in shape, complete with bumps and ridges. Wriggling along it are long, thin, yellow fibres, which can be stripped off easily. Inside the flesh are black stones, wedge-shaped and exactly the texture of pebbles on the beach.

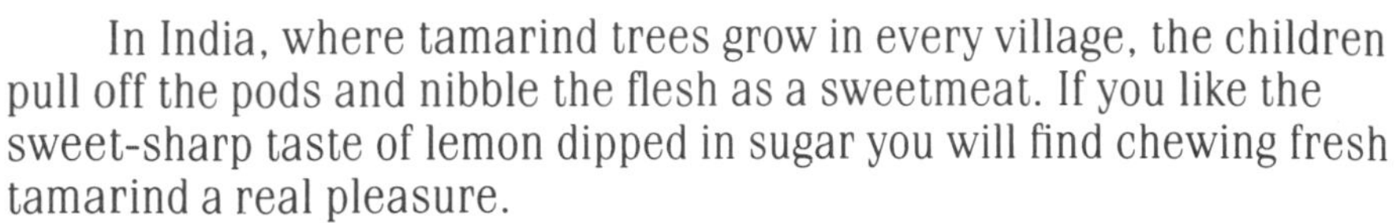

In India, where tamarind trees grow in every village, the children pull off the pods and nibble the flesh as a sweetmeat. If you like the sweet-sharp taste of lemon dipped in sugar you will find chewing fresh tamarind a real pleasure.

The Arabs introduced tamarind to Europe, but it has been little known here until recently. One of its main uses has been as an ingredient in Worcestershire sauce, the recipe for which was brought back from India by Lord Sandys, a former governor of Bengal. In 1835 he took the recipe to be made up at the Worcester pharmacy of John Lea and William Perrins. When they first tasted the results of their efforts, it was quite awful, so they left it in the cellar and forgot about it. Two years later they rediscovered it, tried it again, and found it to be superb, the secret having been the long maturation.

Nutrition

Tamarind is rich in B Vitamins, potassium and calcium.

Buying and storing tamarind

When buying fresh tamarind, make sure that the pods are unbroken.

Fresh tamarind, still in the pods, will keep for up to a month in a cool place, although the flesh tends to harden after a time and it will need longer soaking (see below) before use.

You can also buy semi-dried tamarind pressed into blocks which, well wrapped, keep for up to a year.

Refined tamarind extract is available from Indian shops. It looks like a dark paste, and can be bought plain or spiced.

Tamarind in the kitchen

The texture of tamarind is chewy, but softens if it is soaked in hot water for 2 hours. Then it can be rubbed through a sieve to make a moist purée. The process does remove some of the sherbetty flavour, although the fresh sharpness remains. When sieving, make sure that you scrape all the purée from the underneath of the sieve. A certain amount of the soaking liquid is usually added to the sieved tamarind, the amount depending on the final recipe.

In India, South East Asia, the Caribbean and parts of the Middle East tamarind puree is added to curries and spiced dishes to give a fresh lift to the flavour. Mixed with more of the soaking liquid, it can be used as a marinade. In the Middle East and the Caribbean, tamarind is made into cool drinks and in India it is made into a spiced digestive drink that is served throughout a meal.

Lamb and vegetable curry

2 oz (50 g) fresh tamarind, weighed after removing the pods
¼ pint (150 ml) boiling water
1 lb (450 g) lean, boneless lamb, from the leg or shoulder
1 medium aubergine
1 teaspoon fine sea salt
12 oz (350 g) potatoes
1 medium onion, thinly sliced
3 tablespoons sunflower oil
1 garlic clove, chopped
1 teaspoon ground cumin
1 teaspoon ground coriander
1 teaspoon ground turmeric
½ teaspoon chilli powder, or more to taste
2 oz (50 g) spiced red lentils
½ pint (275 ml) stock
4 oz (125 g) shelled peas, fresh or frozen

A gently spiced curry with the fresh hint of tamarind.

Put the tamarind into a bowl, pour the boiling water over it and leave for 2 hours. Rub it through a sieve and discard the seeds.

Dice the lamb. Dice the aubergine, put it into a colander, sprinkle with the salt and leave to drain for 20 minutes. Run cold water through it and dry with kitchen paper. Dice the potatoes without peeling.

Heat the oil in a large frying pan on a high heat. Brown the lamb. Lower the heat and mix in the onion, garlic and spices. Cook gently, stirring occasionally, until the onion is soft. Mix in the potatoes, aubergine and lentils. Pour in the tamarind purée and the stock. Raise the heat, and bring to the boil. Add the peas, cover the pan, and simmer for 1 hour.

Serve with plainly boiled brown rice.

Serves 4.

Tamarind drink

2 oz (50 g) tamarind, weighed after removing the shells
1 tablespoon honey
1 pint (575 ml) boiling water

An extremely refreshing drink with a delicious tang.

Put the tamarind into a jug with the honey. Pour on the boiling water and leave for 4 hours. Strain the liquid, rubbing the tamarind in the sieve to make it into a soft purée. Either stir the drink very vigorously to break up the tamarind, or liquidize it for a few seconds in a blender.

Serves 3–4.

NUTS AND SEEDS

ALMOND

PRUNUS AMYGDALUS SYN. AMYGDALUS COMMUNIS

THE SWEET FLAVOUR of almonds, and the fact that they can be ground into a fine, moist paste, have been appreciated for many centuries.

The exact origin of almonds is uncertain. Some say that they first grew around the Mediterranean area, and others that they came from much further away, from south-eastern Russia, China and Japan and were brought to the western world by the Phoenicians. Wherever it happened the cultivation of almonds started thousands of years ago, as they are mentioned in Genesis, the first book of the Bible.

The Greeks took almonds to Italy, and the Romans carried them all over their empire. Great quantities were used in medieval kitchens. They were eaten before a meal in the belief that they would prevent diners from getting drunk, and were also blanched, fried and scattered over cooked dishes. Most frequently they were blanched and ground. In this form they were used as a thickening agent in sweet and savoury dishes, and made into almond milk. There were many fasting days in the medieval calendar when no meat or dairy products were permitted and cooks in rich kitchens performed culinary miracles with almonds. When ground almonds were boiled in water and strained, the liquid became almond milk which was used as the base for savoury stews and pottages and for sweet desserts. The paste that was left, was almond butter.

Marchpane, made with ground almonds, was the forerunner of our marzipan. It was first served in Elizabethan times and consisted of a ground almond and sugar mixture on a biscuit base, decorated with small coloured sweets, frosted with sugar and rosewater, and gilded with gold leaf.

Ground almond tarts, made like cheesecakes, were popular in the seventeenth century and at the same time the idea of coating almonds in chocolate came from France. The liqueur known as ratafia was made in the eighteenth century by immersing bitter almonds in brandy and leaving them to stand in the sun.

Although Britain has always consumed such quantities of almonds, they have only very rarely been home-grown. Some trees were cultivated quite extensively in the sixteenth century, but all produced more blossom than fruit. In order to flourish, almond trees need a combination of warmth and a rich, deep soil, conditions which are found mainly in southern Europe and the Middle East. From early times a large percentage of almonds have been imported from Spain, where they are second only to oranges in importance. They now also come from Italy and France, North Africa and California and are grown as well in South Africa, Australia, Iran, Afghanistan and Kashmir.

Almonds are related to the apricot, but the shell is surrounded by a leathery green casing which splits when the nuts are fully ripe. The nuts are dislodged from the trees by sharply tapping or hitting the branches or shaking the trees. The nuts fall on to canvas sheets spread out under the trees, so they can be picked up easily.

The husks are removed and the nuts are immediately laid in the sun for anything up to three weeks, until the kernels are dry enough to break without bending. Some nuts are sold in their shells, mainly for the Christmas market, but most are shelled and graded according to size.

There are two types of almonds, sweet and bitter. Sweet almonds differ in size, shape, oil content and the hardness of their shell. The best are **Jordan** almonds from Spain, called originally 'jardin' or garden almonds because they grew in gardens. Jordan almonds are grown in Malaga and Alicante and are long, flat and slender, rather like fingers. They are mainly sold whole and unblanched and can be used for dessert purposes and also for cooking. Italian **Premice** almonds are very similar.

Valencia almonds are grown mainly in Spain and Portugal, and are heart-shaped and less sweet than Jordan almonds. They have thick, rough skins and are usually sold blanched but still whole, or blanched and flaked or ground.

Californian almonds are flat and medium-sized, and are used in the same ways as Valencia almonds, mainly going for processing.

Besides being sold in the shell, shelled, blanched, flaked, in pieces, nibbed and ground; sweet almonds are also used in the production of almond oil, which is sweet and mild and can be used for both culinary and cosmetic purposes.

Bitter almonds are small, less oily than the sweet varieties, and with very hard, shiny shells. They are grown mainly in Sicily, Sardinia, North Africa and southern France. They are used mainly in the production of almond oil and almond essence, and also to flavour marzipan.

Nutrition

Like most nuts, almonds are high in protein, but must be combined with a whole grain food if they are to produce a complete protein in a meal. They are rich in potassium, calcium, magnesium and phosphorus.

Buying and storing almonds

Almonds in their shells are available mainly in the months around Christmas. Their shells should be clean and unbroken, and they will keep for several months.

When buying shelled almonds, choose the biggest you can find. Shelled almonds, still in their skins, will keep for up to four months in an airtight container.

If you buy almonds in their skins and blanch and process them yourself, you will always get a better flavour and moister texture than when buying them ready-prepared. However, if you need to buy them blanched, get them in sealed packs and keep them for no longer than a month. The same applies to flaked, nibbed (finely chopped) and ground almonds.

Almonds in the kitchen

For some nut roasts, where a robust flavour is needed, almonds can be ground in their skins, but for most dishes they are blanched and skinned first. This process is easier than it sounds. Put the nuts into a shallow frying pan, and just cover them with watcr. Bring to thc boil on a high heat, and drain them immediately. Leave them clustered together so they keep each other damp, then pick them up one at a time and gently squeeze the kernels out of the skins. It takes a while to get the squeeze right, and at first the nuts will either shoot across the room or refuse to burst out, but once you have got the right degree of pressure you will be able to skin them very quickly.

If you nccd flaked almonds for a fruit cake or a Christmas pudding, flake them as soon as they are blanched, holding them in your hand and using a small, sharp knife. Bought flaked almonds tend to be in rather large pieces so, if you are using these for speed, crumble them first.

To chop almonds, use either a long curved blade called a mezzaluna, which fits into a wooden bowl or, much more practical in modern kitchens, a food processor. A coffee grinder or blender can also be used, but these are not as efficient at producing even-sized pieces.

A food processor is also best for quickly grinding almonds, but coffee grinders and blenders can be used, although they will not be able to cope with so many nuts at a time. The very best way of all to grind almonds is to use a pestle and mortar. It makes a smooth, moist paste that is wonderful for marzipan and is also best for making almond milk as it releases more oils.

Whole, unskinned almonds can be added to salads and used as a decoration for cakes and desserts. They can be made into praline by setting them in a caramelized sugar. When grated, praline can be used to flavour mousses, soufflés and ice-cream.

Whole almonds are also excellent in salads, and as decorations.

Fried in oil until brown, and coated in salt, they make an excellent savoury snack. Split into two flat pieces, they can be fried in butter or toasted under a high grill, and sprinkled over meat dishes or fish.

Flaked almonds can also be fried and toasted, or can be sprinkled without cooking first, over Danish pastries and other cakes and desserts.

Ground almonds are used for marzipan, sweetmeats and macaroons. Mixed into cake mixtures they add richness and flavour, while in pastries they give a crumbly texture and nutty flavour. Added to whipped cream, or cream or curd cheese, ground almonds make a base for fruits in a tart. As almonds are so sweet, they are rarely used alone in vegetarian dishes but can be mixed with walnuts and brazil nuts.

The method for making almond milk is given on page 125 (fruit in almond jelly). Almond milk is rich and oily. It makes delicious, rich jellies and blancmanges, and can also be drunk by anyone allergic to cow's milk.

If you need the flavour of almonds without the texture, use almond essence. Make sure it is labelled 'essence' and not 'flavouring', as almond flavouring is chemically made, whereas the essence is extract of bitter almonds. It has a strong flavour, so use it drop by drop. It is mainly used to flavour cakes, rich pastries and desserts.

Almond oil has a light, delicate flavour. It is expensive, but makes a mild and delicate mayonnaise.

Smoked cod with almonds and tomatoes

1½ lb (675 g) smoked cod
1 bay leaf
1 teaspoon black peppercorns
1 blade mace
3 oz (75 g) almonds
1 lb firm tomatoes
1 large onion, thinly sliced
3 tablespoons olive oil
1 garlic clove, finely chopped

A light and colourful fish dish, best served with boiled potatoes tossed with parsley, and a green vegetable such as broccoli or green beans.

Put the fish into a shallow pan with the bay leaf, peppercorns and mace, and cover with water. Cover, and set on a low heat. Bring slowly to the boil, simmer for 1 minute, and remove from the heat. Lift the fish from the water and flake it.

Blanch and split the almonds. Scald and skin the tomatoes and slice into rounds.

Heat the oil in a large frying pan on a medium heat. Cook the almonds, stirring, until they are just beginning to brown. Lower the heat, add the onions and garlic and soften them, stirring occasionally to stop the almonds from over-browning. Raise the heat to high. Add the fish and tomatoes and fork them around to heat through. Serve immediately.

Serves 4.

Wholemeal simnel cake

ALMOND PASTE

8 oz (225 g) ground almonds *(see page 208)*
4 oz (125 g) dark Muscovado sugar
1 egg, beaten
juice ½ lemon
½ teaspoon almond essence

CAKE

8 oz (225 g) wholemeal flour
pinch salt
¼ teaspoon baking powder
1 teaspoon ground mixed spice
2 oz (50 g) ground rice
8 oz (225 g) butter, softened
grated rind 2 lemons
4 oz (125 g) Barbados sugar
4 eggs, separated
4 oz (125 g) raisins
4 oz (125 g) sultanas
4 oz (125 g) currants
4 oz (125 g) glacé cherries, halved

A delicious rich cake to make for Easter or Mothering Sunday.

To make the almond paste, mix the almonds and sugar. Beat the egg with the lemon juice and almond essence, and work it into the almonds and sugar. Divide the paste in half.

Heat the oven to 325F/170C/gas 3. Prepare an 8-inch (20 cm) diameter cake tin. Mix together the flour, salt, baking powder, spices and ground rice. Cream the butter and lemon rind together. Beat in the sugar. Add the egg yolks one at a time, beating well. Stiffly whip the egg whites. Mix a quarter of them into the butter and add a quarter of the flour. Do the same again and mix in all the fruit. Add the remaining whites and flour.

Put half the cake mixture into the prepared tin, building it up slightly at the sides. Shape half the almond paste into a flat round, smaller by about 1½ inches (4 cm) than the diameter of the cake. Put it on top of the cake mixture. Add the remaining cake mixture and smooth the top.

Bake the cake for 2 hours, or until a skewer inserted into the centre comes out clean. Turn it on to a wire rack. Reset the oven to 375F/190C/gas 5. Make the remaining paste into 12 egg shapes for Easter, or 12 flat rounds for Mothering Sunday. Place them round the edge of the cake, pressing down slightly to make them stick. Put the cake, on the rack, back into the oven for 15 minutes or until the paste begins to turn golden. Cool the cake completely on the rack.

BRAZIL NUT

BERTHOLETTIA EXCELSA

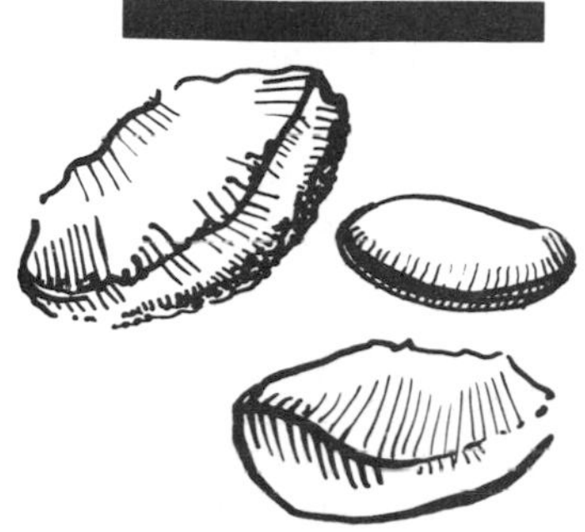

WHEN YOU BUY a pound of Brazil nuts, encased in their rough, brown, segment-shaped shells, you are buying a small part of the Amazon jungle. Brazil nuts, in their country of origin, are not cultivated, but picked wild from managed areas of forest.

Brazil nuts grow mainly in the Amazon area of Brazil, but can also be found in Guiana, Venezuela and Bolivia. Small amounts are now cultivated in Malaysia, Sri Lanka, Java and the West Indies. They remained very much a local nut until 1836, when some arrived in Boston on a Yankee clipper ship. By 1850 Brazil nuts had become an important export, later second only to rubber, and were sent to Britain through the port of Liverpool.

Brazil nut trees tend to grow in colonies which are managed and left to grow as naturally as possible. The trees are tall and thin, branching and leafing only at the top, all their leaves being above the heads of the surrounding trees. The nuts grow in round, woody outer husks, about 6 inches (15 cm) in diameter and looking rather like a bald coconut. Inside this husk, twelve or more nuts fit together perfectly in a circle, with one in the centre. That is why the shells are such an odd wedge shape. The round containers swing from the trees from thin stems and, when they are ripe, crash to the ground.

The local men who collect the nuts, called *castanheiros*, camp out in leafy shelters during the collecting season. The clusters of nuts are taken from the trees as well as from the ground, and broken open with a well-aimed blow from a machete. The single nuts are put into baskets and dipped in a nearby river, so the bad ones float to the surface and can be discarded. After drying on mats, the nuts are once again packed into baskets and taken by canoe to a central depot. From there, larger boats take them on down river to towns, where they are picked over to remove any that are damaged, then graded to size and sold to exporters.

Nutrition

Brazil nuts are high in protein but, if used in a main meal, must be combined with a whole grain product. They are exceptionally high in potassium, manganese and phosphorus and have significant amounts of calcium and sodium and very small amounts of some B Vitamins.

Buying and storing Brazil nuts

When buying Brazil nuts in their shells, make sure that none are broken. They will keep for up to six months.

Shelled Brazil nuts should look fresh and the kernels underneath the skin should be a pale cream colour. Yellowing of the kernels is a sign of age. Once shelled, Brazil nuts quickly become rancid, so they should be stored in an air-tight container and kept for one month only.

If you are buying nuts for grinding or chopping, buy pieces instead of whole nuts. There is no difference in freshness and quality, and they are usually cheaper.

Brazil nuts in the kitchen

Coarsely chopped Brazil nuts can be added to salads and sprinkled over fruit salads and other fruit desserts. They go exceptionally well with chocolate flavours. When finely chopped, they can be added to stuffings and to nut roasts, in which they have a creamy savoury flavour. Ground, they can be added to pastries, for either sweet or savoury pies and tarts; or to crumble, cakc or pudding mixtures.

Chocolate and Brazil nut oat tart

4 oz (125 g) Brazil nuts
6 oz (175 g) porridge oats
4 oz (125 g) plain chocolate
2 oz (50 g) dark Muscovado sugar
2½ oz (65 g) butter
2 tablespoons cold water
4 drops vanilla essence
2 eggs, separated
¼ pint (150 ml) Greek-style natural yoghurt

Brazil nuts go beautifully with chocolate and, mixed into oats, make a crunchy substitute for pastry in a tart base.

Heat the oven to 400F/200C/gas 6. Finely chop the Brazil nuts and mix them into the oats. Grate 1 oz (25 g) of the chocolate into the oats and add the sugar. Melt the butter and stir it in well. Press the mixture into the base and sides of an 8-inch (20 cm) diameter tart tin. Bake for 10 minutes and cool in the tin.

Break up the remaining chocolate and put it into a saucepan with the water and vanilla essence. Stir until the mixture is creamy and hot but not boiling. Take the pan from the heat and beat in the egg yolks, one at a time. Stiffly whip the egg whites. Fold the yoghurt, and then the egg whites, into the chocolate mixture.

Spoon the mixture on to the oat base and leave it in a cool place to set. Remove the tart from the tin just before serving.

Serves 6.

Brazil nut croquettes

8 oz (225 g) Brazil nuts
4 tablespoons sunflower oil
2 medium onions, finely chopped
1 garlic clove, finely chopped
4 oz (125 g) burghul wheat
3½ fl oz (100 ml) stock
2 tablespoons tomato purée
2 tablespoons chopped parsley
1 tablespoon chopped thyme
1 tablespoon chopped marjoram
2 teaspoons chopped rosemary
2 oz (50 g) wholemeal flour
1 egg, beaten
oil for deep frying

Deep-fried croquettes with a light, crumbly texture and crispy outside.

Grind the nuts. Heat the oil in a frying pan on a low heat and soften the onions and garlic. Add the wheat and cook, stirring, for 5 minutes. Pour in the stock and cook very gently, stirring frequently, for 10 minutes. Take the pan from the heat and mix in the nuts, tomato purée and herbs.

Form the mixture into 12 oval shapes. Coat in the flour, dip in the beaten egg, and coat again in the flour.

Heat the oil in a deep fryer to 375F/190C. Drop in the croquettes, 4 at a time, and cook for about 2 minutes, or until golden brown.

Serves 4.

CASHEW NUT

ANACARDIUM OCCIDENTALE

SWEET, CRUMBLY CASHEW nuts grow in the tropics. They are native to Brazil and the West Indies, where they were found by Portuguese explorers in the sixteenth century. The Portuguese took them to India, East Africa, Mozambique and Kenya. The trees quickly became established in their new countries, where a large percentage of the world's crop now originates. The name cashew comes from the Portuguese *caju*, which is in turn a shortened version of the Brazilian name, *acaju*.

Cashew nuts are the seeds of a small, evergreen tree which bears bright orange pear-shaped fruits known as 'cashew-apples'. The nuts are externally borne seeds attached to the base of the fruit and enclosed in a bean-shaped, olive, leathery, two-layered shell. Between the layers is a honeycombed membrane containing a powerful irritant oil which protects the nuts from insects. It can also irritate and burn the skin but is driven off when heated, so, before shelling, the nuts are roasted, a process which also improves the flavour.

Roasting was once carried out by either burying the nuts in hot sand, tossing them in a pan over an open fire or heating them in perforated iron pots. Nowadays, they are mostly put into rotating drums over fires fuelled with the discarded shells.

The cashew nut kernels are extracted by hand, a skilled job as the nuts are very brittle. They then have a few hours in a drying chamber, after which their thin yellow skins can be easily rubbed off. After this they are put into sweating chambers so that they can absorb more moisture and become less brittle. Cashew nuts are then graded and packed for export.

Because of the skilled handling needed during all stages of processing, cashew nuts are expensive. Only a small percentage come to Britain, as 90 per cent of all those produced are taken to the United States.

Nutrition

Cashew nuts contain some protein and have a high oil content. Unlike other nuts, they contain a small amount of Vitamin C.

Buying and storing cashew nuts

Cashew nuts should be pure white, plump and brittle, with an even, kidney-shape, not twisted. Whole nuts, halves, and broken pieces all taste the same, but the whole nuts are by far the most expensive. Unless for some reason you need the appearance of the whole nuts, there is no need to buy them. For cooking and for salads the halves will do very well and for recipes where the nuts need to be chopped or ground, buy pieces.

Cashew nuts keep for up to two months in an air-tight container.

Cashew nuts in the kitchen

Whole salted cashew nuts are a favourite pre-dinner snack in the United States and are also available here. They are excellent in salads and sprinkled over cooked meats.

Unsalted nuts, either whole or in half, are often mixed with raisins and other dried fruits and eaten as sweets. They are good in side salads, and also in salads of poultry or cooked dried beans. They are excellent in stir-fried dishes with vegetables or meat, cooked in mild sauces flavoured with ginger. They are good for adding bite to curries and spiced meat stews, and can be ground and added to spiced mixtures for making meat balls or to smooth sauces for chicken or turkey. Ground cashew nuts can be added to biscuit mixtures and beaten into batter for making waffles.

Mushroom and salted nut strudel

PASTRY

8 oz (225 g) wholemeal flour
pinch fine sea salt
1/4 pint (150 ml) water
3 fl oz (90 ml) corn oil
1 egg, beaten

FILLING

8 oz (225 g) open mushrooms
4 tablespoons olive oil
1 medium onion, finely chopped
1/4 pint (150 ml) soured cream
3 tablespoons chopped parsley
2 oz (50 g) pine kernels
4 oz 125 g) cashew nut pieces
1 teaspoon fine sea salt

Salted cashew nuts add a contrasting texture and flavour to a rich mushroom filling.

For the pastry, put the flour and salt into a bowl. Bring the water to the boil in a saucepan and add the oil. Boil until the mixture begins to look opaque and the oil and water are well incorporated. Pour the mixture into the flour and beat with a wooden spoon until it forms a soft dough. Knead the dough to make it smooth and shiny. Cool, wrap in foil, and chill for at least 30 minutes. Heat the oven to 400F/200C/gas 6.

For the filling, finely chop the mushrooms. Heat 2 tablespoons of the oil in a frying pan on a low heat and soften onion. Raise the heat to medium. Cook the mushrooms, stirring, for 2 minutes. Take the pan from the heat, and mix in the soured cream and parsley.

Heat the remaining oil in another frying pan on a medium heat. Cook the pine kernels and nuts, stirring, until they are golden brown. Tip on to a double thickness of kitchen paper, spread out, and sprinkle with the salt. When cool, add to mushroom mixture. Leave to cool completely.

Roll out half the pastry to a large, very thin, rectangle. Spread with half the mushroom mixture. Roll up the pastry from one short side and place the roll on a floured baking sheet. Do the same with the remaining pastry and filling. Brush with beaten egg.

Bake for 25 minutes, or until the pastry is golden brown. Serve hot.

Serves 4.

Marrow with cashew nut and peanut stuffing

one 2½ lb (1.25 kg) marrow
4 oz (125 g) cashew nuts
2 oz (50 g) peanuts
4 tablespoons sunflower oil
1 large onion, finely chopped
1 garlic clove, finely chopped
4 oz (125 g) fresh, wholemeal breadcrumbs
2 tablespoons chopped parsley
1 tablespoon chopped marjoram
1 tablespoon tomato purée
3 fl oz (90 ml) dry white wine
sea salt and freshly ground black pepper

When marrows are not in season, this stuffing can be used for tomatoes or green peppers.

Heat the oven to 400F/200C/gas 6. Cut off and reserve both ends of the marrow. Scoop the seeds from the main part and discard. Put all the parts of the marrow into lightly salted boiling water, and simmer for 5 minutes. Drain well.

Grind the nuts. Heat the oil in a frying pan on a low heat and soften the onions and garlic. Take the pan from the heat and mix in the breadcrumbs, nuts, herbs, tomato purée, wine and seasonings. Fill the marrow with the stuffing, and anchor the ends in place with cocktail sticks.

Put the marrow into a large, lightly oiled casserole, cover, and bake for 1 hour. To serve, discard the ends of the marrow and cut the main part into 4 thick slices.

Serves 4.

SWEET CHESTNUT

CASTANEA SATIVA

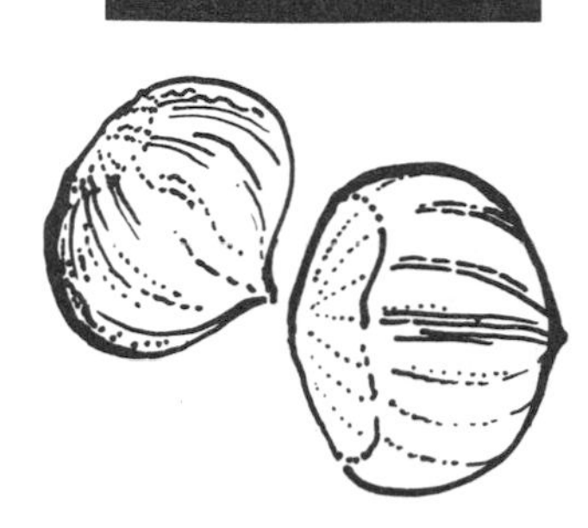

CHESTNUTS ARE THE odd ones out among the nuts. Although crisp, milky and rather pleasant when first picked, they soon become harder and drier so are seldom eaten raw. When cooked, however, they develop a soft, floury texture, and pleasant musty flavour that can blend with both sweet and savoury ingredients.

Chestnuts have grown wild in Britain for many centuries, but are not indigenous to this country. They thrive best in warmer climates, and originated around the eastern Mediterranean. The Greeks took chestnuts to southern Europe, and the Romans spread them northwards through France and eventually to Britain, where they quickly became established in the south of the country. In Britain they have always been essentially a wild tree, as the nuts are small and the crops unreliable, but a few varieties were once developed for cultivation in gardens and parks.

British chestnuts fall from the trees in late October and early November. Their outer husk is bright green and spiky but, if the nuts inside are ripe enough, it either splits as it falls or can be split by being stamped on. Inside each case are two, or sometimes three round nuts with pointed tops and flat sides, one of which can be up to twice as big as the rest. The nuts are enclosed in leathery, shiny, brown shells, which can be easily peeled away. Wrapping completely round the nut, and sticking fast to it, is a very thin, pale brown, slightly furry skin, and this presents the problem. Its flavour is very bitter and it can completely mask the crisp, creamy flavour of the nut inside if it is not completely scraped away.

Chestnuts imported from Italy, France and Spain are larger, and so there is more nut in relation to the amount of skin. There are also fewer fissures on the surface of the nut for the skin to burrow into, as it does with English wild chestnuts.

There are over 200 varieties of these larger European chestnuts, but two main types, the **marron** and the **chataigne**. The marron is the best, being large and fat with a sweet, creamy flavour, and it is this type that is used to make *marron glacé*. The chataigne is smaller, but widely grown, especially in France.

In chestnut-growing areas, the nuts are left in the hot sun for a few days or put into drying sheds or kilns. This improves their keeping qualities and prevents them from going mouldy. It does, however, harden the raw nuts.

In Britain, chestnuts have mainly been used in savoury dishes, added to pottages and broths, gravies, sauces and stuffings. For many centuries the favourite way with chestnuts has been to roast or boil them in their skins, to be served quite plainly with butter and salt.

Nutrition

Unlike most nuts, chestnuts are low in oil and high in carbohydrates, and this is what gives them their floury texture. They contain small amounts of B Vitamins, and are high in potassium, with significant amounts of calcium, magnesium and phosphorus.

Buying and storing chestnuts

Chestnut shells should be a glossy dark brown. If they have a slight grey bloom, they are beginning to age. Chestnuts in their shells can be kept for up to two weeks in a cool place. After that, the nuts begin to shrivel and harden.

Out of season, you can buy shelled dried chestnuts, and these keep for up to four months in an airtight container.

Chestnut flour keeps for up to a month, and canned whole chestnuts or chestnut purée keep for a year or more when unopened. When opened, use as quickly as possible.

To freeze chestnuts, peel them first (see below) and pack them whole into rigid containers. They will keep for up to six months, and can be cooked from frozen. You can also freeze chestnut purée for up to three months.

Chestnuts in the kitchen

Chestnuts must be shelled and skinned before use. If you have a microwave oven, now is the time to make use of it. Slit the tops of the chestnuts with a small, sharp knife and arrange them, six at a time, around the edge of a microwave dish. Microwave on High for 2 minutes, and both skins and shells will slip off easily, leaving a firm nut which can be eaten as it is or used in cooking.

Without a microwave oven, the chestnuts must be blanched. Slit the tops first, put them into a saucepan and cover with water. Bring to a good boil, and take them from the heat. Take the chestnuts out of the water one at a time, and hold with folded kitchen paper while you peel off the shell and skin.

To reconstitute dried chestnuts, soak in cold water for three hours, and simmer in the soaking water for three minutes. For 1 lb (450 g) chestnuts weighed in their shells, substitute 6 oz (175 g) dried chestnuts, weighed before reconstituting. When using canned chestnuts, weigh them after draining. You will need 12 oz (350 g) drained, canned chestnuts for every 1 lb (450 g) fresh chestnuts weighed in their shells.

Whole skinned chestnuts can be added to casseroles of meat or beans, and also to braised vegetables. They can also be chopped, and added to stuffings, mixtures for nut roasts, and soups.

To soften chestnuts for making into a purée, skin them and simmer for 20 minutes in water, stock or milk, or a mixture. Drain, and either mash with a potato masher, or purée in a blender or food processor. Mixed with savoury ingredicnts, chestnut purée can be made into stuffings, nut roasts and savoury patties. It can also be thinned with stock, to make a savoury sauce for meats or vegetarian dishes.

A sweetened chestnut purée can be used as a filling and topping for cakes or meringues. For a quick dessert, add a little ground cinnamon and some chopped stem ginger, pile into bowls, and top with whipped cream. The purée can also be beaten with a little brandy and whipped cream, or natural yoghurt, to make a chestnut syllabub.

There is nothing so cosy as roasting chestnuts over an open fire in winter. To do this you will need a proper chestnut roaster, like an open frying pan, perforated and with a long handle. Slit the tops of the chestnuts first and place each one over a hole in the pan. Hold over the fire until they start to sing, which will be in about seven minutes. To roast chestnuts in the oven, again slit them first. Put them on to a baking sheet and roast at 400F/200C/gas 6 for 15 minutes. According to Mrs Beeton, 'Chestnuts, the brightest and prettiest of all the nuts, are invariably served, after boiling and roasting, in a napkin, with one corner folded back to show its contents.'

Chestnut flour can only be bought in Britain from specialist shops. It can bc used in cakes, biscuits and bread, to make sweet and savoury pancakes and fritters, or to thicken soups and stews.

Chestnuts and prunes

A delicious side dish to serve with roast poultry and game.

12 prunes
½ pint (275 ml) cold tea
1 lb (450 g) chestnuts
1 oz (25 g) butter
2 medium onions, thinly sliced
¼ teaspoon cayenne pepper
½ pint (275 ml) dry white wine

Soak the prunes in the tea overnight. Drain, halve and stone them. Skin the chestnuts.

Melt the butter in a saucepan on a low heat and soften the onions. Add the chestnuts and sprinkle in the cayenne pepper. Pour in the wine and bring to the boil. Simmer, covered, for 10 minutes. Add the prunes, and simmer for a further 5 minutes, or until the wine is reduced to a glaze.

Serves 6.

Chestnut and cranberry castles

MAIN MIXTURE

1 medium onion, finely chopped
1 tablespoon sunflower oil
4 oz (125 g) hazelnuts
3 oz (75 g) Brazil nuts
8 oz (225 g) unsweetened chestnut purée
6 sage leaves, chopped
1 tablespoon chopped savory
4 tablespoons dry red wine

STUFFING

2 oz (50 g) cranberries
1 tablespoon sunflower oil
1 small onion, finely chopped
2 oz (50 g) fresh, wholemeal, breadcrumbs
1 tablespoon chopped marjoram
1 teaspoon chopped savory
3 tablespoons dry red wine

SAUCE

2 oz (50 g) cranberries
1 tablespoon sunflower oil
1 small onion, finely chopped
7 fl oz (200 ml) vegetable stock
3 fl oz (90 ml) dry red wine
6 oz (175 g) unsweetened chestnut purée
bouquet garni

These colourful little striped 'puddings' are served in a pool of rich sauce. They make a good vegetarian main course.

Heat the oven to 400F/200C/gas 6. For the main mixture, soften the onion in the oil on a low heat. Take the pan from the heat, and thoroughly mix in all the remaining ingredients.

For the stuffing, finely chop the cranberries. Heat the oil in a frying pan on a low heat and work the onion and cranberries until the onion is soft. Take the pan from the heat, and mix in the remaining ingredients.

Line 6 dariole moulds with oiled greaseproof paper. One-third fill each one with the main mixture. Put a layer of the cranberry stuffing on top, and finish with the remaining main mixture. Bake the castles for 30 minutes, or until they feel firm and the tops have browned. Leave to rest for 30 minutes, and turn out on to a flat surface.

For the sauce, finely chop the cranberries. Heat the oil in a saucepan, on a low heat and cook the onion and cranberries until the onion is soft. Pour in the stock and wine, and bring to the boil. Add the chestnut purée and bouquet garni. Cover, and simmer for 15 minutes. Remove the bouquet garni, and rub the sauce through a sieve. Return it to the cleaned pan, and reheat it gently.

To serve, put a portion of the sauce on to each of 6 dinner plates, and carefully lift the castles on to the sauce.

Serves 6.

COCONUT

COCOS NUCIFERA

THERE IS AN old Sanskrit saying: 'If man were placed on earth with nothing else but the coconut tree, he could live in happiness and contentment.' The coconut, the largest of all the nuts, with its crisp, pure white, creamy flesh, provides food, drink and oil. The leaves of the coconut tree are used for making shelters, and the mid-ribs of the leaves for brooms. A drink is brewed from its sugary sap, and the fibrous husk round each nut is made into ropes, mats and brushes. The shells are used as bowls, and burned to make charcoal. *Valpa vriksha* is the Sanskrit name, meaning 'the tree that provides all the necessities of life.'

Coconuts, however, have never been as popular in the West as they are in their countries of origin, mainly because other, home-produced, ingredients have provided our necessities. Ask anyone what they would do with a coconut in Britain, and you will probably get the answer: 'throw a wooden ball at it', for fairs would never be the same without the coconut shy. What a thrill it is to win one, to drink the fresh 'milk' and eat the crisp kernel. Only rarely, however, would we buy the coconut to eat, which is a shame, as they are highly versatile and available all the year round.

The coconut tree is a tall palm that grows on shores of tropical islands. It probably first came from islands in the Indian Ocean, but its absolute origins have been lost. When Portuguese explorers first found coconuts, they called them *macaco*, which means monkey, since when looked at from the top, the coconut has a little monkey face, with three eyes and a nose.

The main producers of coconuts are now the West Indies, Kenya, the Ivory coast, the Philippines, Malaysia and Sri Lanka. The nuts, each encased in a thick, outer husk, grow right in the tops of the trees, and harvesting is different in each country. The most common method is for the climber to fasten a sling round both himself and the trunk of the tree, which supports him and can be used as a climbing aid. In Sumatra, tame monkeys were once used to loosen the ripe nuts. Once the nuts have been cut, the thick, green outer husk is removed, leaving the round or oval nut encased in a hard, fibre-tufted shell.

Coconuts are either exported in the shell, or made into desiccated coconut, which is popular in the West both for baking and for making confectionery. For this, the nuts are shelled and the brown outer skin is removed. The flesh is either grated, shredded, or flaked, spread out on sieves, and put into hot air dryers. When it comes out, it is still pure white with a distinctive coconut aroma and flavour, but all the moisture has evaporated and the small pieces are dry and separate. Three whole coconuts are needed to make 1 lb (450 g) of desiccated coconut.

Coconut oil is also produced in the countries of origin. It is thick and pale, with a sweet, coconut flavour. It is likely to set in a cool temperature, which indicates that it contains a large proportion of saturated fats even though it is technically a vegetable oil.

Coconuts are also made commercially into coconut milk, used mainly for cooking in many tropical countries, and into coconut cream. Coconut cream, also called creamed coconut, looks a bit like lard and can be bought in 7 oz (200 g) blocks. It is like a cooking fat but harder, and has a sweet coconut flavour and almost granular texture.

Nutrition

Coconuts are rich in potassium and have significant amounts of phosphorus and magnesium. They have traces of B Vitamins, and are a good source of protein, although they must be eaten with a whole grain product if they are to be made into a main protein dish.

Buying and storing coconuts

When buying a whole coconut, give it a good shake. If it sounds as though there is plenty of 'milk' in it, it will be fresh and sweet. The less milk, the drier the flesh, and the more likelihood there is of the flavour having deteriorated. A fresh coconut should keep for up to two weeks in a cool place.

Coconuts in the kitchen

To remove the shell from a coconut, pierce through the eyes with a sharp, thick skewer, and hold the nut over a cup or bowl for the juice to run out. This juice is not the coconut milk that is used in cooking. It is much thinner and has a fresh, sweet flavour. Drink it as it is.

To open a coconut, bake it fifteen minutes in an oven, preheated to 400F/200C/gas 6. Place it on a hard, firm surface (concrete is ideal), and smash it open with a hammer. Baking the coconut first makes the shell split easily, and also helps the nut to come away easily. Cool the coconut, and peel away the brown skin with a potato peeler.

Grated fresh coconut can be added to curries, and other spiced meat and vegetable dishes. It can also be used to make a dressing for raw vegetables (see recipe, page 223). Use it alone, or mixed with yoghurt or cream, to top fresh and cooked fruits. In the Far East grated coconut is added to cake mixtures and made into a pancake filling.

Ambrosia is the name of a traditional American dish, originally made with oranges, sugar and grated fresh coconut. Small, sweet oranges, such as blood oranges, are the best, and desiccated coconut will not do. The oranges are sliced, layered in a bowl with the coconut and sugar, and chilled for about 2 hours. It is as simple as that. The coconut picks up the sugary juices and becomes soft and creamy, and the dish is fit for a king.

Coconut milk is used as a cooking liquid in many spiced, Far Eastern dishes. It gives flavour and richness to curries, and rice can be cooked in it. To make coconut milk, soak the grated flesh of one fresh coconut or 3 oz (75 g) desiccated coconut in 1 pint (575 ml) boiling water for one hour, and then strain through muslin, squeezing well. A quick way of making coconut milk is to use coconut cream. Add 1 oz (25 g) to ½ pint (275 ml) boiling water, and stir well until it dissolves.

Coconut cream can be added to vegetable curries to give a rich flavour and texture. It can also be made into desserts.

Coconut oil is used as a cooking oil, and gives a light coconut flavour to meat or vegetables cooked in it.

Desiccated coconut is used mainly for making cakes, macaroons and biscuits. Soaked in yoghurt for a time, it makes a delicious topping for soaked dried fruits.

Indonesian salad

A crunchy salad with a rich dressing, best served as a first course.

½ small fresh coconut
1 tablespoon tomato ketchup
½ teaspoon chilli powder
1 garlic clove, crushed with a pinch sea salt
juice ½ lime
½ Chinese cabbage
12 radishes
2 large carrots
½ cucumber

Remove the brown rind from the coconut, and grate the flesh. Mix the tomato ketchup, chilli powder, garlic and lime juice, and mix in the coconut.

Shred the cabbage, thinly slice the radishes, grate the carrots and dice the cucumber. Mix in a salad bowl, and fold in the coconut dressing.

Serves 4.

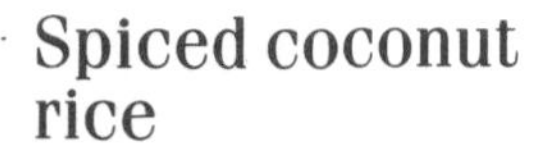

Spiced coconut rice

8 oz (225 g) long grain brown rice
3 tablespoons sunflower oil
1 medium onion, finely chopped
1 garlic clove, finely chopped
3 oz (75 g) desiccated coconut
juice 1 lime
¼ teaspoon chilli powder
1 mango (optional)

An excellent rice dish to serve as an accompaniment to curry.

Cook the rice in 1 pint (575 ml) lightly salted water for 40 minutes, or until tender and all the water is absorbed. Keep warm.

Heat the oil in a frying pan on a high heat and stir-fry the onion and garlic for 1 minute. Add the coconut and cook it, stirring all the time, until it turns a pale gold colour. Mix in the lime juice and chilli powder. Toss the coconut into the rice.

If you are using the mango, chop the flesh and mix it into the rice.

Serves 4.

Coconut cookies

6 oz (175 g) wholemeal flour
1 teaspoon ground mixed spice
4 oz (125 g) butter, softened
4 tablespoons concentrated apple juice
3 oz (75 g) desiccated coconut

These sweet, crumbly biscuits are sugar-free.

Heat the oven to 325F/170C/gas 3. Mix the flour with the mixed spices. Cream the butter, and beat in the flour alternately with the concentrated apple juice. Beat in the coconut.

Roll out the mixture to a thickness of ¼ inch (6 mm), and cut it into circles using a 2-inch (5 cm) cutter. Lay the circles on floured baking sheets, and bake for 20 minutes, or until firm but not coloured.

Makes about 24.

Coconut mousse

one 7 oz (200 g) bar creamed coconut
15 g (½ oz) gelatin
4 tablespoons water
¾ pint (425 ml) natural orange or pineapple juice, or a mixture

Cut the creamed coconut into thin slices. In a small saucepan, soak the gelatin in the water. Put the coconut and fruit juice into another saucepan, and stir on a low heat for the coconut to melt. Melt the gelatin on a low heat, and stir it into the coconut and fruit juice. Take the pan from the heat, pour the mixture into a bowl, and cool until it is on the point of setting.

Whisk the mixture well, preferably with an electric beater, until it looks pale and fluffy, and the coconut and juice are well mixed together. Pour into a serving dish, and refrigerate to set.

Serve plain, or decorated with chopped nuts or fresh fruit.

Serves 6.

HAZEL NUT, COB NUT AND FILBERT

CORYLUS SPECIES

HAZEL NUTS, COB nuts and filberts are all small, round nuts that grow enclosed in a leafy, shaggy-edged casing that looks like a frilled bonnet. Their generic name comes from the Greek, *korys*, which means a hood, and 'hazel', the name for the British wild nut, comes from the Anglo-Saxon *haesil*, meaning head-dress. The nuts have their origins in Britain, Europe, north Africa, Asia and north America. They still grow wild in these countries and, over the years, many varieties have been developed, differing in size, the shape of the husk, the thickness of the shell and also in their keeping qualities.

Hazel nuts, *Corylus avellana*, grow wild in southern Britain. They are very small and round, and their shells are thinner than those of cultivated nuts. They grow in clusters of two or three, each cluster hanging down under an umbrella-like leaf. Hazel nuts ripen in late August and September, and as they are so small they are best eaten fresh, before they have started to dry and shrivel. Do not pick too many at once, since squirrels and dormice rely on them for food.

In medieval and Tudor times, hazel trees were cultivated in gardens, and orchards, but later they were superseded by the improved cultivated types, which are the cob nuts and filberts. **Cob nuts** are round in shape, and their hood does not cover the whole nut. **Filberts** are generally larger and oval, and the hood covers the nut completely. Confusingly, in England the main commercial variety of this type of nut is the **Kent Cob**, which in fact is not a cob at all, but a filbert. It was developed in about 1830 by Mr Lambert of Goudhurst in Kent, and has the charming alternative name of Lambert's Filbert.

Cobs and filberts have always been grown mainly in Kent, but the acreage is a diminishing one. Existing nut plantations, many of which are over 100 years old, give low yields and are uneconomic. The grubbing up of trees to make way for more profitable crops started during the last war, and has carried on ever since.

When Kent Cobs are available, for a few weeks in October, they are sent to the shops exactly as they are when they fall from the tree, still inside their long hoods, and with their thin shells still tinged with green. The nuts fill the shells and are crisp, moist and creamy tasting.

In the weeks coming up to Christmas, the larger varieties of cob nuts, imported mainly from Sicily, fill the shops. They are round, with shiny brown shells, and the kernels are drier than those of locally grown cobs, with a more musty flavour. These are from trees developed in Italy and Spain, which produce larger nuts in warmer climates. The Spanish nuts are said to be of the best quality, with a high oil content which improves their flavour and allows for better storage. According to Spanish legend, lightning can never strike the trees, neither can reptiles hide underneath them, since a hazel tree once gave shelter to the Virgin Mary.

The nuts that we buy ready-shelled are also from this type of tree and, although they are either cobs or filberts, they are still referred to as hazel nuts in the shops. Shelling has little effect on them, and if they are stored well and used quickly shelled hazel nuts taste much the same as those bought in the shells.

Hazel nuts can be bought chopped, in sealed packets, and also chopped and toasted. Hazel nut oil can be bought in specialist shops.

Nutrition

Hazel nuts have a high calcium content, which can be important to vegetarians who eat few dairy products. They also have significant amounts of phosphorus and Vitamin B1. When freshly picked, they also contain some Vitamin C.

Buying and storing hazel nuts

Fresh Kent Cobs, if you are lucky enough to be able to buy any, are best eaten as soon as possible, as the fresher they are the crisper the texture. If you would like to store them for Christmas, strip off the hoods and layer the unshelled nuts in a box between layers of dry sand. If no sand is available, screwed up newspaper makes a good substitute.

Imported nuts, still in their shells, can be kept for several months. Shelled hazel nuts should be stored in an airtight container for no longer than a month.

The chopped and toasted nuts can be kept in their sealed packets for up to a month. Once opened, however, they quickly go rancid, so use them up as soon as possible.

Hazel nuts in the kitchen

Wild hazel nuts and Kent Cobs are used mainly as dessert nuts and one grower has recommended that you should eat them 'in the connoisseurs's way – with port and Stilton cheese'. He is right. They are now so rare that it would be sacrilege to do anything else with them.

Hazel nuts have a good, strong flavour that is excellent with savoury dishes, but which also complements both fruit and chocolate. They can be put whole into salads, but can be very crunchy, so use sparingly. They are excellent with celery and celeriac, with grated carrot and also with apples. The whole nuts make excellent garnishes, both for small salads and for desserts.

Chopped hazel nuts, either bought, or chopped at home using a mezzaluna and bowl or a food processor, can be mixed into salad dressings, and added to mixtures for biscuits, cakes and tea breads. They also add flavour and a crunchy texture to crumble mixtures. Ground hazel nuts can be added to sweet and savoury pastry mixtures, and to cakes. They can also be used as a coating for fish. They are excellent in all vegetarian nut dishes, such as nut roasts and patties, and also in sauces for pasta.

Chopped toasted hazelnuts are used mainly as a garnish for desserts and cakes and can also be added to muesli and crumble mixtures.

Hazel nut oil has a fine, nutty flavour, and is best kept for salads.

Jum-Jills

2 oz (50 g) hazelnuts
2 oz (50 g) Brazil nuts
1 medium onion, finely chopped
3 tablespoons sunflower oil
4 oz (125 g) wholemeal breadcrumbs
1/4 pint (150 ml) stock
2 oz (50 g) sunflower seeds
1 tablespoon chopped thyme
4 sage leaves, chopped
4 oz (125 g) green cabbage, in one piece
3 oz (75 g) Cheddar cheese, grated

In a childrens' story by Wanda G'ag, Bobo, the little old man of the mountains, feeds what he calls Jum-Jills to a vain monster to prevent him from eating dolls. The ingredients were: 'seven nut cakes, five seed puddings, two cabbage salads, and fifteen little cheeses.'

At a request from my daughter, we made up something like them. They won't make your spines grow bigger and your tail grow longer, but they are rather delicious. Serve them like nut cutlets, with potatoes and salad or a green vegetable.

Heat the oven to 350F/180C/gas 4. Finely grind the hazel and Brazil nuts. Heat the oil in a large saucepan on a low heat and soften the onion. Stir in the ground nuts and breadcrumbs. Pour in the stock, and bring it to the boil. Simmer for 1 minute, and take the pan from the heat. Mix in the sunflower seeds and herbs and let the mixture cool.

Cook the cabbage in lightly boiling water for 2 minutes. Drain well, and chop finely. Mix the cabbage and the cheese into the nut mixture. Form the mixture into 16 small balls. Lay them on a greased baking sheet, and bake for 25 minutes, or until golden brown.

Serves 4.

Hazel nut and carob florentines

3 oz (75 g) butter, plus extra for greasing
3 oz (75 g) demerara sugar
4 oz (125 g) hazel nuts, finely chopped
2 oz (50 g) glacé cherries, quartered
1 oz (25 g) candied peel, finely chopped
7 oz (200 g) plain sugar-free carob bar

Serve these rich biscuits at tea time, or after a meal. Sugar-free carob has a very rich flavour, but it is not as sweet and sickly as chocolate. You can, however, substitute plain chocolate.

Heat the oven to 350F/180C/gas 4. Cover 2 large baking sheets with buttered greaseproof paper. Melt the butter and sugar gently together in a small saucepan, and gradually bring to the boil. Take the pan from the heat and mix in the hazel nuts, cherries and candied peel. Divide the mixture into about 20 well-spaced heaps on the greaseproof paper and flatten them slightly. Bake for 10 minutes. They will have spread out considerably, so cut them into perfect rounds with a 3-inch (7.5 cm) biscuit cutter while they are still warm and flexible. Take the biscuits off the trays and lay them, smooth side up, on a clean sheet of greaseproof paper.

Break up the carob, and put it into a double saucepan or into a bowl standing in a saucepan of water. Melt very gently on a low heat, never letting the water underneath boil. Also, be careful not to splash any water into the bowl as this will give the carob an unpleasant, granular texture.

Using a pastry brush, brush a thin layer of carob over the smooth side of each biscuit. Let it cool and set, keeping the rest of the carob warm. Brush on a second layer of carob and leave to set completely.

Makes about 20.

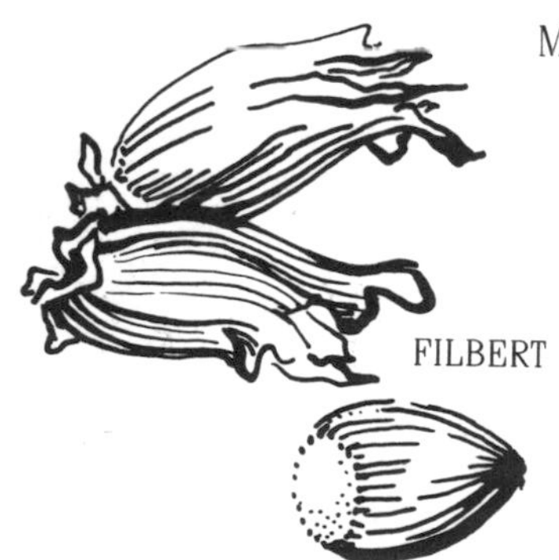

MACADAMIA NUT

MACADAMIA TERNIFOLIA

THE SMALL, ROUND, skinless macadamia nut is a native of Queensland and New South Wales in Australia. It is well known in the United States, but little used in Britain and Europe.

Macadamia nuts have long been collected by the Aborigines, whose name for them is *kindal kindal*. Early settlers first discovered the tall, many-branched trees around 1860, and planted them around their farm houses for shade and for their pink blossoms, as well as for their nuts. The nuts, in their shiny brown shells each covered in a green husk, are quite round.

It was not long before the macadamia nut was taken to other countries with suitable climates, including the West Indies, South Africa, south east Asia, countries around the Mediterranean, the southern United States and also Hawaii, where it has been cultivated on a large scale since 1892.

After picking, the nuts are first dried and then mechanically cracked and graded. Some are sold as they are, and others are very slightly salted.

The kernels of macadamia nuts have no skin and, after shelling, are about the size of large hazel nuts; a rich, creamy colour and quite round, with a very small point on top. When you bite into them, macadamia nuts have a light, crumbly texture but a rich, creamy flavour, and a few will go a long way.

Nutrition

Macadamia nuts have a low protein content, but are rich in oil.

Buying and storing macadamia nuts

Macadamia nuts are mostly available in specialist shops, and can be bought plain or slightly salted. The plain ones are sold loose, and the salted ones often come in sealed foil packs. Use loose nuts within a month. Foil-packed ones will keep for several months unopened, but, once opened, should be used as soon as possible.

If you are unable to buy plain nuts, the salted ones can be used instead as the salting is very light, and the creamy colour and flavour of the nuts is preserved.

Macadamia nuts in the kitchen

Macadamia nuts are very rich, and should be used sparingly. In the United States and Australia, they are a popular accompaniment to pre-dinner drinks. They are excellent in salads, and a few can be ground and added to salad dressings. In south east Asia, ground macadamia nuts are used to thicken soups and spiced savoury dishes. They can be added to creamy textured sauces as a thickener, and also to stuffings for poultry.

Macadamia nuts go well with sweet flavours. They can be added to fruit salads, and the ground nuts can be added to rich pastries, to custards and to custard-based pies such as pumpkin pie. The flavour also goes exceptionally well with chocolate.

Macadamia nut and chickpea salad

8 oz (225 g) long grain brown rice
½ medium honeydew melon
3 oz (75 g) macadamia nuts
6 oz (175 g) chickpeas, soaked, cooked and drained
4 tablespoons natural yoghurt
2 tablespoons olive oil
1 teaspoon curry powder
1 garlic clove, crushed

Chickpeas and macadamia nuts look very similar, and their flavours go together well. The melon in this salad gives a contrasting freshness.

Cook the rice in lightly salted boiling water for 40 minutes, or until tender. Drain, run cold water through it, drain again and cool completely.

Remove rind and seeds from the melon, and dice the flesh. Mix the rice, macadamia nuts, chickpeas and melon. Beat the remaining ingredients together to make the dressing, and fold it into the salad.

Serves 4.

Cauliflower with spiced macadamia nut sauce

1 medium cauliflower
1 bay leaf
4 tablespoons sunflower oil
2 oz (50 g) macadamia nuts, finely chopped
1 teaspoon ground cumin
¼ pint (150 ml) natural yoghurt

An attractive vegetable dish, best served with plainly cooked meats such as grills.

Steam the cauliflower whole, with the bay leaf, for 20 minutes, or until just tender. Remove bay leaf, put the cauliflower on to a serving dish, and keep warm.

Heat the oil in a frying pan on a medium heat. Cook the nuts and cumin, stirring, until the nuts are golden brown. Take the pan from the heat, and cool the nuts for about 30 seconds or until no longer sizzling. Stir in the yoghurt. Pour the hot sauce over the cauliflower.

Serves 4.

PEANUT

ARACHIS HYPOGAEA

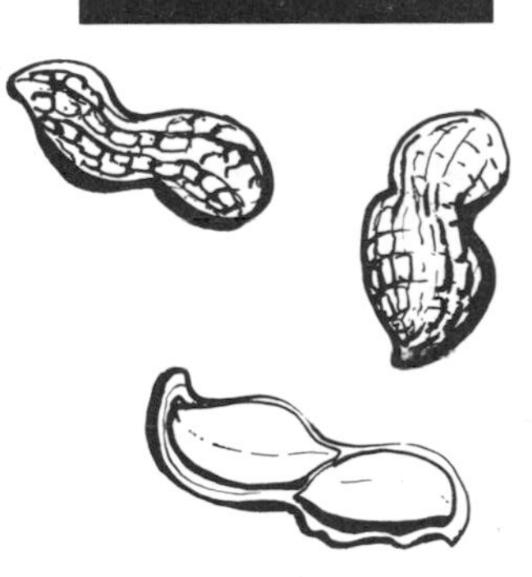

PEANUTS ARE THE most extensively used, and most widely grown, of all the nuts. They are a favourite snack in some countries and a staple food in others, and are eaten whole; ground; and in the form of butter and oil. In fact, they are not nuts at all, but the fruit of a leguminous plant, related to the pea and bean, that grows underground, hence their other names of ground nut and earth nut.

Peanuts have never been found growing wild, but are thought to have originated in South America. They were grown by the Peruvian Incas, and the first Westerners to discover them were the Portuguese, in the sixteenth century, who used them as rations on slave ships and were responsible for taking them to Asia, the Pacific Islands and India and Africa. Peanuts are highly nutritious and easy to grow, and their cultivation rapidly became established wherever the climate was suitable.

In the eighteenth century, peanuts travelled to America with African slaves, who grew them round the doorways of their cabins. Salted peanuts were first eaten in the southern states, and a liking for them was carried home by northern soldiers after the Civil War.

The main peanut producing countries are India, the United States, East and West Africa, and parts of the Far East. All processing, from digging to packing, is mechanically done. The plants are loosened in the soil and pulled up with the nuts still attached. The nuts are stripped from the stems, cleaned, sorted, graded, shelled and packed.

There are many varieties of peanuts, differing in oil content, size, flavour and colour of their skins. Some are small and plump, others long and thin, and some very small and only used locally. Peanuts used for oil production do not have as good a flavour as those that are sold whole. Oil-producing peanuts account for a large percentage of the total world crop.

Half the US crop goes into the the making of peanut butter, and for this a nut with an excellent flavour is required.

Peanuts for the confectionery and snack trade are larger. A few of these are roasted in their shells to give them a rich, toasted flavour, and it is this type that has often been sold along seaside esplanades and at fairs. Shelled, unskinned nuts are often sold in health food shops. For salting and dry roasting, the nuts are skinned.

Nutrition

Peanuts are high in protein, and rich in potassium, calcium, phosphorus and magnesium. They also have significant amounts of Vitamins B and E.

Buying and storing peanuts

For culinary use, buy peanuts that have been shelled but not skinned. The larger the nuts the better, since there will be more kernel in proportion to skin. Shelled peanuts keep for up to two months in an airtight container.

Peanuts in the kitchen

Peanuts are an extremely versatile and cheap ingredient to have in store.

They add interest, flavour, texture and extra protein to salads and hot dishes of cooked grains and can be stir-fried with vegetables or meat. Peanuts can be chopped or ground for mixing into vegetarian dishes such as nut roasts, or using in pastry and crumble mixtures, biscuits, cakes and tea-breads.

There are both smooth and chunky versions of peanut butter, and you can buy these or make your own. Spread 8 oz (225 g) of shelled peanuts on a baking tray, and roast at 250F/120C/gas ½ for 20 minutes. Cool, and rub off all the skins. Put the nuts into a blender or food processor, and work them until they are finely ground, easing them from the sides when necessary. Add two tablespoons of ground nut oil, and work again to a smooth paste.

Peanut butter sandwiches are always popular with children, and you can add chopped dates or a smearing of yeast extract. Peanut butter can also be used to make richly flavoured salad dressings. Put one tablespoon into a bowl and gradually work in four tablespoons ground nut oil and two tablespoons vinegar.

Peanut oil, called ground nut oil, is pale and clear with a very mild flavour. Use it for stir-frying, for frying the ingredients in curries and other spiced dishes, and for salad dressings.

Gala nut loaf

8 oz (225 g) shelled, unroasted peanuts
4 oz (125 g) Brazil nuts
4 oz (125 g) hazelnuts
8 oz (225 g) wholemeal bread
4 tablespoons sunflower oil, plus extra for greasing
2 medium onions, finely chopped
1½ tablespoons yeast extract
2 tablespoons tomato purée
6 fl oz (175 ml) stock, boiling
1 tablespoon dried mixed herbs
4 small eggs, hard-boiled

A delicious vegetarian equivalent to the gala pork pie.

Heat the oven to 350F/180C/gas 4. Grind the nuts and the bread together. Heat the oil in a frying pan on a low heat and soften the onions. Mix in the nuts and breadcrumbs and herbs, and take the pan from the heat. Dissolve the yeast extract and tomato purée in the stock. Stir the mixture into the nuts.

Put about one-third of the mixture into the bottom of a greased, 2-lb (900 g) loaf tin. Place the eggs in a row on top and cover them completely with the remaining mixture. Bake the loaf for 30 minutes, or until browned and set. Cool in the tin, before carefully turning out.

Serves 6–8.

Stir-fried beef with peanuts

1 small head celery
1 tablespoon crunchy peanut butter
¼ pint (150 ml) tomato juice
1 garlic clove, crushed with a pinch sea salt
pinch cayenne pepper
2 large oranges
2 tablespoons ground nut or sunflower oil
1 large onion, finely chopped
2 oz (50 g) shelled, unroasted peanuts
1 lb (450 g) minced beef

A rich, quickly prepared and economical dish.

Finely chop the celery. Mix the peanut butter, tomato juice, garlic and cayenne pepper. Cut the rind and pith from the oranges. Quarter the flesh lengthways, and cut the quarters into thin slices.

Heat the oil in a large frying pan on a high heat and stir-fry the onion, celery and peanuts for 2 minutes. Add the beef, and stir-fry until browned. Lower the heat, and cook for 2 minutes more. Pour in the peanut butter mixture, and bring to the boil. Mix in the oranges, and stir for 1 minute for them to heat through.

Serves 4.

PECAN NUT

CARYA PECAN

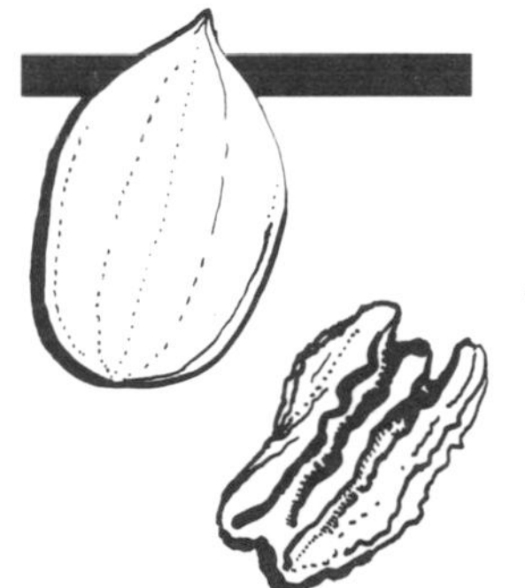

THE PECAN IS essentially an American nut and its name comes from an American Indian word meaning 'nut with a hard shell to crack'. Its kernel is like an elongated walnut kernel, but the flavour is sweeter than that of a walnut. Its shell is long and oval, completely smooth, and a deep red-brown.

Pecan trees came originally from the Mississippi Valley, and were semi-cultivated by many Indian tribes who, according to one sixteenth century Spanish explorer, lived on nothing but the nuts for two months in the year. The Indians were nomadic, but always returned to the same camp sites where they planted pecan seedlings, to ensure good nut supplies in future years.

Early settlers in America soon discovered pecan nuts for themselves. At first they gathered the wild nuts, and later established their own nut plantations. Commercial production began around 1800.

The shell of the original pecan nut was, as the Indians had described it, thick and hard to crack. What was needed was a thin shelled nut with the same sweet kernel. Various attempts were made at producing this, but they were unsuccessful until a freed negro slave by the name of Antoine perfected the technique of grafting in Louisiana in 1846 and produced a variety known as Centenniel. All the modern, thin shelled varieties were developed from this. The wild pecan is now known as the Seedling Pecan, and can still be found growing along river valleys.

Pecans are now grown commercially throughout the southern half of the United States, as well as in Australia and South Africa. When the nuts are ripe, canvas sheets are laid under the trees and the trees are beaten or shaken so the nuts drop off. They are partially dried before the outer husks, which are split into four pieces, are removed. The nuts are then polished by steel brushes rotating in drums of sand and, to make the outer shell more attractive, are bleached and then dipped in a red-brown dye.

Nutrition

Pecan nuts are high in protein, but must be combined with a whole grain product or other first class protein such as eggs or cheese, if they are to be the base of a vegetarian meal. They have significant amounts of some B Vitamins plus iron, calcium, potassium and phosphorus.

Buying and storing pecan nuts

Pecan nuts in their shells can be bought around Christmas time. The shells should be shiny and undamaged, and the nuts will keep for up to two months in a cool place.

Shelled pecan nuts are usually sold in halves, although broken nuts, which are excellent if they are to be chopped or ground, are also available.

Shelled pecans should be kept for no longer than one month in an air-tight container.

Pecan nuts in the kitchen

With their dark brown colour and attractive long shape, halved pecan nuts are often used as a garnish for both desserts and savoury dishes, such as nut roasts, pâtés and salads. The traditional American pecan pie is made with the halved nuts baked in pastry in a rich custard mixture.

Chopped pecan nuts can be used like walnuts, in salads, stuffings, cakes, tea-breads and biscuits, and also in ice-cream, toffee and fudge. Ground, they can be added to nut roast mixtures.

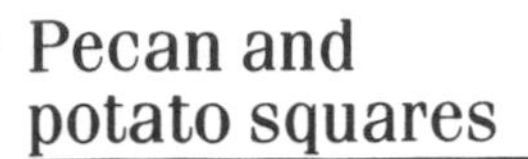

Pecan and potato squares

4 oz (125 g) pecan nuts, plus 12 extra for garnish
1½ lb (675 g) potatoes
2 oz (50 g) butter, plus extra for greasing
3 oz (75 g) Cheddar cheese, grated
1½ oz (45 g) wholemeal flour
1 teaspoon bicarbonate of soda
1 egg, beaten
1 medium onion, finely chopped
4 oz (125 g) mushrooms, finely chopped
8 oz (225 g) French beans
1 tablespoon chopped thyme
2 tablespoons chopped parsley

An all-in-one vegetarian meal that is excellent served hot, or which can be cooled and put in a lunch box. Serve it with a salad.

Heat the oven to 400F/200C/gas 6. Grind the pecan nuts. Peel, boil and drain the potatoes. Mash them, and beat in half the butter, the cheese, flour, bicarbonate of soda and egg. Mix in the nuts.

Melt the remaining butter on a low heat and soften the onion. Add the mushrooms, and cook for 2 minutes more. Cook the beans in lightly salted water for 7 minutes, or until just tender, and chop finely. Mix the onion, mushrooms, beans and herbs into the potato mixture.

Put the mixture into a buttered 8 by 10 inch (20 by 25 cm) tin and score it into 12 squares. Put a pecan half on each square.

Bake for 30 minutes, or until set and browned.

Serves 4.

Honeyed pecan pie

shortcrust pastry made with 6 oz (175 g) wholemeal flour
4 eggs, beaten
1 tablespoon wholemeal flour
1 oz (25 g) butter, melted and cooled
¼ teaspoon fine sea salt
1 teaspoon vanilla essence
6 oz (175 g) honey, melted
8 oz (225 g) pecan halves

There is no better use for pecan nuts than to put them into a traditional American pecan pie. The creamy nuts are set in a sweet, thick custard mixture.

Heat the oven to 375F/190C/gas 5. Line an 8-inch (20 cm) diameter tart tin with the pastry.

Using an electric beater if possible, beat the eggs and then beat in all the remaining ingredients, apart from the pecan halves. Lay the pecan halves in the pastry base and pour the egg mixture over them.

Bake for 40 minutes, or until the filling is set, but not too browned on top.

Serves 6.

PINE NUTS

PINUS PINEA

THE SMALL, AROMATIC, creamy textured pine nut is the edible seed of a pine tree. It is the most expensive nut in the world, second only to saffron and truffles when priced according to weight.

There are about eighteen pine trees that have edible nuts, and these can be found in central and southern Europe, India, Mexico, the United States, Korea, China and Siberia. The seeds vary in size and taste, but the most favoured are the mild seeds of the Stone Pine tree, which grows in Italy and Spain and looks, in silhouette, like an enormous umbrella. The nuts are about ½ inch (1.3 cm) long and tear-drop shaped, cream in colour, and with a smooth, crumbly texture.

Pine nuts have been gathered all over the world since the Mesolithic Age, 12,000 years ago. They have been found, unshelled, in the tombs of the Pharaohs; preserved in honey in the ruins of Pompeii; and the empty cones have been found in Britain, on sites of Roman rubbish tips. American Indians valued the pine nut. They gathered it not only from the tree, but by raiding the stores of the pack rat and replacing the pine nuts they found there with maize.

The cones of the Stone Pine are 4–6 inches (10–15 cm) high, and look exactly like miniature pineapples. On the outside, the cone is patterned like a pineapple, and the kernels are nestling inside each tightly closed section. As the cone ripens, the sections gradually open to reveal the tiny nuts in light brown shells.

The cones are difficult to collect, as they grow in the tops of the trees at the ends of the strongest branches. The trees grow on steep slopes, so any form of mechanisation is impossible. In Spain, the cones are gathered between November and March during periods of dry weather, and left in small heaps throughout the spring and summer so the sun can fully open them and make the seeds accessible. In Italy, the cones are left to dry in sheds. The seeds are removed either by hand or machine, but the kernels are always extracted mechanically.

Each metric tonne of cones yields only 38 kg of shelled kernels. Because of this, the difficult picking, and the fact that the trees are highly susceptible to forest fires, pine kernels will remain a luxury.

Nutrition

Pine kernels are rich in oil, protein and carbohydrate, and contain significant amounts of B Vitamins.

Buying and storing pine nuts

Pine nuts should smell fresh, sweet and aromatic, and should have a crumbly, fairly soft texture. They should be kept for no longer than one month, in an air-tight container. If kept for too long, they may become resinous and unpleasant.

Pine nuts in the kitchen

Pine nuts are normally used whole, rather than ground or chopped. They can be added to salads and sprinkled over fruit. They are good in quiches, vegetable pies and nut roasts, and can be sautéed with chicken, and added to savoury rice dishes.

Pine nut sauce for pasta

A rich, tomato flavoured sauce, that turns plain pasta into a main meal.

6 tablespoons (90 ml) olive oil
1½ lb (675 g) onions, thinly sliced
2 garlic cloves, finely chopped
1 pint (575 ml) tomato juice
2 tablespoons chopped basil
4 oz (125 g) pine nuts

Heat the oil in a saucepan on a low heat. Mix in the onions and garlic. Cover, and cook very gently for 30 minutes, stirring occasionally, so they soften but do not colour. Pour in the tomato juice, and bring to the boil. Add the basil. Simmer, uncovered, for 5 minutes. Finely grind the pine nuts, and mix into the sauce just before serving.

Serves 4.

Pine nut shortbreads

These are rather like a cross between pastries and biscuits; sweet, light and crumbly.

8 oz (225 g) wholemeal flour
1 teaspoon baking powder
1 teaspoon ground cinnamon
grated rind 1 lemon
5 oz (150 g) butter
4 oz (125 g) golden caster sugar
1 egg, beaten
3 tablespoons clear honey
3 oz (75 g) pine nuts

Heat the oven to 350F/180C/gas 4. Put the flour into a bowl with the baking powder, cinnamon and lemon rind. Add the butter, in small pieces, and rub it into the flour until the mixture resembles fine breadcrumbs. Mix in the sugar and bind everything together with the beaten egg. Knead the dough with your hands, until it becomes smooth and elastic. Leave it in a cool place for 30 minutes.

Divide the dough into two. Roll one portion into a 10 inch (25 cm) square and lay it on a baking sheet (it will spread as it cooks). Spread it with the honey, and scatter the pine nuts over the top. Roll out the second piece of dough into a 10 inch (25 cm) square, and lay it over the pine nuts. Trim the edges to neaten.

Bake the shortbread for 15 minutes, or until golden brown. Cut it into 2-inch (5 cm) squares as soon as it comes out of the oven, but leave it on the baking sheet to cool.

Makes about 36 squares.

PISTACHIO NUT

PISTACIA VERA

SMALL, GREEN PISTACHIO nuts are an ancient symbol of happiness, and lovers meeting under the trees were said to have lasting joy. They have also been much coveted and fought over by nomads, claiming rites of collection.

The pistachio tree has its origins in the mountainous regions of Afghanistan, Russian Turkestan and parts of western Asia, and it has also been cultivated around the Mediterranean for many thousands of years. The nuts have been greatly prized by nomadic peoples in Afghanistan and northern Iran, where they have been an important winter food.

Pistachio nuts were enjoyed by the Queen of Sheba, and were taken to Rome by Lucius Vitellius, the governor of Syria. The Romans were quick to cultivate pistachio trees, and their cultivation spread to Spain and North Africa. They are still grown in the same areas, as well as in Turkey, Greece, Sicily, France, India and the United States.

There are only a few varieties of pistachio nut, differing in the size, colour and shape of the nuts. The nuts are small, about ½ inch (1.3 cm) long when shelled, slightly curved, and with a green skin flushed with purple. The kernels of the best nuts are also green, although some are paler than others. Pistachio nuts have a soft texture, and mild flavour. In all cases, the cultivated nuts are considered superior to the wild kinds, which can be small and have a turpentine flavour. Those from Iran are said to be the best of all.

Pistachio trees are small, shed their leaves in winter and bear sweetly scented blossoms before the new leaves appear in the spring. The green-shelled nuts look rather like olives and grow in grape-like clusters. As they ripen, the husk begins to shrivel and turn yellow, and finally splits open so the nuts look as though they are laughing. Once picked, the nuts are spread out in the shade to dry, and the husks turn a pale biscuit colour.

Nutrition

Pistachio nuts contain less protein than peanuts. They have a small Vitamin A content.

Buying and storing pistachio nuts

Pistachio nuts can be bought both shelled and unshelled. Those still in the shell may be salted, so read the label if you need plain ones for cooking. Unshelled nuts are used mainly for savoury snacks. If you need the nuts for cooking, buy shelled ones if you can, to save time and trouble.

Pistachio nuts keep for up to a month in an air-tight container.

Pistachio nuts in the kitchen

Because they are tiny, soft and colourful, pistachio nuts are used as much for their appearance as for their flavour. They are often added to savoury rice dishes, pâtés and terrines, meat loaves and stuffings, as well as fruit jellies and ice-creams. In Greece they are used as a filling for pastries and in Europe in confectionery such as nougat.

In the Middle East, pistachio nuts either plain, roasted and salted or fried in butter are served as a snack in bars and sold in the streets.

Pork, apricot and pistachio nut terrine

A simple, tasty terrine, that can be served as a main dish, or as part of a cold buffet.

4 dried whole apricots
¼ pint (150 ml) dry cider or natural apple juice
2 lb (900 g) lean boneless pork
1½ oz pistachio nuts
1 tablespoon chopped marjoram
1 tablespoon chopped thyme
2 tablespoons chopped parsley
½ teaspoon ground mace
½ teaspoon ground allspice

Soak the apricots in the apple juice or cider for 8 hours. Drain and chop finely.

Heat the oven to 375F/190C/gas 5. Mince the pork, and mix it with the remaining ingredients. Put the mixture into a 2 lb (900 g) loaf tin, and cook for 1 hour, or until the terrine is cooked through and slightly browned on top. Cool completely in the tin before turning out.

Serves 6–8.

Pistachio and honey ice-cream

3/4 pint (425 ml) double cream
1/2 teaspoon vanilla essence
1/2 pint (275 ml) Greek-style natural yoghurt
4 egg yolks
3 oz (75 g) honey
3 fl oz (90 ml) water
2 oz (50 g) pistachio nuts, skinned

A very rich ice-cream for special occasions.

Lightly whip the cream with the vanilla essence. Mix it with the yoghurt. Whip the egg yolks until thick. Put the honey and water into a saucepan, and set on a low heat for the honey to dissolve. Bring to the boil, and boil for 2 minutes. Take the pan from the heat and wait until the syrup has stopped bubbling. Whisk the syrup, in a thin stream, into the egg yolks. Whisk in the cream and yoghurt.

To freeze, either use an ice-cream machine, or put the mixture into a freezing tray and put it into the coldest part of the freezer, or into the ice compartment of the refrigerator set at the coldest temperature. Freeze for 2 hours. Whip again, and mix in the pistachio nuts. Put the ice-cream into a rigid plastic container, cover, and freeze for 3 hours.

Serves 6.

WALNUT

JUGLANS REGIA AND OTHER SPECIES

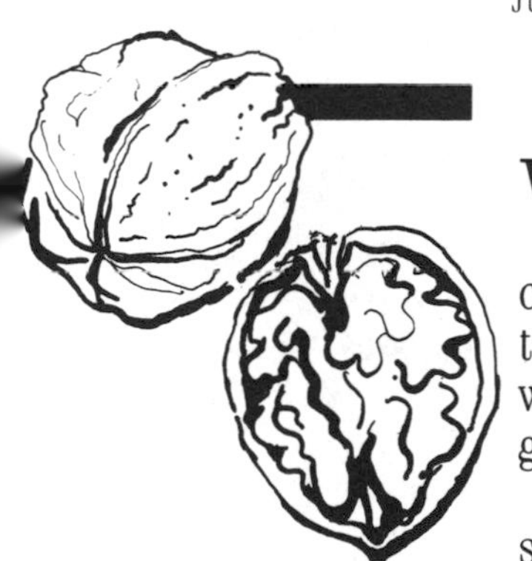

WALNUTS, TOGETHER WITH almonds, have been the nut most widely used in European countries since early times. The trees thrive in temperate climates, although a certain degree of warmth is needed if the nuts are to be large and of good quality.

Walnuts came originally from an area stretching from south eastern Europe through to Afghanistan and India. There is also a type native to the United States.

Walnuts were much loved by the ancient Greeks and Romans. The Greeks dedicated them to Diana, and held feasts beneath the trees. They called the nuts 'caryon nuts' from their word *kara* which means head, because of the likeness of the shell and convoluted kernels to the skull and brain.

Walnuts have always been a sign of fertility and happy marriage, because the two halves of the shell are so closely united. Roman bridegrooms threw them to young boys at weddings to ensure fertility, and show that they had left childish things behind.

It was the Romans who first introduced the walnut tree to France and Britain and, although it quickly became established here, the Anglo-Saxons still called it the 'wealh-nut', meaning foreign nut. Walnuts have never been planted in vast quantities in Britain. In medieval times, some were grown with fruit in orchards but they have mainly been a farm and garden tree, grown near dwellings and outbuildings for family use. Many also became wild, but these are becoming increasingly difficult to find.

In medieval times, eating walnuts at the end of a meal was thought to close the stomach and aid digestion, and walnut milk, made like almond milk, was given to babies after weaning besides being used in the kitchen. Walnuts were candied in sugar, and crushed with garlic, pepper and breadcrumbs to make a sauce for salt fish. When young, soft and green, the nuts were pickled in their outer husks to be eaten with bread and cheese and, in the eighteenth century, they were an ingredient in spiced ketchups. In Victorian times, the freshly picked nuts, still in their shells but with their outer husks removed, were piled high on decorative dishes and served with the dessert. The anti-scorbutic properties of the green husks have been known for centuries, and in country districts they have been boiled with honey to make a cure for sore throats and coughs.

English walnuts have never grown as prolifically as those in warmer climates. Even in medieval times, some nuts had to be imported and those that we find in the shops at Christmas come from France, Italy, China and California. Walnuts are also commercially grown in Roumania. Even in these countries, walnuts are not grown over large acreages.

English nuts are small, and slightly more oval than foreign varieties. Their shells are a light buff colour, with dark stains from the outer husks which are usually removed by hand. Few reach the general market but some arrive in local shops. They are mainly sold 'wet', that is, untreated and with the kernels still white, milky and crisp, and are an absolute treat.

In warmer countries, harvesting does not take place until walnuts are fully ripe and their thick, outer husks begin to split. If the season has been too dry and this does not happen, they are referred to as 'sticktights'. In machines, ethylene gas helps in the removal of the husks, and the nuts are then washed. They are dried either in the sun or, mostly, in hot air dryers, immersed in a bleaching solution and then graded.

Commercially dried nuts, still in their shell, have a mustier flavour than home-grown 'wet' ones, and their kernels are pale yellow. They are still quite crisp, however, and have a fresher flavour than nuts that are sold shelled.

Jars of pickled, immature walnuts, still in their husks are produced in Britain. The oil made from walnuts is expensive, but has a very fine flavour. It was once only available in specialist shops, but an own-label brand is now being stocked by a large supermarket chain.

Nutrition

Walnuts are high in oil and protein, but must be combined with a whole grain if they are to make a protein meal. They contain large amounts of potassium and phosphorus and some B Vitamins. 'Wet' walnuts contain a little Vitamin C but this disappears when the nuts are dried.

Gathering, buying and storing walnuts

If you are lucky enough to be able to gather fresh walnuts, you can either pick them young for pickling or wait until they are ripe enough for the kernels to be eaten alone. Walnuts for pickling should be gathered in early July, when the husks are green, and you can easily stick a pin right through to the centre of the nut without meeting any resistance from the shell.

If you want the ripe kernels, wait until late September or early October when the nuts fall naturally from the trees. Shaking the branches or beating the tree is the traditional way to make them fall off. To remove the outer husks, wear protective gloves or else your hands will be stained brown. Slit the husks all around with a small, sharp knife and gently prise them away from the shells. Using a soft nailbrush and warm water, scrub off any pieces that remain as they can go mouldy.

If you wish to store nuts until Christmas, layer them in a box with dry sand, sawdust or screwed up newspaper, sprinkling salt over each layer. This will keep them moist.

Commercially grown walnuts can be bought in November and December and, if stored in a cool place until needed, will stay in good condition for up the three months.

Shelled nuts quickly lose their flavour and may become rancid. Store them in an air-tight container for no longer than a month. Buy half nuts for garnishing, and pieces for any recipe where they need to be chopped or ground.

Walnuts in the kitchen

'Wet' walnuts are usually kept for dessert purposes, but, if you have enough and have the time to shell them first, they can be used in any recipe that calls for walnuts. They are particularly good in salads and in France are chopped and mixed with chopped shallots, vinegar and the juice of green grapes.

Half walnuts make attractive decorations for cakes and desserts and can be used to garnish salads, savoury pies and quiches. Chopped walnuts can be mixed into ice-creams, cakes, breads, biscuits and tea-breads, and added to salads, stuffings, meat stews and sauté dishes.

Ground nuts make an excellent addition to nut roasts and other similar vegetarian dishes, and can also be used in pastry and shortbread mixtures. Pounded with walnut or olive oil, vinegar and herbs, they make a rich dressing for salads or pasta which is particularly good when made with 'wet' walnuts.

Pickled walnuts are excellent with cheese and beer. They can be used as a garnish for cold meats, and chopped and added to salads, stuffings and sauté dishes.

Walnut oil has a rich, nutty flavour and is best kept for salads. It can be pounded with the nuts to make a dressing.

Avocados with walnut filling

2 ripe avocados
10 wet walnuts, or 2 oz (50 g) shelled walnuts
1 garlic clove, finely chopped
2 tablespoons walnut oil (or olive oil)
2 tablespoons white wine vinegar
freshly ground black pepper
2 tablespoons chopped parsley

A recipe for 'wet' walnuts, although shelled ones may be used.

Cut the avocados in half and remove the stones. Put each one into a small dish. Shell the walnuts. Reserve 4 of the best halves and chop the rest. Using a pestle and mortar, pound the chopped walnuts to a paste, adding the garlic when they begin to break up. Add the oil, vinegar and pepper. Pound again to mix well, and mix in the parsley.

Fill the centres of the avocados with the walnut mixture. Top with the remaining walnut halves.

Serves 4 as a first course; 2 as a main course with a salad.

Chicken liver, bacon and walnut pâté

4 oz (125 g) chicken livers
4 oz (125 g) streaky bacon rashers, rinds removed
2½ oz (65 g) walnuts
1 garlic clove
freshly ground black pepper
1 tablespoon brandy
1 teaspoon dried sage

A very rich pâté, best served with a salad or bread for lunch rather than as a first course.

Heat the oven to 350F/180C/gas 4. Either put the livers, bacon, nuts and garlic twice through the coarse blade of a mincer; or chop very finely in a food processor. Beat in a liberal amount of pepper, the brandy and sage.

Put the mixture into a small, earthenware terrine or other small ovenproof dish, and cover. Stand the dish in a roasting tin filled with water to come half way up the sides. Bake for 1 hour.

Serves 6.

Mackerel with pickled walnuts and anchovies

2 medium-large mackerel
approximately 4 tablespoons wholemeal flour
freshly ground black pepper
1½ oz (45 g) butter
¼ pint (150 ml) dry red wine
2 anchovy fillets, pounded to a paste
4 pickled walnuts, finely chopped
2 tablespoons chopped parsley

A dish with the flavour of the eighteenth century. The walnuts add a slight sharpness but, once simmered, are far less vinegary than when eaten from the jar.

Fillet the mackerel. Season the flour with the pepper and use it to coat the fillets.

Melt half the butter in a frying pan on a moderate heat. Cook two of the mackerel fillets, skin side down first, until they are golden brown. Turn, and cook the other side. Remove to a serving dish and keep them warm. Cook the others in the same way. Pour the wine into the pan. Bring it to the boil and stir in the anchovies, walnuts and parsley. Simmer the sauce for 1 minute, and spoon over the mackerel.

Serves 4.

Spiced honey and walnut cake

4 oz (125 g) butter, softened, plus extra for greasing
8 oz (225 g) honey
2 eggs, beaten
8 oz (225 g) wholemeal flour
1 teaspoon ground cinnamon
3 oz (75 g) walnuts, chopped
2 oz (50 g) sultanas

A sweetly spiced, moist cake that needs no decoration.

Heat the oven to 325F/170Cgas 3. Butter a 1-lb (450 g) loaf tin. Cream the butter, beat in the honey and then the eggs, a little at a time. Mix the flour with the cinnamon, and beat it into the butter and eggs. Fold in the walnuts and sultanas.

Put the mixture into the prepared tin. Bake the cake for 50 minutes, or until a skewer inserted into the centre comes out clean. Turn on to a wire rack to cool completely.

SEEDS

Poppy seeds,
Pumpkin seeds,
Sesame seeds,
Sunflower seeds,
Water melon seeds

MANY SMALL SEEDS are grown throughout the world, which are just as nutritious as nuts. Some are used locally, others can be bought in Britain in specialist shops and health food shops.

POPPY SEEDS

PAPAVER SOMNIFERUM

The poppy seeds used in cooking are the seeds of the opium poppy, which is probably a native of central Europe. A resin produced by slitting the seed heads has been used as a sleep-inducing drug since classical times, but the seeds have no such effect and have been eaten since 800 AD in India and China.

There are two types of poppy seed, both very tiny and round, with a creamy, nutty flavour. One is dark grey-blue and the other a pale cream colour.

The dark poppy seeds are used most often for sprinkling over bread and pastries, and can also be added to cheesecake mixtures. The pale types are used more in India. They are ground and added to curry powders and spice mixtures such as garam masala, and are also used as a thickening agent in savoury dishes.

PUMPKIN SEEDS

Special pumpkins are grown to produce edible seeds, which do not have thick husks. The seeds are dark green, flat and oval and have a rich, creamy flavour. They can be eaten as they are, or fried in a little oil and rolled in salt. Used whole, they make an interesting ingredient in loaves made with ground nuts. They can also be added to salads.

SESAME SEEDS

Sesame seeds are probably the best known of all the seeds. They are very tiny, only about ⅛ inch (1.5 mm) long, pale brown or cream coloured and almond-shaped. They came originally from Africa, but have been grown for many centuries in India and China, and are now grown in tropical and sub-tropical climates all over the world.

Sesame plants are about 6 feet (2 metres) high, and are cut down when the seeds are ripe and arranged upright in stacks. When they have dried, the plants are turned upside down so that the seeds can be shaken free.

Sesame seeds are often sprinkled over breads and buns, and can be added to pastry mixes. Use them in savoury stuffings, in fillings for baked apples, or press them all over a nut roast. Mix them into rice or grains just before the end of the cooking time.

For use in salads, sesame seeds are best toasted to draw out their nutty flavour. Put them into a heavy frying pan without any fat, and stir them on a medium heat until they brown, smell rich and start to jump. Tip them on to a plate to cool.

Roasted with an equal portion of sea salt and then ground, sesame seeds make sesame salt. It can be used in salads and cooked dishes as a salt substitute.

In Greece and the Middle East, sesame seeds are ground to make a rich nut butter known as tahini. There are two kinds, one dark grey and one a pale biscuit colour. The paler one has the finer flavour.

Tahini is added with lemon juice and garlic to mashed chickpeas, to make the dip known as hummus. It can also be added to nut roasts. Tahini can be used plain as a spread for bread, very much like peanut butter, or can be mixed in equal amounts with soy sauce. To make a rich salad dressing, put one tablespoon of tahini into a bowl, and gradually beat in four tablespoons of sesame or olive oil, and two tablespoons of vinegar. Tahini is an ingredient of the sweetmeat known as halva, which is made in Greece.

Sesame seeds contain around 50 per cent oil, and this is extracted by cold pressing. Unrefined sesame oil is a rich, golden colour with a nutty flavour and is high in polyunsaturates. It keeps well because it contains a natural preservative known as sesamolin. It is used for cooking savoury dishes in India and Mexico, and in China a few drops are poured over certain dishes to flavour and enrich them after they are cooked. It is also an excellent salad oil, and can be used in baking.

SUNFLOWER SEEDS

HELIANTHUS ANNUUS

Sunflower seeds cannot be extracted from the sunflowers that grow in British gardens, but come from a particular species that is commercially grown. The origin of the sunflower is unclear, but it could have come originally from South America. It has been cultivated in Europe since the sixteenth century, and large quantities of the seed-producing types have been grown in Russia since then, mainly for oil.

Sunflower seeds are about ⅜ inch (1 cm) long, flat, grey and almond-shaped. They have a soft texture and sweet, mild flavour. They are popular in Spain, where they are salted and eaten like peanuts.

Sunflower seeds can be scattered into salads, mixed into biscuits, and added to nut roast mixtures. They can also be sprinkled over fruit salads and other desserts as a garnish. Ground, they can be used in a pastry mix. To roast sunflower seeds to serve as a snack, stir them in a bowl with a little soy sauce, just enough to coat them. Spread on a baking tray, and roast in a medium oven for 10 minutes or until dry. Tip them out to cool, and eat like salted peanuts.

Sunflower oil, because of its high level of polyunsaturated fats, has recently become one of our most popular cooking oils. It has a pleasant, mild flavour, and can be used for stir-frying, sautéeing, deep frying and even for frying eggs. It does not have the same rich flavour as olive oil, for salad dressings, but does make an excellent mayonnaise. It can also be used in cake and pastry mixtures.

WATER MELON SEEDS

CITRULLUS VULGARIS

Water melon seeds are popular in southern China, Java and tropical west Africa, where the melons are grown solely for their seeds. Special varieties of water melon have been developed for seed collection. When ripe, they are placed in heaps until the pulp ferments and the seeds can easily be extracted.

There are various types of melon seeds, white, yellow, black and red. The white and black types are those usually found in Britain, and they can be bought in health food shops and Chinese shops.

Cheese and poppy seed savouries

3 oz (75 g) wholemeal flour
2 oz (50 g) butter, softened
2 tablespoons poppy seeds
3 oz (75 g) Cheddar cheese, finely grated

Thin, crumbly biscuits to eat as a snack.

Heat the oven to 375F/190C/gas 5. Put the flour into a bowl. Add the butter, in small pieces, and rub it into the flour. Add the poppy seeds. Mix in the cheese, and press the mixture together to make a dough. Chill for 30 minutes.

Roll out the dough very thinly, and cut it into small triangles or squares. Lay them on floured baking sheets, and bake for 10 minutes or until golden brown. Cool on a wire rack.

Makes about 50.

Poppy seed rolls

6 oz (175 g) wholemeal flour
4 oz (125 g) strong, plain flour
1 teaspoon fine sea salt
3 fl oz (90 ml) milk
1 oz (25 g) butter
½ oz (15 g) fresh yeast, or 1 tablespoon dried
4 tablespoons honey
2 eggs, beaten separately
2 oz (50 g) poppy seeds

Semi-sweet, yeasted pastry rolls that are good eaten for breakfast, or as a mid-morning snack.

Mix the flours and the salt. Gently warm the milk, add the butter and, off the heat, stir for it to dissolve. Tip the milk mixture into a bowl and, when it has cooled to blood heat, stir in the yeast. If you are using dried yeast, add 1 teaspoon of the honey. Leave the yeast in a warm place to froth. When ready, tip it into the flour and add one of the eggs and 2 tablespoons of the honey. Mix to a dough. Turn on to a floured board and knead until smooth. Return to the bowl, make a cross-cut in the top, and cover with a clean tea cloth. Leave in a warm place for 1 hour to double in size.

Heat the oven to 400F/200C/gas 6. Knead the dough again, and roll out into a rectangle about 16 inches by 8 inches (40 cm by 20 cm). Mix the poppy seeds with the remaining honey and spoon them in a thin line down one long side of the dough. Roll up the dough from that side, brush with the remaining egg, and cut into 1-inch (2.5 cm) thick slices. Lay on a baking sheet. Leave in a warm place for 30 minutes to prove. Bake for 15 minutes, or until beginning to brown but still soft in the middle. Cool on a baking sheet.

Makes 16.

Gently curried mango

2 ripe mangoes
½ pint (275 ml) thick yoghurt
1 teaspoon hot Madras curry powder
2 oz (50 g) melon seeds

A simply prepared but exotic first course, to freshen the palate before a meal.

Dice the mango flesh (for how to prepare a mango, see page 131) and divide it between four small bowls. Spoon the yoghurt over the top and sprinkle with the curry powder. Scatter the melon seeds over the top.

Serves 4.

Satsuma and sesame salad

1 small lettuce
4 satsumas
4 celery sticks
2 tablespoons tahini
4 tablespoons olive oil
2 tablespoons white wine vinegar
1 garlic clove, crushed with pinch sea salt
freshly ground black pepper
2 tablespoons sesame seeds

A refreshing and crisp first course salad, with a nutty dressing.

Arrange a bed of lettuce on four small plates. Pull the satsumas into segments and finely chop the celery. Pile on top of the lettuce.

Put the tahini into a bowl and very gradually beat in first the oil, and then the vinegar. Mix in the garlic and pepper. Spoon over the satsumas and celery, and scatter the sesame seeds over the top.

Serves 4.

Sunflower and leek pudding

12 oz (350 g) leeks
1 oz (25 g) butter
4 eggs, beaten
½ pint (275 ml) milk
3 oz (75 g) Cheddar cheese, grated
2 tablespoons tomato purée
½ teaspoon mustard powder
4 oz (125 g) fresh wholemeal breadcrumbs
4 oz (125 g) sunflower seeds

A substantial, all-in-one family meal. Serve it with a salad.

Heat the oven to 400F/200C/gas 6. Chop the leeks, and soften in the butter on a low heat. Beat the eggs and mix with the milk. Mix in all the remaining ingredients, including the leeks.

Put the mixture into a heatproof dish and bake for 25 minutes, or until set, risen and golden brown on top.

Serves 4.

Pumpkin seed omelette

2 oz (50 g) Brazil nuts
2 oz (50 g) hazel nuts
6 eggs
2 oz (50 g) pumpkin seeds
1 tablespoon tomato purée
1 tablespoon chopped thyme
1 tablespoon chopped marjoram
2 tablespoons chopped parsley
1 oz butter
1 medium onion, finely chopped

A thick, substantial omelette for a main course.

Grind the Brazil nuts and hazel nuts together. Beat the eggs together. Beat in the tomato purée and herbs. Stir in the nuts and pumpkin seeds.

Heat the grill to high. Heat the butter in a frying pan on a low heat and soften the onion. Pour in the egg mixture and cook it, tipping the pan and lifting the edges of the omelette so that as much liquid egg as possible gets to the sides and base of the pan. When the underside is brown and the omelette beginning to set, put the pan under the grill, and cook until the top of the omelette is set and golden brown.

Cut the omelette into quarters in the pan before serving.

Serves 4.

Vegetable and sesame crumble

1 lb (450 g) aubergines
2 teaspoons fine sea salt
1 large green pepper
1 lb (450 g) courgettes
1 lb (450 g) tomatoes
4 tablespoons olive or sesame oil
2 medium onions, finely chopped
1 garlic clove, finely chopped
1 teaspoon ground coriander
1 teaspoon whole cumin seeds
2 oz (50 g) sesame seeds
2 oz (50 g) wheatgerm

Succulent, spiced vegetables topped with a toasted brown crumble of sesame seeds and wheatgerm.

Heat the oven to 400F/200C/gas 6. Cut the aubergines into ½-inch (1.3 cm) slices. Place in a colander, scatter with the sea salt and leave to drain for 20 minutes. Run cold water through them, and dry with kitchen paper. Cut into ½-inch (1.3 cm) dice. Core, seed and dice the pepper. Cut the courgettes into ½-inch (1.3 cm) dice. Scald, skin and thinly slice the tomatoes.

Heat the oil in a large frying pan on a low heat. Cook the pepper, onions and garlic until the onion is soft. Mix in the aubergines, courgettes, coriander and cumin seeds and cook for a further 2 minutes.

Take the pan from the heat, and put half the contents into a large pie dish. Put half the tomato slices on top, then the remaining aubergine mixture, and finally the rest of the tomatoes. Mix the sesame seeds with the wheatgerm, and scatter over the top. Bake the crumble for 30 minutes, or until the top is golden brown. Serve with long grain brown rice.

Serves 4.

Apricot and sunflower pancakes

BATTER

4 oz (125 g) wholemeal flour
½ teaspoon ground mace
pinch fine sea salt
1 egg
1 egg yolk
½ pint (275 ml) milk
½ oz (15 g) butter, plus extra for frying

FILLING

6 oz (175 g) dried whole apricots
½ pint (275 ml) natural orange juicc
4 tablespoons natural yoghurt
2 oz (50 g) sunflower seeds

Pancakes with a sweet apricot filling, both of which can be prepared in advance.

Soak the apricots in the orange juice for 8 hours. For the batter, put the flour, mace and salt into a bowl, toss together, and make a well in the centre. Add the egg and egg yolk, and start to beat in flour from the sides of the well. Gradually beat in half the milk, the melted butter and then the remaining milk. Beat the batter until there are bubbles on the surface, then leave in a cool place for 30 minutes. Make 8 pancakes with the batter, using a moderate heat and turning each one with a fish slice when the underside is browned and the top is set. Cool completely.

Heat the oven to 400F/200C/gas 6. Drain the apricots, reserving the juice. Liquidize with the yoghurt, and mix in the sunflower seeds. Put a portion of the apricot mixture on each pancake, roll up and place in a heatproof dish. Sprinkle with about 4 fl oz (125 ml) of the reserved juice. Heat through for 10 minutes.

Serves 4.

INDEX